AF324237

As we see it

Aida Amoako

As we see it

Artists Redefining Black Identity

Contents

Introduction

The unassuming prefix "re" became a source of unexpected insight while researching this book. "Re" can mean simply doing something again, but it can also mean more than mere repetition – it can mean undertaking an action again but with a view to a (hopefully) better outcome. Words like reimagine, reconsider, rewrite, reconceptualize, reread and rework frequently popped up in relation to the work of the Black artists and photographers featured here. The better outcome? A fuller representation and more nuanced appreciation of the lives and artistic output of Black people.

These artists from across the globe explore new ways to represent the humanity of Black people, upend persistent myths that denigrate them, and also demonstrate the multiplicity of Blackness. In their endeavours they engage with, pay tribute to and expand upon older bodies of work: like that of the greats of the twentieth century like Malick Sidibé, Gordon Parks and Carrie Mae Weems. The so-called canons of Western art and photography and the collective cultural imaginations, primarily but not exclusively, of the West that once excluded these artists are also simultaneously the playgrounds and contested territories in which these artists experiment.

The photographs, short films, sculptures and paintings not only insist on a Black point of view but that that point of view is also always in flux and evolving. There's an aversion to being boxed in. This point of view could be called the "Black gaze", one that decentres the white gaze, that rejects stereotyping and exploitative, paternalistic ethnographic perspectives. Black feminist theorist Professor Tina M. Campt's recent book *A Black Gaze: Artists Changing How We See* (2021) is perhaps the most prominent recent discussion in art academia of the Black gaze and defines it as the idea of what Blackness specifically brings to both the creation and viewing of video art.

The current cultural and socio-political landscape has more than merely coincided with what feels akin to a Black artistic renaissance. The insistence on seeing the humanity of Black people in society, it could be argued, has contributed to a demand to see Black perspectives in all creative fields, with an awareness that the images we consume play a large part in how Black people are perceived and then treated. Take, for example, the discourse around hooded jumpers which became a major part of conversations about the killing of teenager Trayvon Martin by George Zimmerman or the persistent linking of du-rags with criminality. Several young Black artists have engaged with this question, wanting to flip those associations on their heads. The emergence of social media platforms such as Instagram and Tumblr has enabled much of these artists' work to be disseminated further than glossy magazines, newspapers and exhibitions might have allowed in the past. These platforms have also provided the opportunity for collaboration and lateral network building, a way in through the side door, dodging the gatekeepers. I would not go so far as to group the artists featured in this book into a particular movement, but at the same time I would say a climate has emerged – or let's be more accurate and say has been fought for and cultivated – in which Black artists are able to have a much more prominent voice at a much younger age than many of their artistic predecessors.

Just as these artists are able to reach back to draw from these pioneers, their own work will

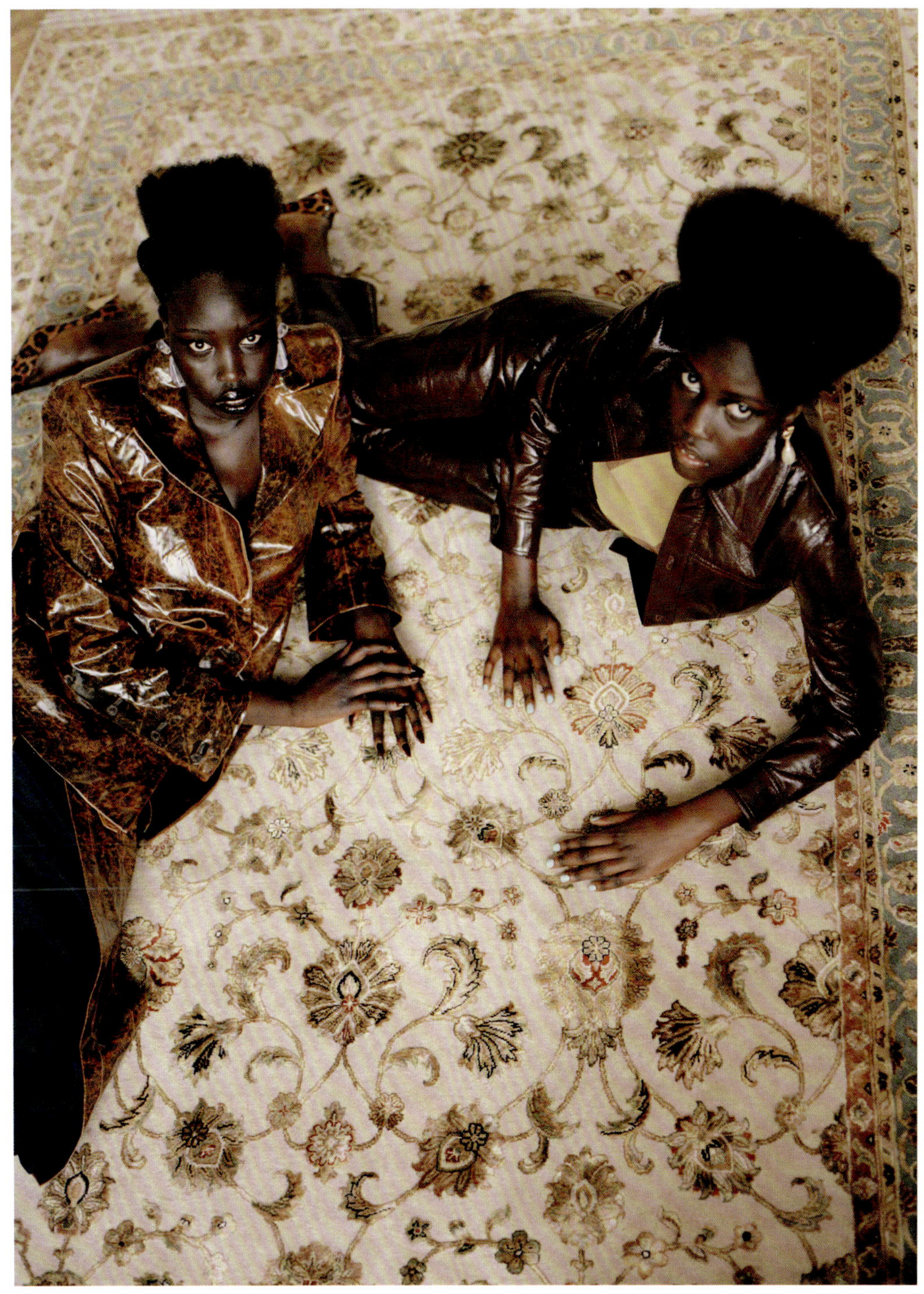

Ronan Mckenzie, *Present, Finally: AJ and Akuac*, 2019

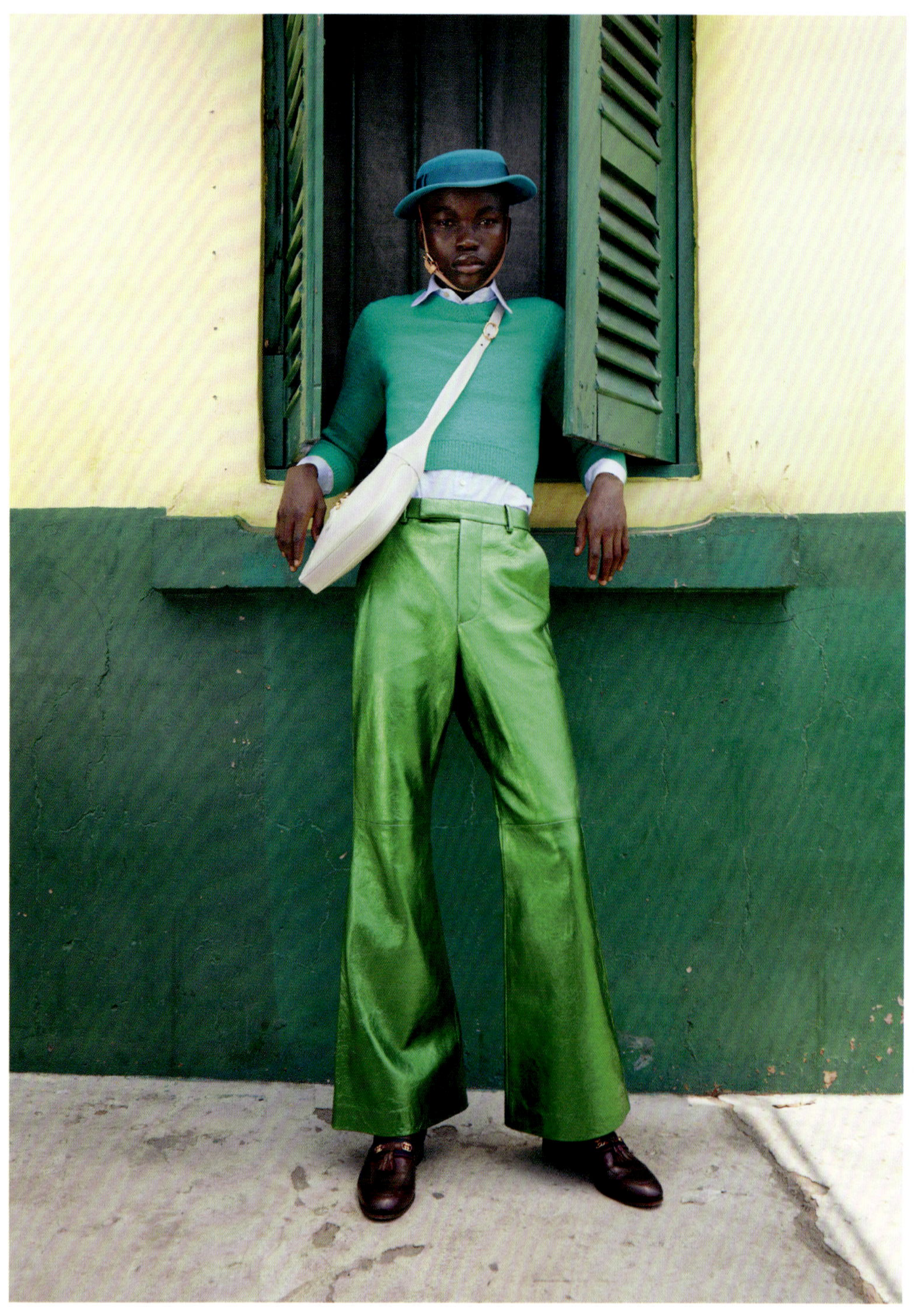

Above: David Nana Opoku Ansah, from *We Are They*, 2020
Opposite: Ronan Mckenzie, from *Small Island*, 2019

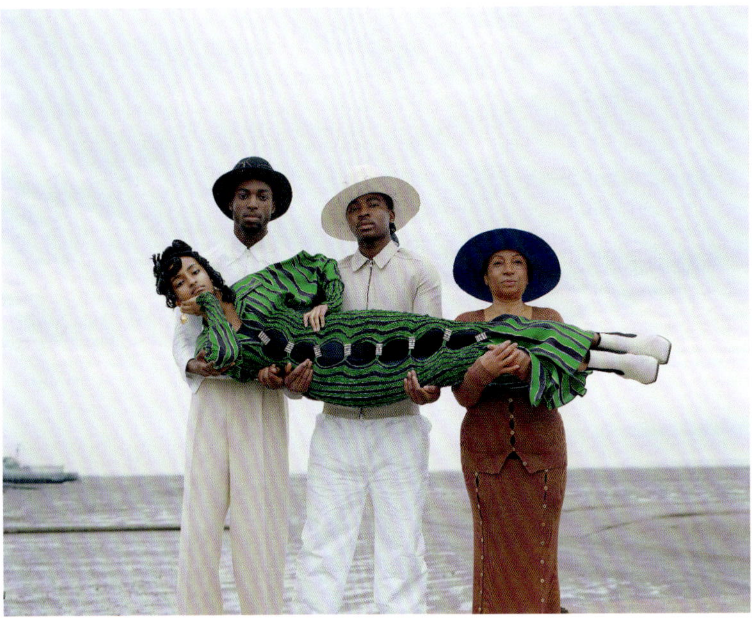

potentially form part of an artistic archive on the myriad Black experiences of the late twentieth and early twenty-first centuries.

Speaking of cultural precedents, this book itself draws inspiration from, and would likely not exist were it not for, books such as Antwaun Sargent's *The New Black Vanguard* (2019) and Ekow Eshun's *Africa State of Mind* (2018), which have deftly highlighted the innovative work of important Black artists.

An interest in mythology and modern mythopoeia – that is, mythmaking in popular culture – also partly influenced this text, specifically how cultural myths are expressed in the cultural products of an age. Where do people get their perceptions of New Yorkers from? Of inner-city British youth? Of LGBTQ+ Africans? How do the creators of those cultural outputs contribute to these ideas? Conversely, how do they challenge them? Telling the undertold stories and celebrating their subjectivities – those of the artists and the subjects – has the potential to provide something new. The result in so many of these artist portfolios is work that advocates for open communication as opposed to projection. Evident in this work and also in how the artists talk about it are concerns about power dynamics, a hyper-awareness of how photography has traditionally been seen as an exploitative tool and a desire not to replicate those relationships.

These artists tackle questions of accountability and artistic freedom while openly acknowledging the amalgamation of the sense of responsibility they feel in representing sections of minority communities and the fear of being placed into a box from which they cannot escape, a box where Black artists are hired due to outside pressure and not because their perspectives are truly respected and seen as vital, a box where "Black artist" becomes a limiting descriptor instead of an empowering one or even, simply, a factual one.

This book is not just about looking *at* Black people; it is also about seeing the world through their varying perspectives. It is not just about presenting counter-narratives through photographs; it is about emphasizing that any photo is just the beginning, the entry point, and the wealth of emotion, artistry, humanity you encounter in the photo is just the tip of the iceberg. The goal is to afford Black people the fullness of their humanity.

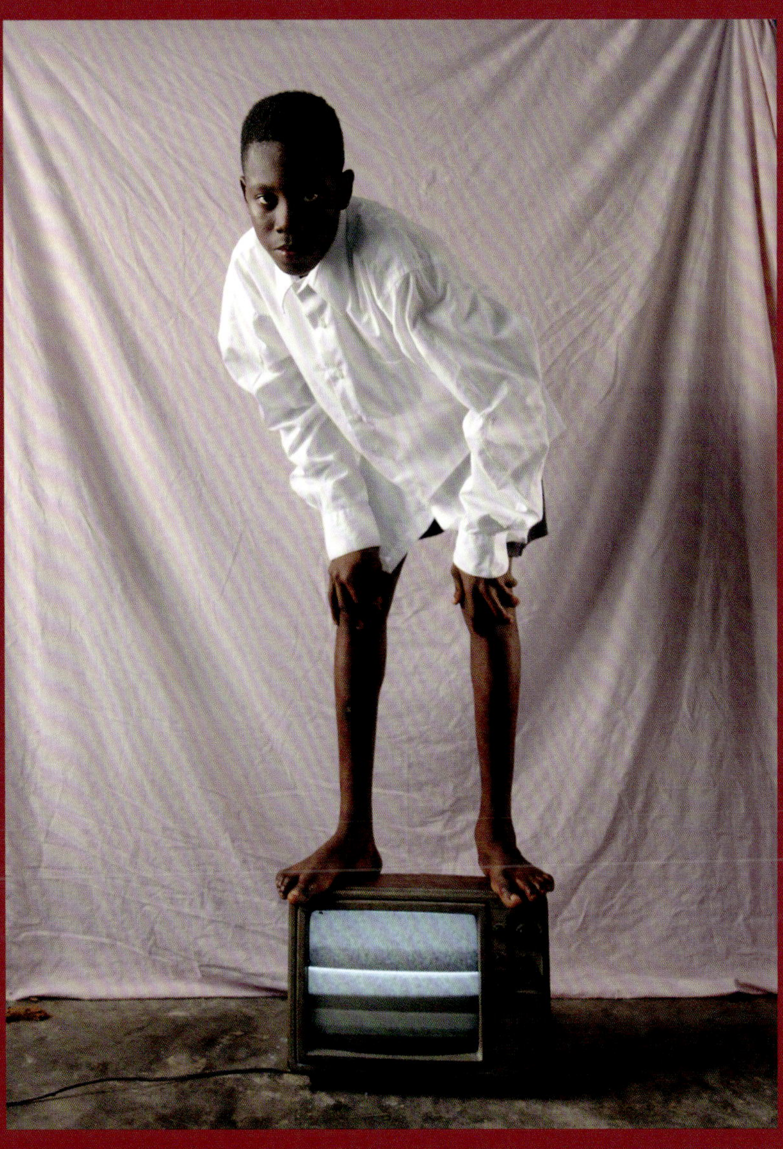

David Nana Opoku Ansah, *Family Property*, from
Where I live I will Grow, 2019

Prince Gyasi

A Divine Assignment

Prince Gyasi, born Prince Gyasi Nyantakyi, lives and works in Accra, Ghana. He began taking photographs with a camera in 2011, and in 2014 started shooting using an iPhone. His mild form of synaesthesia – a neurological condition that can be described as the overlapping of two senses – expresses itself in his signature usage of bright colours and high saturation. Dark skin looks incredibly rich, as though illuminated from within; waters are impossibly blue and sands are a fantastic hot pink. Colours are connected to moods and words: blue is calming; red connotes not only blood and sacrifice but also labour. His manipulation of colour lends an otherworldliness to some of his photographs that curiously doesn't take away from Gyasi's documentarian approach but instead complements it.

Gyasi sees himself as both a photographer and a conceptual artist creating works where themes such as the bonds of friendship and familial relationships are explored. However, *potential* could be described as the overarching theme of many of the images. For his series *Boxed Kids*, which he began in 2016, Gyasi photographed the young people of a small fishing community in Jamestown, a district that is simultaneously one of Accra's poorest and an up-and-coming tourist hotspot. Many of the more underprivileged children living there are kept out of school to learn the local trade and supplement their parents' incomes. Gyasi's photographs highlight their circumstances without creating the "poverty porn" that has come to influence the images of many African countries in the collective cultural imaginations of the West. An intimate understanding of just how powerful photography is as a tool to shape narratives about people and places informs Gyasi's work and, while challenging stereotypes about Ghana and countering the image of Africa as a "negative space" is important to the artist, it is also clear that his works are not merely for the consumption of others but also for the subjects of the images themselves.

In an interview published in *The Fader*, he revealed he feels it is his "divine assignment" to "empower these kids to help them see themselves as lights". In one image featuring these young children, they stand in the ocean holding a fishing net between them, their backs to the camera, looking out at a pink horizon, as though transported to another world mid-task. For Gyasi, education is the way out of what he sees as a persistent generational cycle. It is for this reason that he began his non-profit, also called BoxedKids, to help provide that education to Accra's creative youth, an act that emphasizes his conviction about the connection between art and social change.

> "His manipulation of colour lends an otherworldliness to some of his photographs that doesn't take away from Gyasi's documentarian approach but instead complements it"

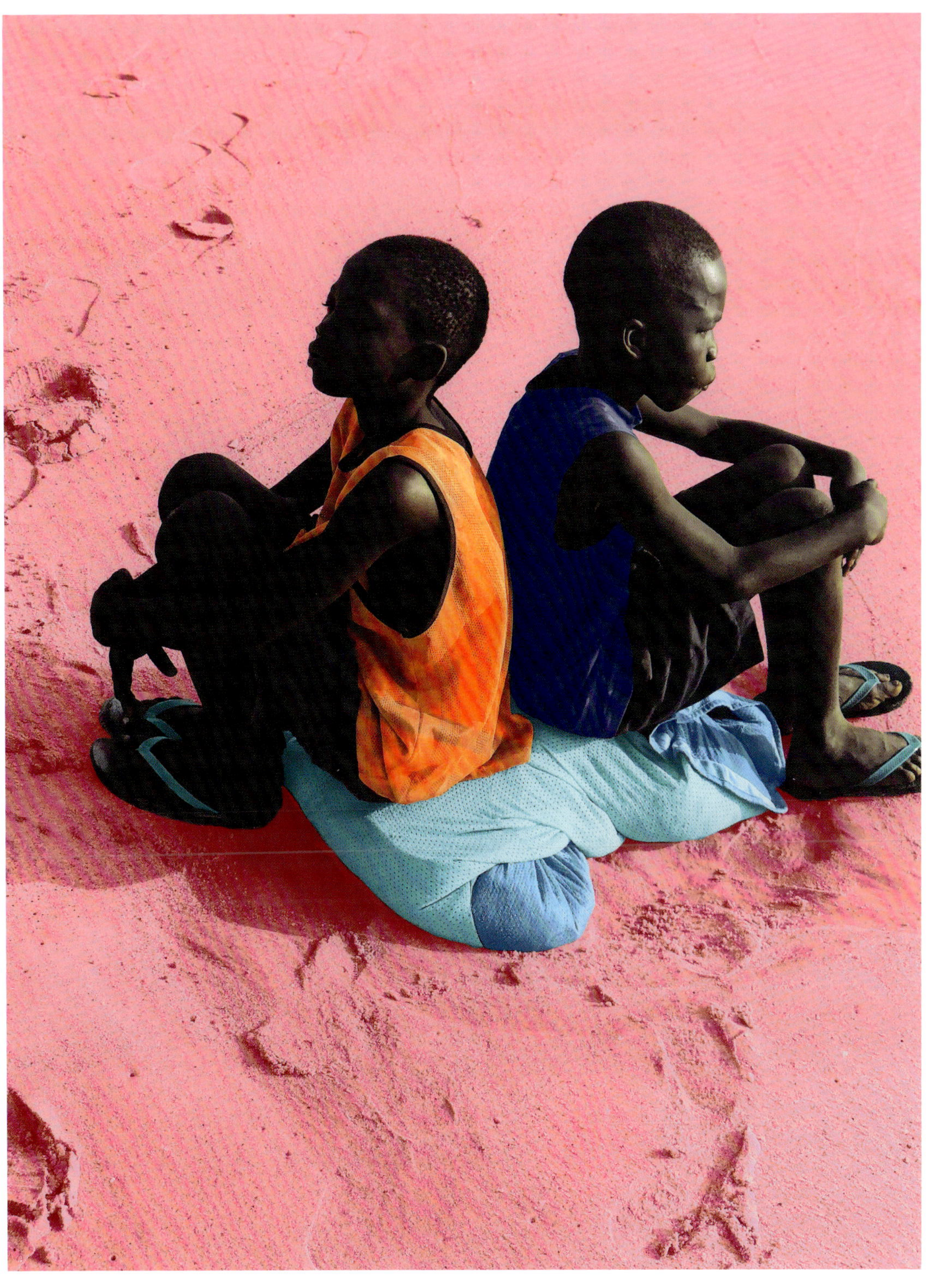

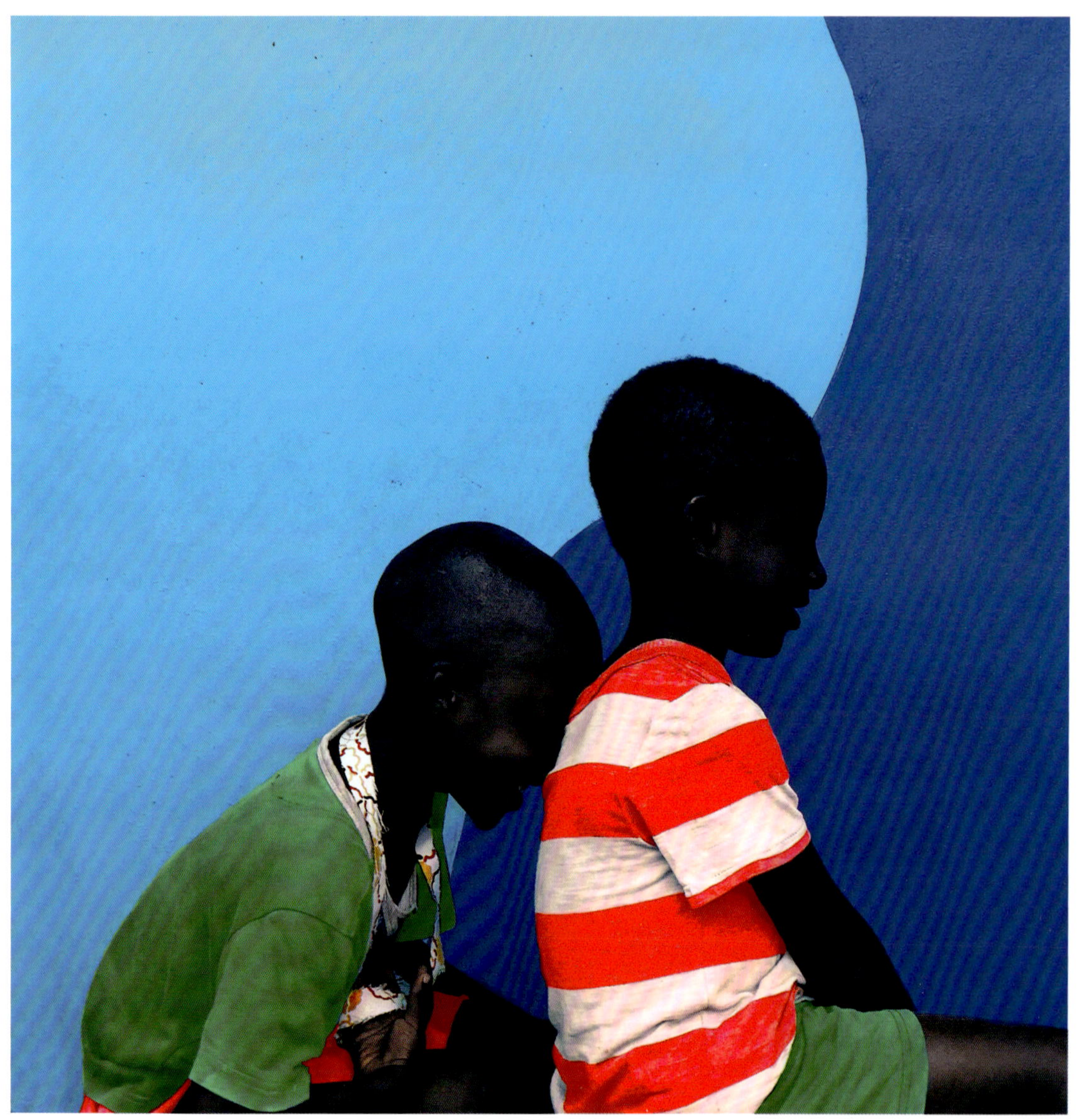

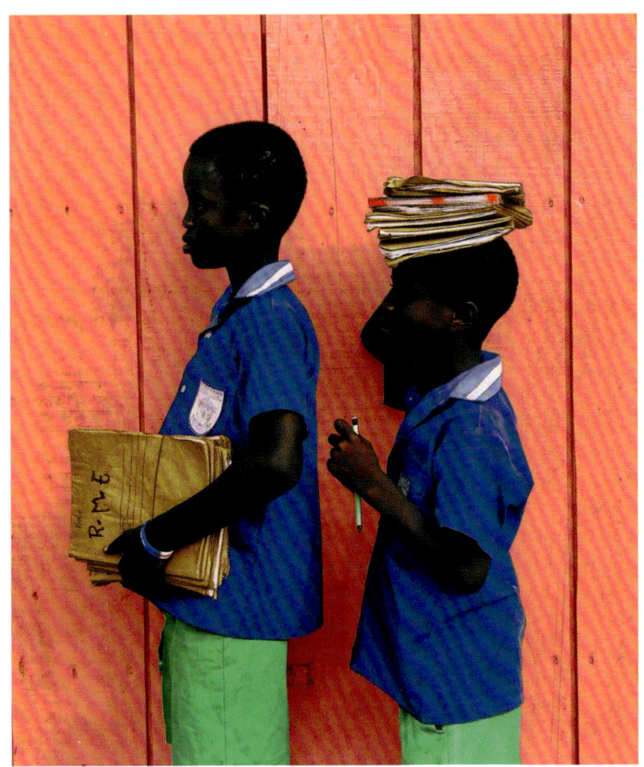

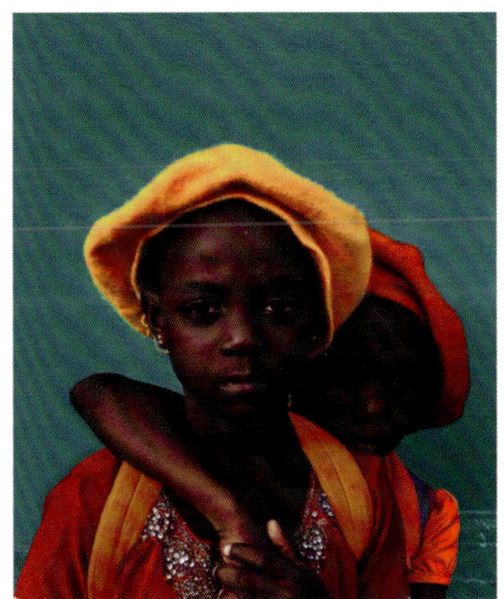

Previous spread:
The Wait 1, from *Boxed Kids*, 2018
These pages, from left:
The Art of Appreciating Little Things, from *Phases*, 2019
Ignorance Costs Money Too, from *Phases*, 2019
Twins Edition, from *Boxed Kids*, 2018

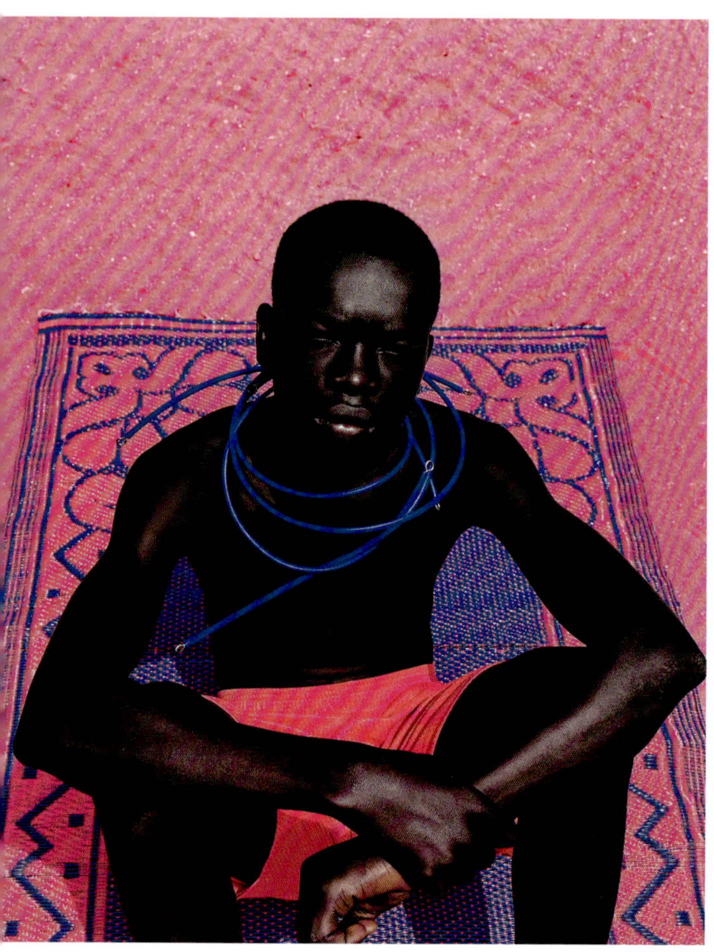

This page, from top:
Projection, 2019
The Last One, 2020
Opposite:
The Wait 2, from *Boxed Kids*, 2018

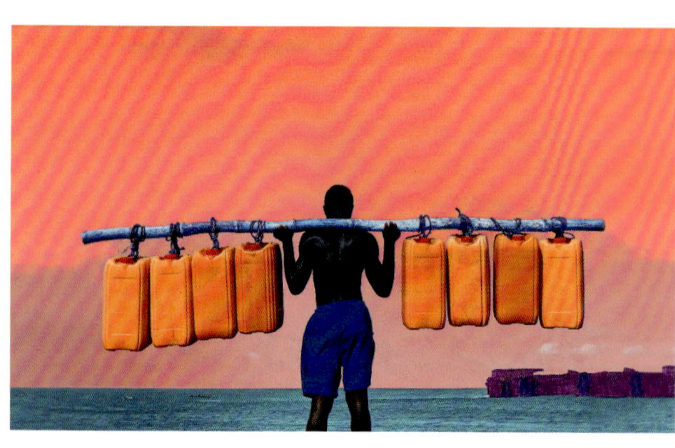

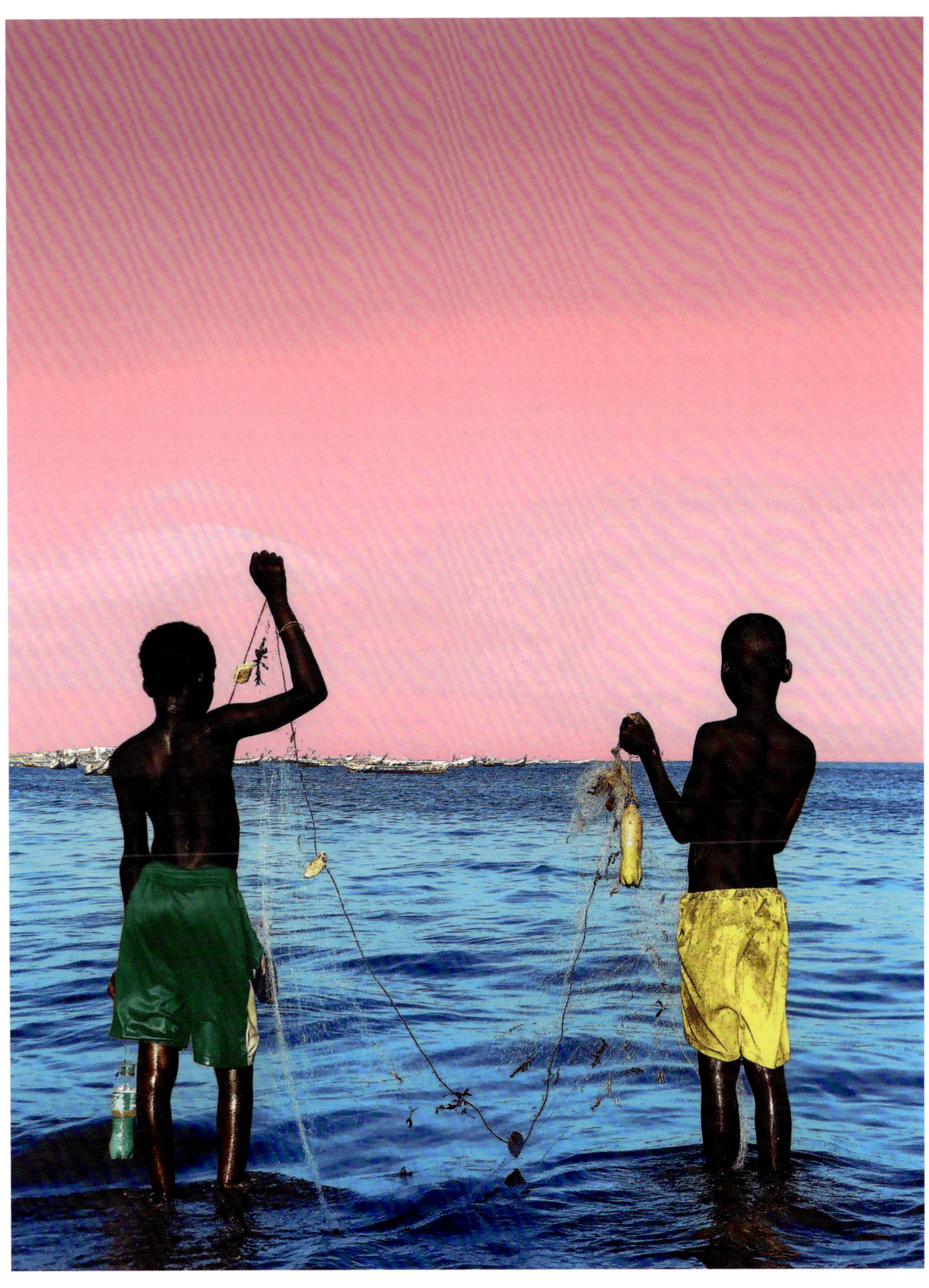

Nadine Ijewere

The Misrepresentation
of Representation

Southeast London-born photographer Nadine Ijewere eschewed more traditional paths to professional photography and instead used social media as both a tool and a platform. It was on Instagram that Ijewere met her earliest collaborators and also cast her models; this allowed her to include those she felt were both underrepresented and misrepresented in mainstream media. In an interview with British *Vogue*, Ijewere said of her work's focus on disrupting fashion editorial's staid and exclusionary beauty standards: "Now, we're sending a message that everyone is welcome in fashion. There are so many different types of beauty in the world. Let's celebrate them all." In 2019, Ijewere became the first woman of colour in the magazine's then 103-year history to shoot the cover for British *Vogue*, and, in 2021, she also became the first Black woman to shoot a cover for US *Vogue*.

Ijewere has cited a mix of portrait photographers and social documentarians, from Richard Avedon and Seydou Keïta to William Eggleston and Gordon Parks, as influences. Her images are vibrant; her use of film often produces a soft grain that mutes the colours into dreamy tones without diminishing them. The 2018 *i-D* magazine series *Joy as an Act of Resistance* expresses both the psychology of colour and clothing and their power to connote and influence emotions. The diverse group of models featured are pictured on the beach at Brighton, southeast England. Close-up portrait shots focus attention on freckles and fuller lips. In other images, glittery cloth, tulle and feathers frame long limbs.

While Ijewere is predominantly known for her fashion photography – having helmed editorial shoots for fashion's biggest magazines and brands – the artist moves with ease between the worlds of commercial and fine art. In 2016, Tate Britain exhibited images from her *Same/Difference* series which explored the similarities and idiosyncrasies of a range of siblings of various ethnicities. In 2021, *Beautiful Disruption*, her first solo show showcasing at C/O Berlin, looked back at her work so far. The exhibition featured *Tallawah*, a more personal project, for which the half-Nigerian, half-Jamaican artist travelled to Jamaica for the first time. Working with noted editorial hairstylist Jawara Wauchope, Ijewere presented the creative self-expression of the local men and women through their hair and clothing with the hope of countering pervasive negative stereotypes of the Caribbean island. Ijewere's London College of Fashion dissertation was titled "The Misrepresentation of Representation" and sought to reveal and challenge Western stereotypes of non-Western features and cultures. But ultimately, what Ijewere is working towards, along with many other artists of her generation, is a landscape of photography where inclusivity of people of colour is a given. As she said in her interview with *Vogue*: "For Black people to be present, why must something have to be disturbed?"

> "What Ijewere is working towards, with many other artists of her generation, is a landscape of photography where inclusivity of people of colour is a given"

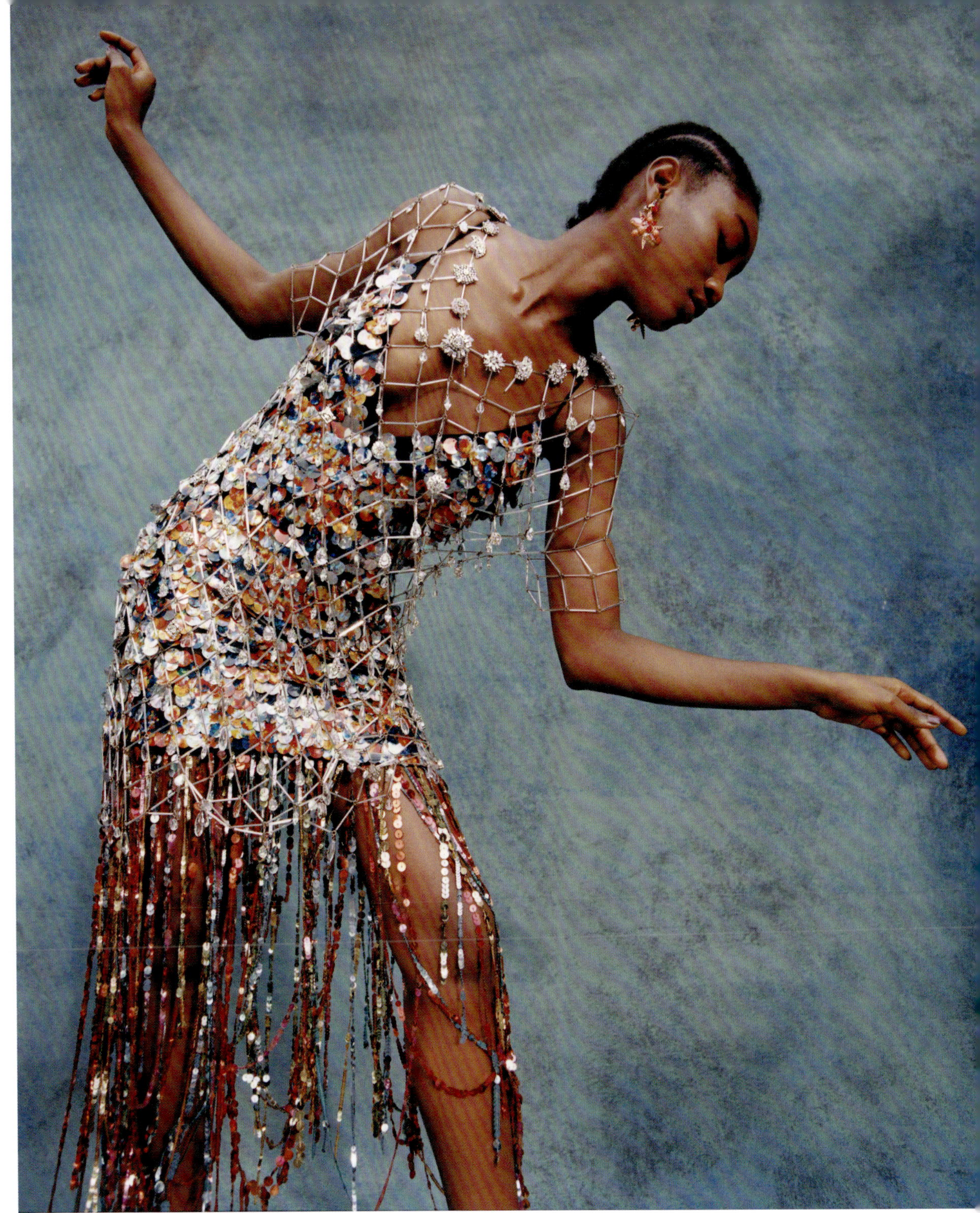

Swarovski x Garage Magazine, Book of Dreams, Vol. III

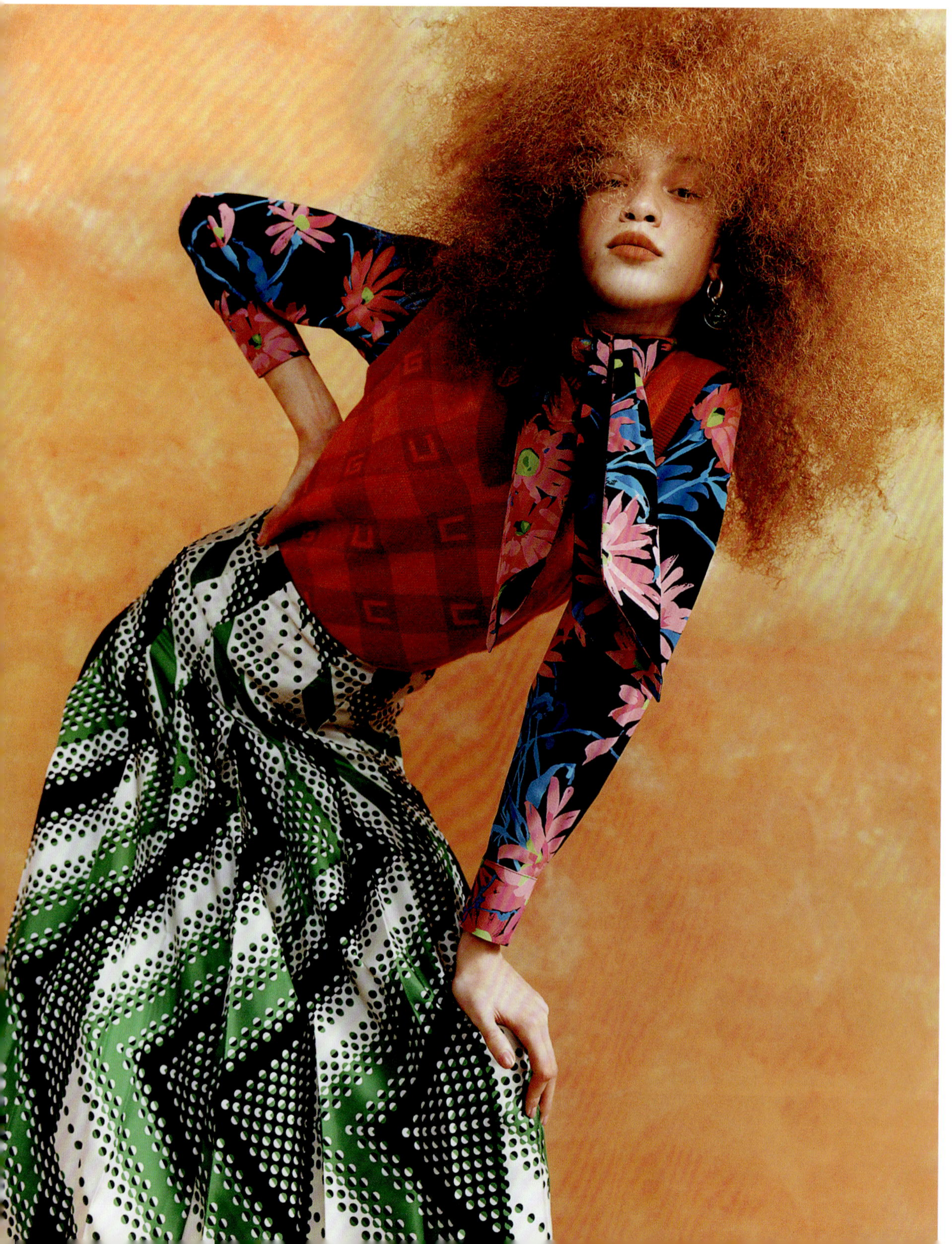

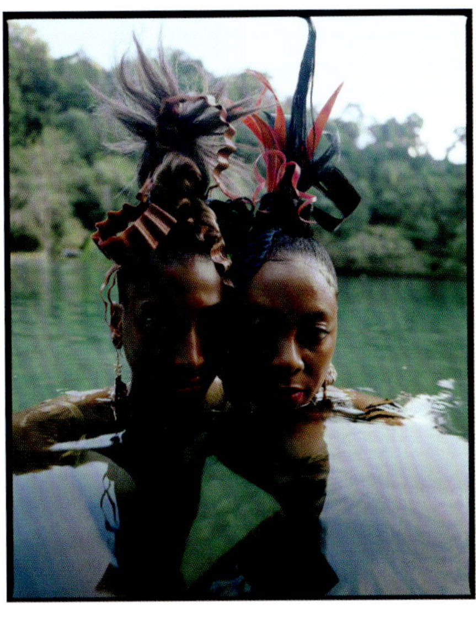

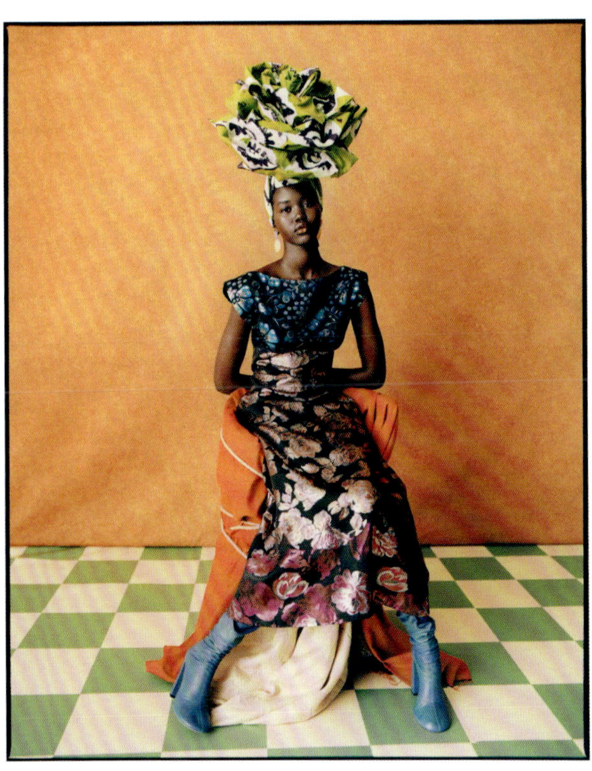

This page, from top:
For US *Vogue*, January 2020
For US *Vogue*, December 2020
Opposite:
For the *Wall Street Journal*, February 2021

Campbell Addy

Seeking and Finding

In 2016, while still studying fashion communication at Central Saint Martins in London, photographer and filmmaker Campbell Addy founded *Niijournal*, an independent print publication, with the tagline "here to educate, not irritate". He had discovered a penchant for photography while visiting his mother in Ghana, but it was after witnessing a memorial in Harlem, New York, for people who had died in police custody that Addy decided he wanted to use photography to educate. In 2017, Addy collaborated with Getty Images to create a series of 42 stock photography portraits with a diverse range of models handpicked from his own casting agency, also called Nii. Just as the casting agency aims to provide a solution to the lack of representation in the fashion industry, so the creation of the stock imagery was a response to the lack of non-white faces in this realm. For Addy, and for other artists featured in this volume, this impulse to diversify photography comes from an understanding that minds are shaped by what they see and that the pervasiveness of some images can create narratives that are damaging and hard to counter. But it isn't just about what others see but also how one views oneself.

In 2020, Addy began creating *In the Waiting*, an ongoing series for which he takes one self-portrait a day to document his experience of the COVID-19 pandemic, this in-between time. Inspired by Kina Grannis's song of the same name, as well as Irving Penn's series of nudes shot between 1940 and 1950, in one image Campbell kneels naked, legs slightly contorted to reveal the sole of his bare foot. But there is no awkwardness. Instead the image evokes both vulnerability and strength, the grace of a dancer and the fluid lines of marble statuary too. One leg in dark shadow, the other gently illuminated, the photograph feels like a painting.

Challenging popular notions of modern masculinity is a prevalent idea in Addy's artistic pedagogy. In a video for Nowness.com, Addy uses expressive dance to explore this topic, and rather than merely opposing an idea of exaggerated muscularity, rigidity and toughness with delicacy and sensuality, he blurs the lines between such simplistic oppositions. His first solo show in 2017, *Matthew 7:7–8*, was, evidently, inspired by religion. Addy was raised as a Jehovah's Witness, where another opposition was set up between homosexuality and religion: "everyone assumes if you're gay, you're not religious," Addy told *Out* magazine. The show set up a coming-of-age narrative exploring faith and organized religion, something embodied in the use of this particular scripture that continues to hold significance for Addy, despite him no longer being a practising Jehovah's Witness. The thread that runs through the photo series is the desire to expand the images that certain notions – from what it means to be gay and have faith to what it means to be a Black man – seem to evoke for people beyond the images with which mainstream media and art have been saturated.

> "There is a desire to expand the images that certain notions – from what it means to be gay and have faith to what it means to be a Black man – seem to evoke for people"

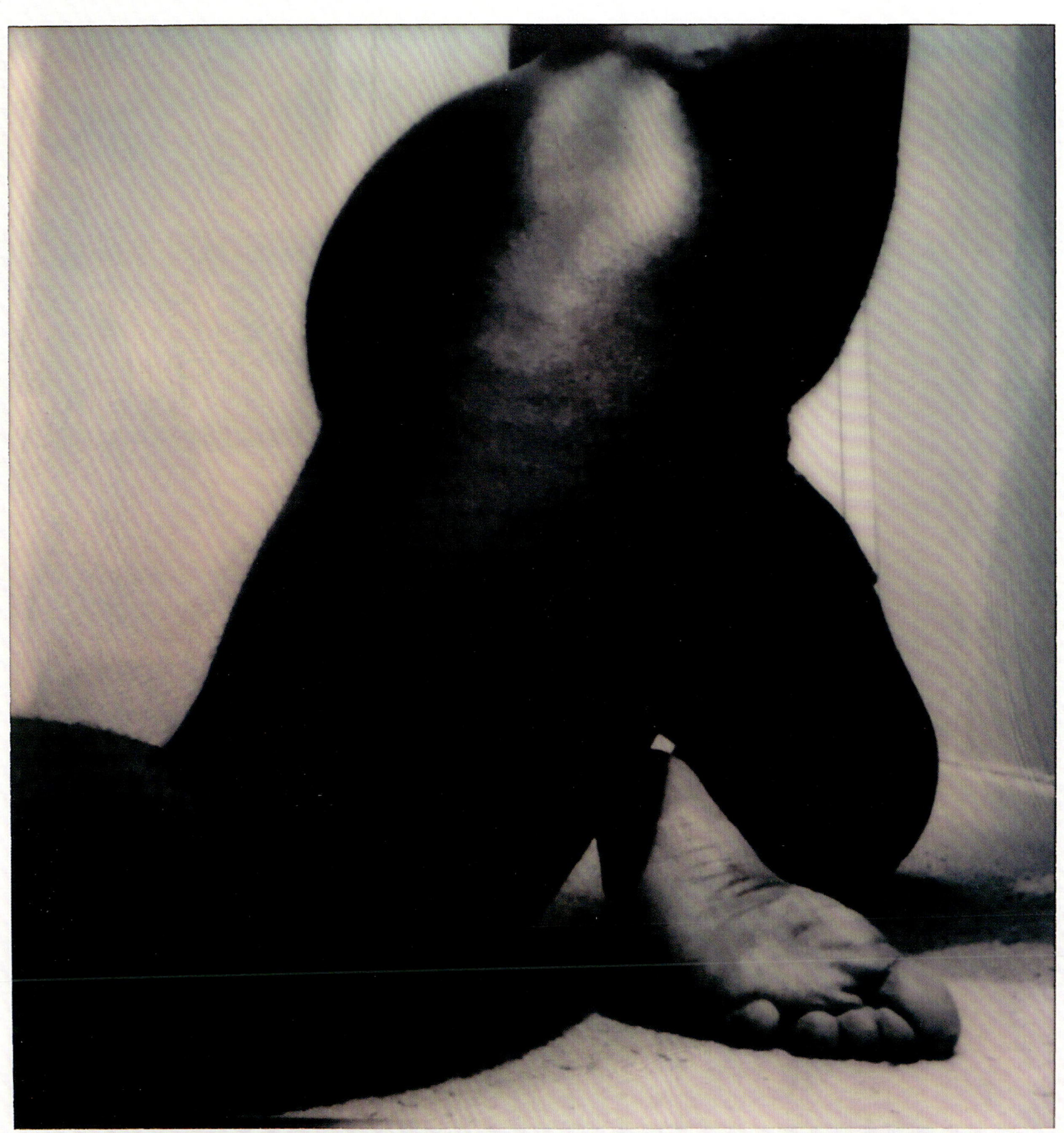

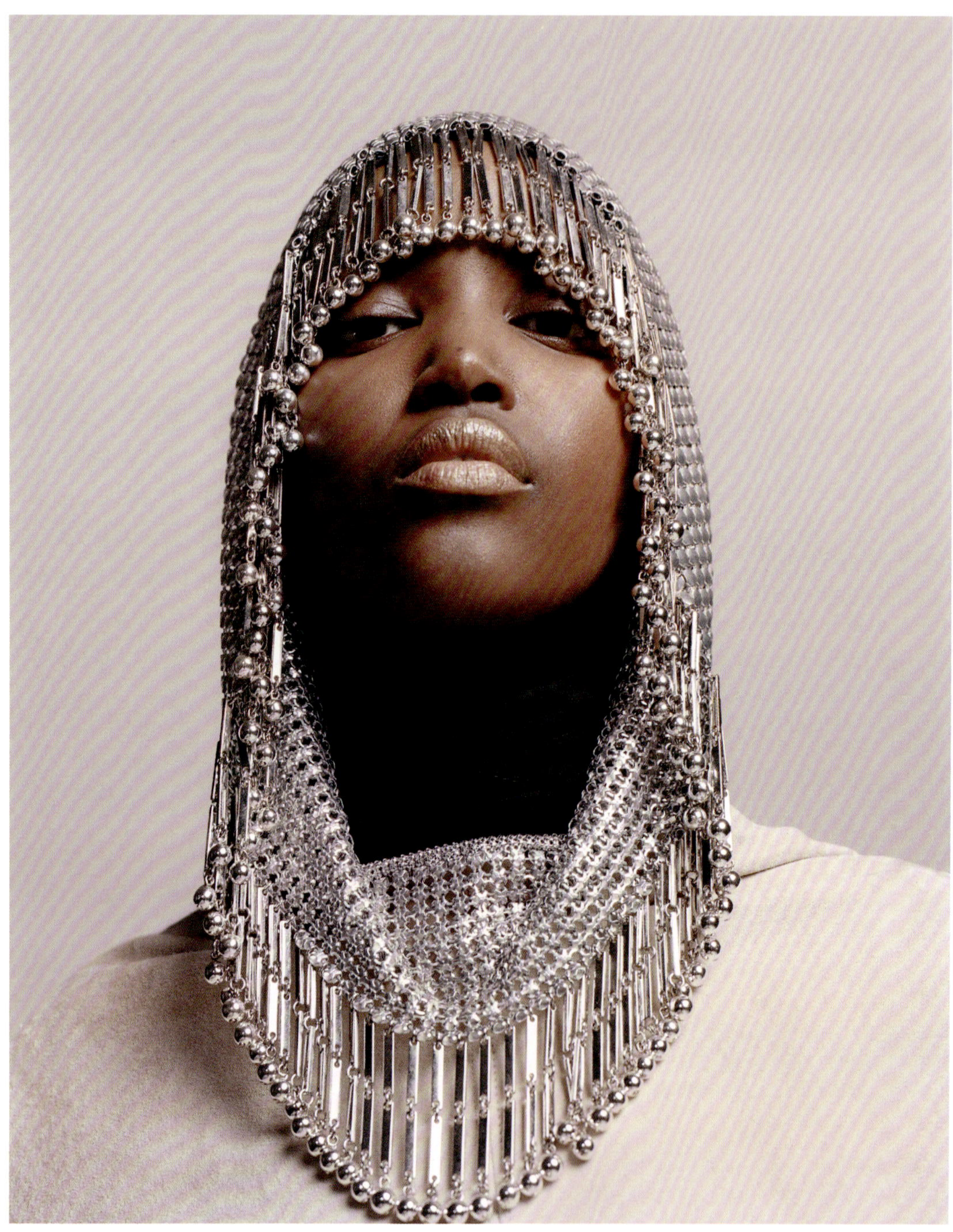

Previous spread: from *In the Waiting*, 2020
Above: Fadhi Mohamed for *W* magazine, 2020

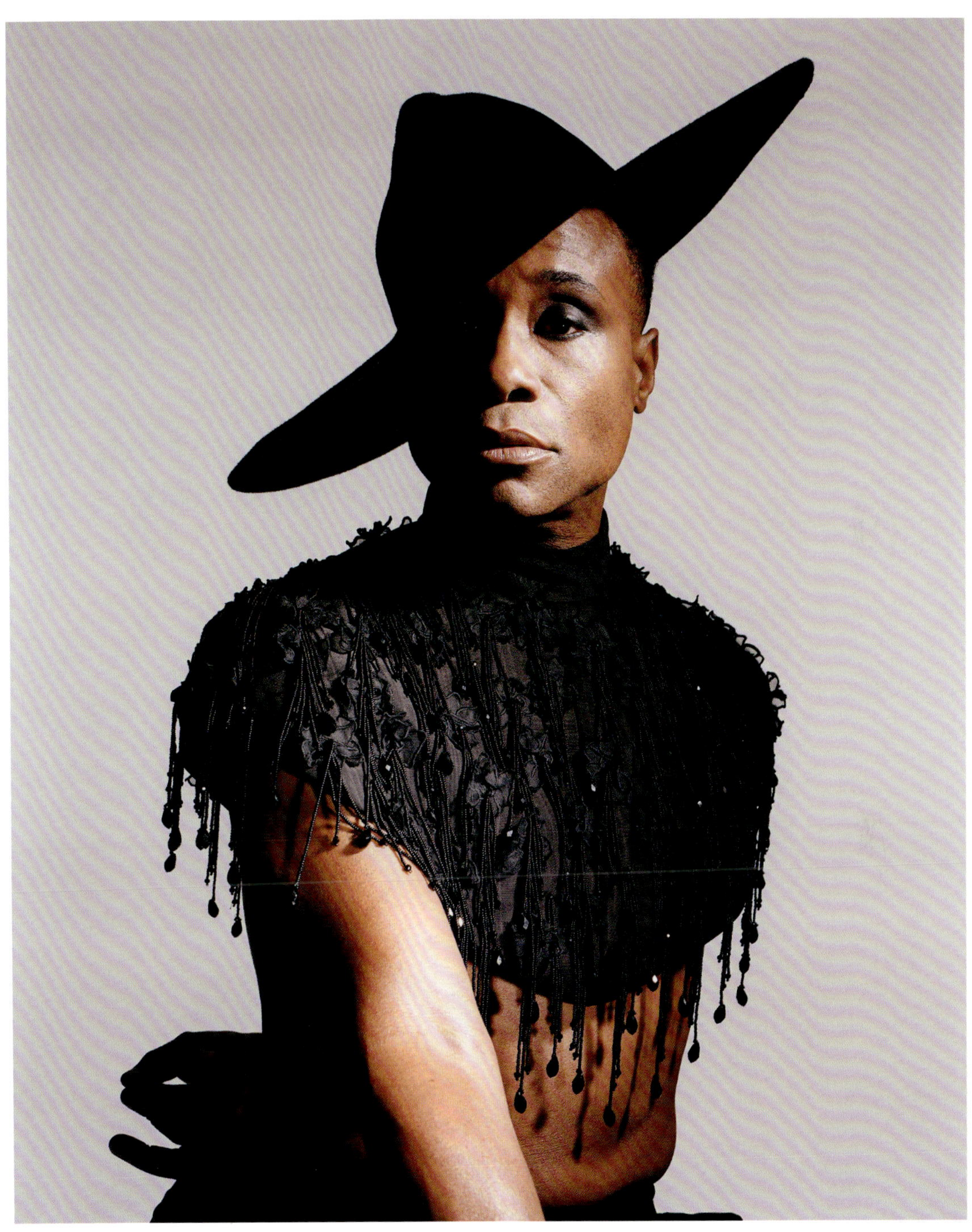

Billy Porter for *The Cut*, 2019

Chris Facey

The New York Eye

North Carolina-based, New York City-born-and-raised photographer Chris Facey trained his "New York Eye" at the School of Visual Arts. He was inspired by the likes of Gordon Parks and Roy DeCarava to be a documentary photographer whose work centres on Black communities.

Facey was working on *#Dadduty*, a series about fathers and their children aimed at breaking stereotypes about ethnic-minority fathers, when George Floyd was killed in May 2020 and protests erupted worldwide. Moved by the anger felt by so many at the time, Facey attended protests outside the Barclays Center and in Union Square in New York. In an article accompanying his photographs for the *New Yorker*, Facey talks about his work as a documentary photographer being affected by his heightened awareness of his race in the presence of police officers, which has even influenced how quickly he moves, wary of his gear being mistaken for a weapon. His black-and-white series documenting both the protests and the way COVID-19 has affected day-to-day living depicts protestors, their signs, lines of police, and activists caught mid-motion in an attempt to capture the heightened tension of that summer.

In one photograph, a woman is surrounded by masked NYPD officers, the fingers of a disembodied hand, most likely that of an officer, digging into her bare shoulder. In a colour photograph, a cardboard box covered in tape marked "fragile" and "handle with care" fills up the entire frame. Only the protestor's eyes and fingers are visible through the cardboard, on which "live animal" is written.

What Facey's photographs also capture is the tension between subjects and the photographer. There is a sense of unwitting collaboration with some of the protestors, a subconscious awareness, perhaps, of the powerful protest image they could potentially create together. However, Facey has also spoken about the uncomfortable question hanging in the air concerning the protest photographer's presence and their assumed detachment from the crowd, which asks: "Just *why* exactly are you here? To take pictures or to be part of the movement?" "If my photographs have a mission," says Facey, "it would be to combat false narratives and negative stereotypes of Black people in America while showcasing their strength and resiliency."

> "Facey's photographs capture the tension between subjects and photographer. There is a subconscious awareness, perhaps, of the powerful protest image they could create together"

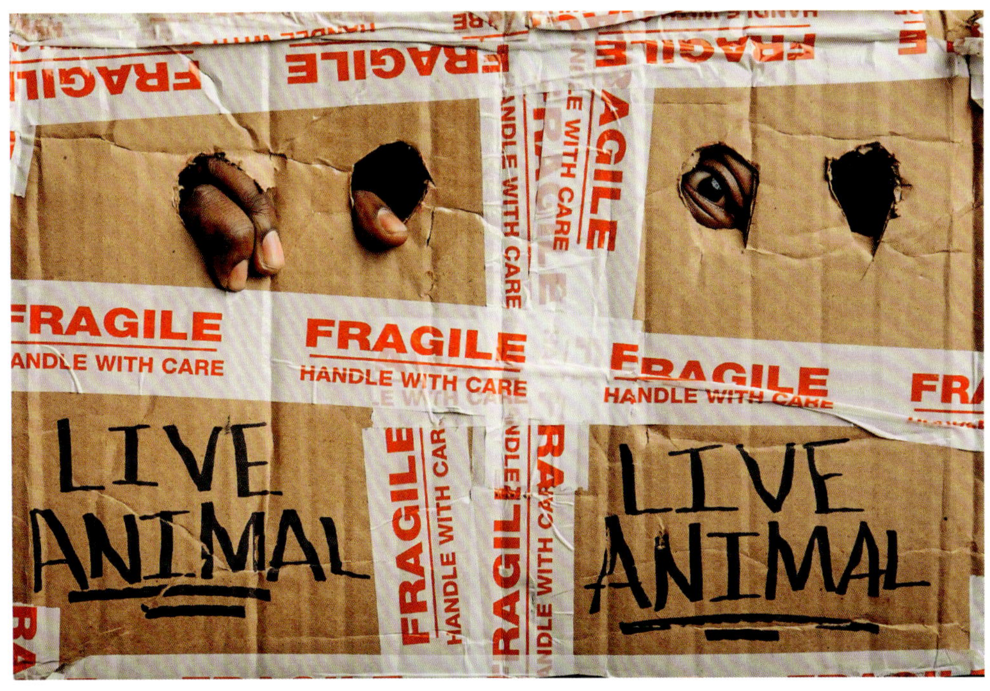

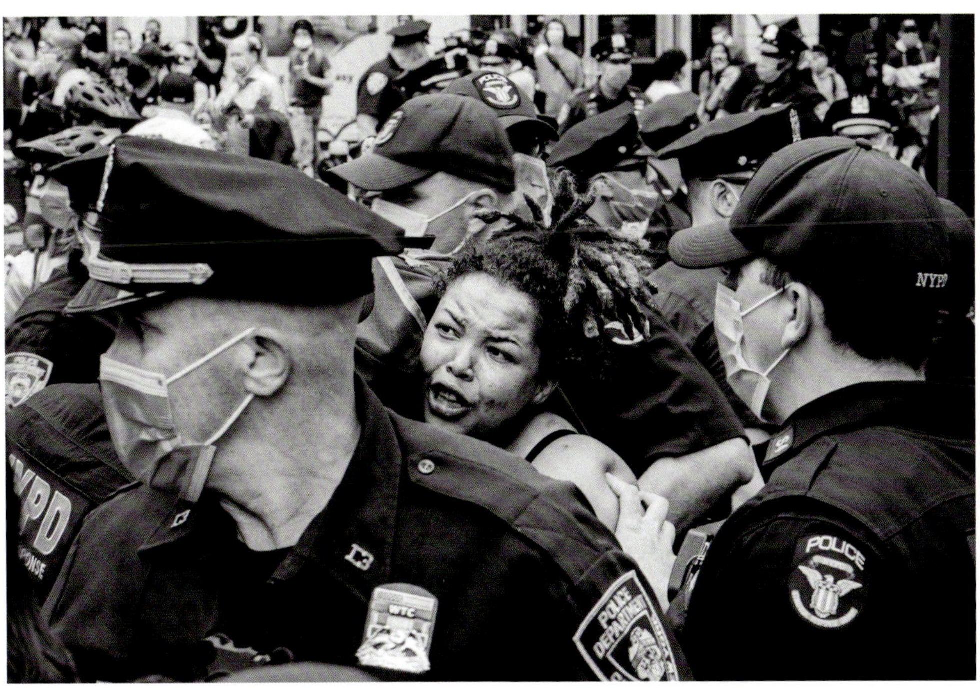

From top: *Self-Portrait*, 2019
Protestor Surrounded and Arrested by NYPD Police
Officers during a Black Lives Matter Protest, 2020

As We See It

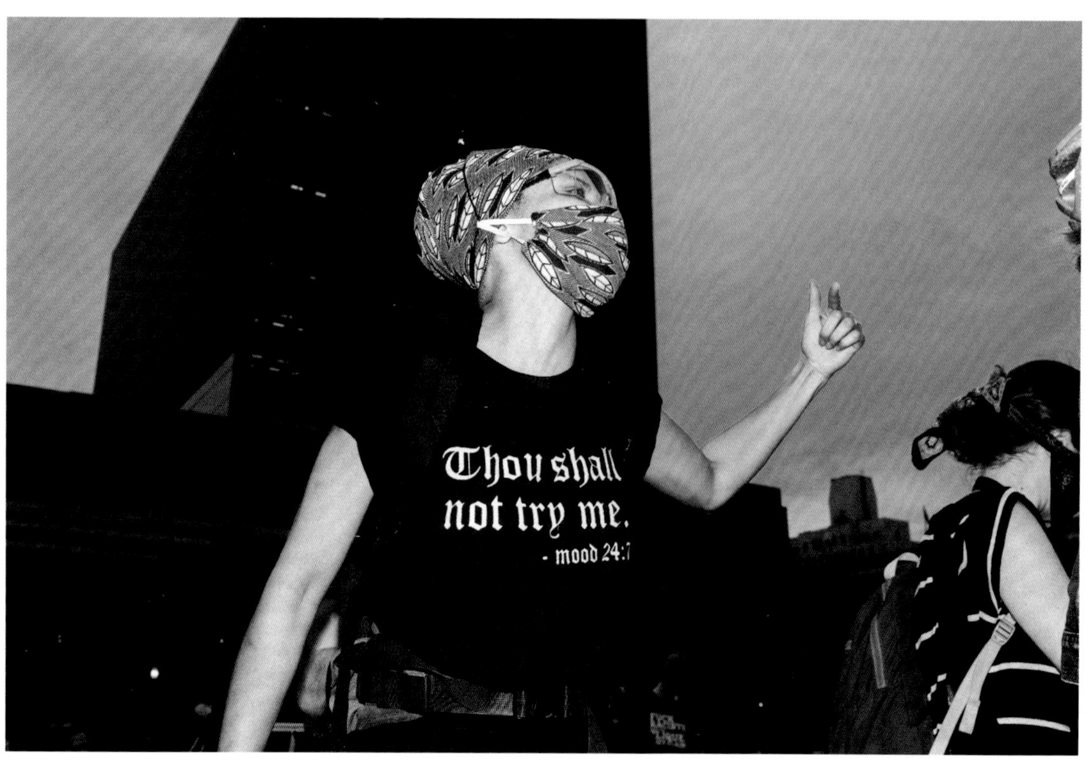

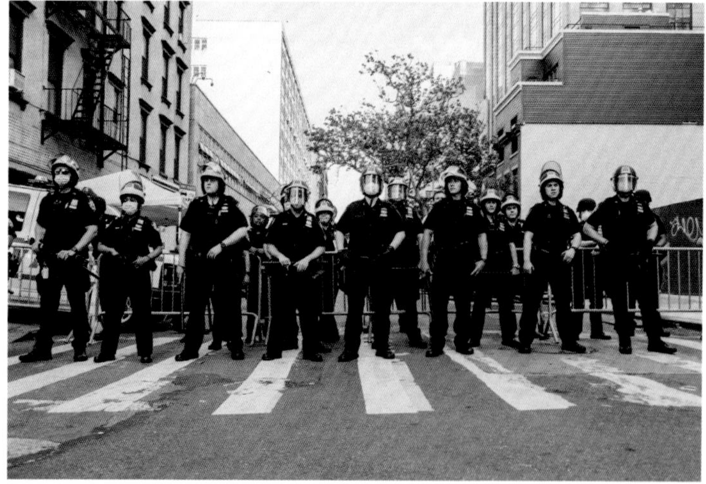

From top:
Photo of a Protestor during a Black Lives Matter Protest in Brooklyn, NY, 2020
A Line of NYPD Police Officers Stand Ready as Protestors Prepare to March By, 2020

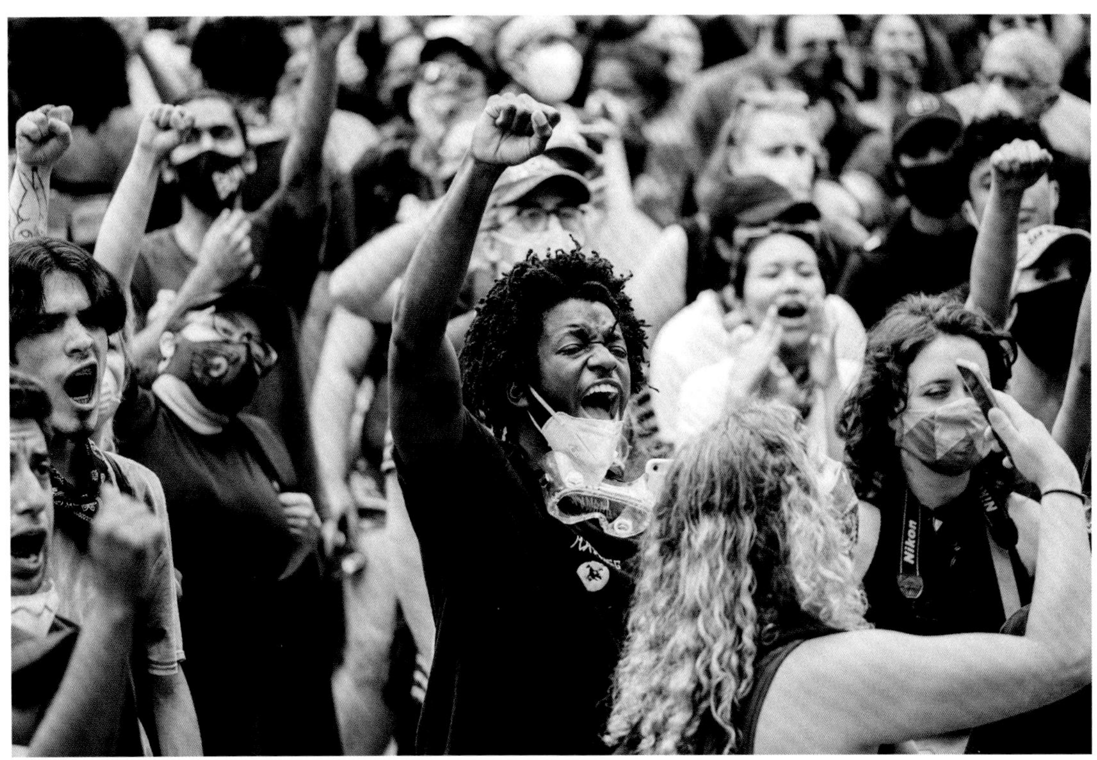

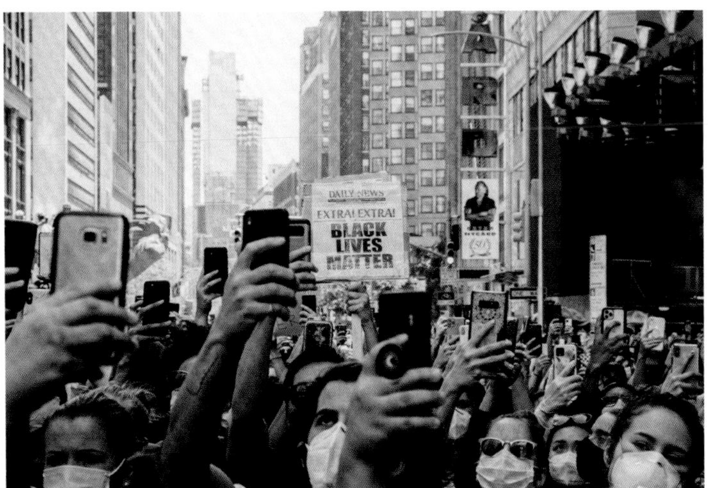

From top: *Protestor at a Black Lives Matter Rally Screaming*
"Black Lives Matter" during a Call and Response, 2020
Black Lives Matter Newspaper Cover Used as a Sign during
a Black Lives Matter Protest, 2020

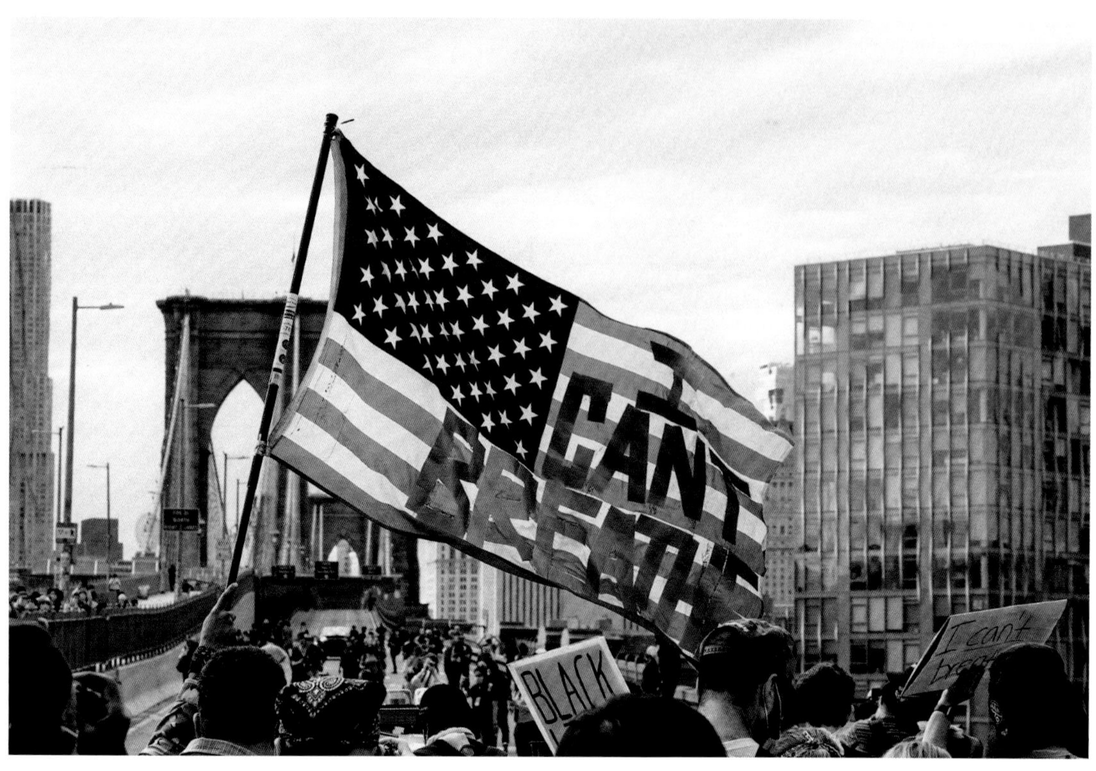

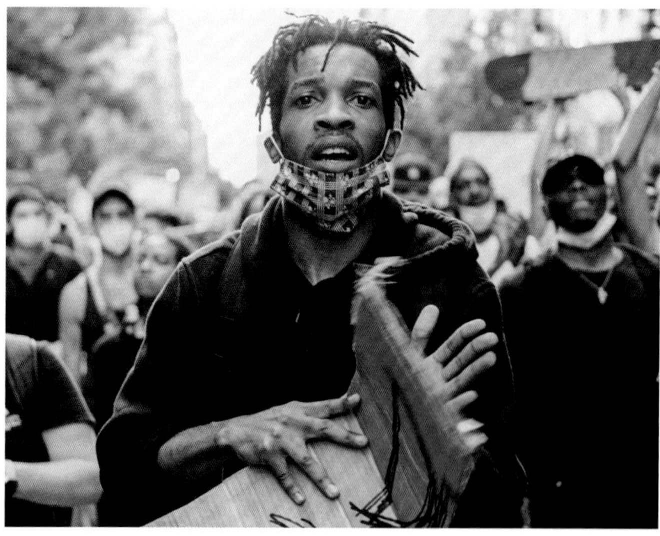

This page, from top:
*An American Flag with the Words "I Cant Breathe" Flown during a Black Lives
Matter Protest on the Brooklyn Bridge in Brooklyn, NY, 2020*
Black Lives Matter Protestor Chanting during a March in Manhattan, NY, 2020
Opposite: *Young Child at a Black Lives Matter Rally Holds a Sign That Reads
"Don't Kill My Dad!!!", 2020*

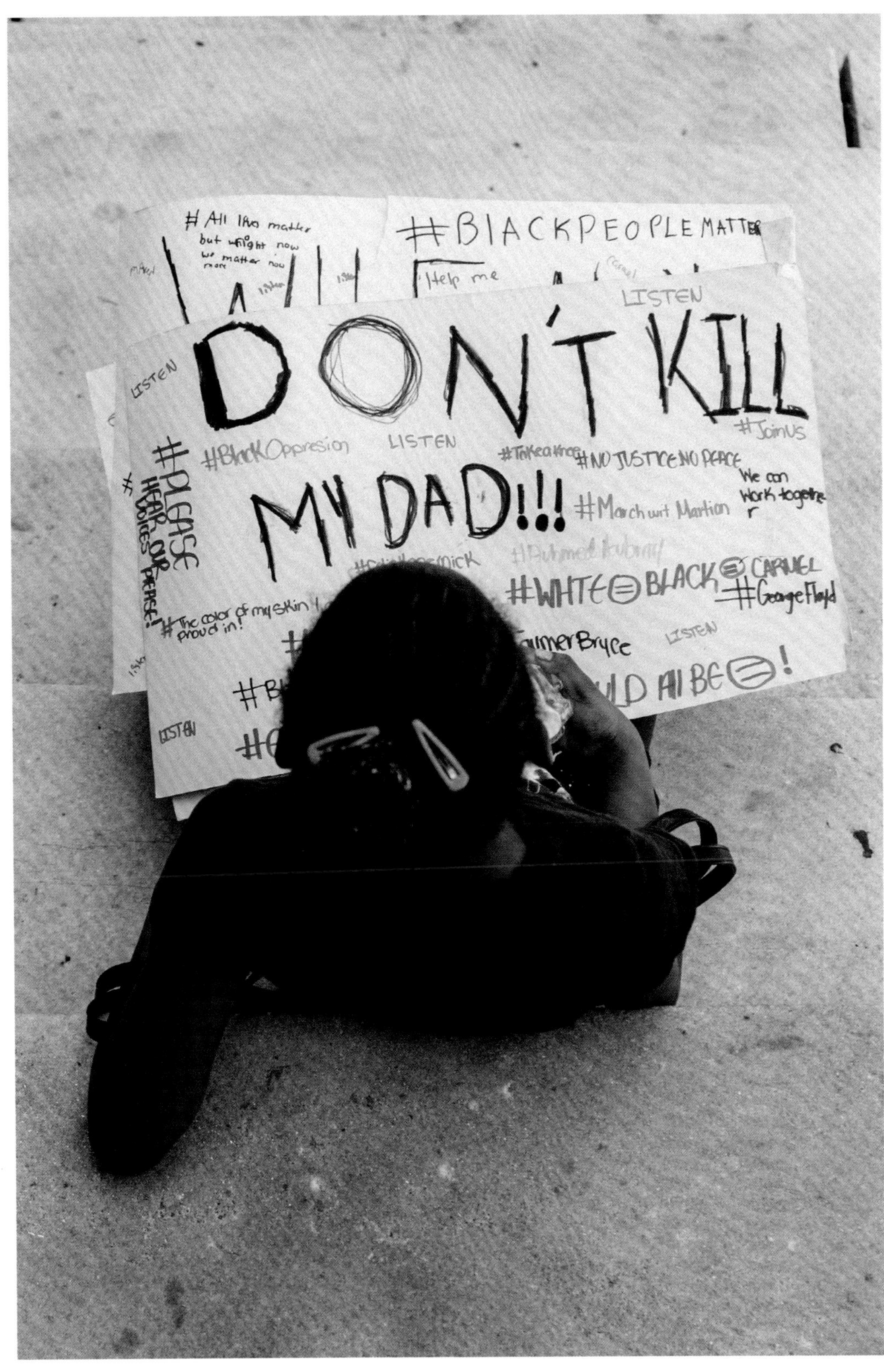

All lives matter but right now we matter now more
#BLACKPEOPLEMATTER
Help me
LISTEN
DON'T KILL
#JoinUs
LISTEN
#Black Oppresion
LISTEN
#Takeaknee
#NO JUSTICE NO PEACE
We can work together
#PLEASE HEAR OUR VOICES PLEASE!
MY DAD!!!
#March wit Martian
#George Floyd
#WHTE = BLACK = CARMEL
#The color of my skin I proud in!
#Aumer Bryce
LISTEN
LD All BE =!
LISTEN

Emeka Okereke

How to Reimage Blackness

In 2019, Lagos and Berlin-based multidisciplinary artist Emeka Okereke held an exhibition called *Reimaging Futures: A Trans-Nigerian Conversation*. What is the difference between "reimagining" and "reimaging"? The former means to conceptualize something in a different way; in the context of art created by underrepresented or marginalized communities, reimagining is a word that pops up often. To reimage, however, is to specifically create a new *image* of something.

Okereke's multimedia approach, which involves not only photography but also filmmaking and even academia, is all about creating new images of Blackness and Africanness. In an essay written for Invisible Borders, the artist-led photography initiative he created with fellow artist Uche Okpa-Iroha in 2009, he discusses the subjectivity of Blackness. He writes that while the word "Black" connects the diaspora, he is concerned that it threatens to become too narrow and synonymous with one experience, creating a hierarchy of Blackness around the globe. He refers to a perceived dominance of African American experiences and narratives when it comes to what is often called Black art. Instead, he advocates for a constant artistic and intellectual interaction between all Black peoples and an engagement with Africa not only as an idea but a reality, writing: "Africa as a location cannot be an abstraction."

This longstanding idea is what pushed Okereke while studying at the École Nationale Supérieure des Beaux-Arts in Paris to base his final-year project in Mozambique as a challenge to his tutors and what he saw as an overbearing insistence on a Western perspective.[8] His ongoing series *As We Recede* focuses on the past, present and future of Nigeria. It looks at the events that shaped the country, including its naming in 1914, its independence in 1960 and the Nigerian-Biafran war. Collecting personal memorabilia such as documents, money, jewellery, clothes and photographs, Okereke makes relics of them, preserving the stories from the 14 states he travelled through during his trans-Nigerian road trip.

Here We Think Only of the Beginning of Things (2016) is a triptych that depicts the River Benue bridge, symbolizing Nigeria's "amalgamation" but also the enduring regional tensions, which makes Okereke's use of "amalgamation" over "unification" a poignant choice.[9] In the third photo, a couple looks out towards the water. Are they hopeful, wistful, sad, nostalgic? We cannot see their faces, only the head of the female leaning on the shoulder of the male, with the title giving us an impression of their thoughts. We can also ask, considering the history of the place in which the figures stand, if we are being invited to see the title as an expression of innocence.

> "He advocates for a constant artistic and intellectual interaction between all Black peoples and an engagement with Africa not only as an idea but a reality"

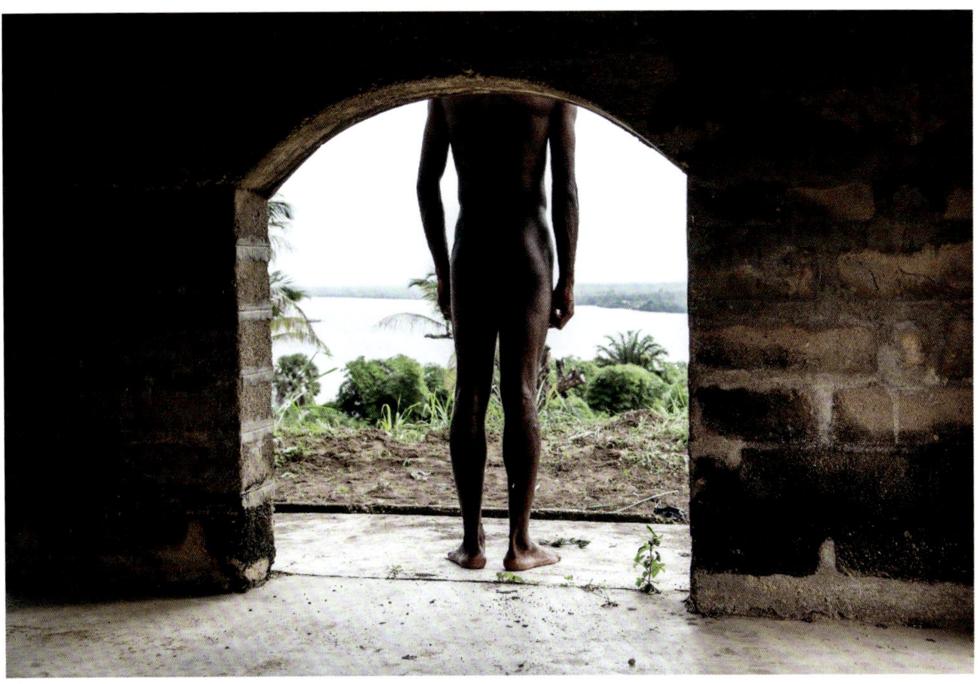

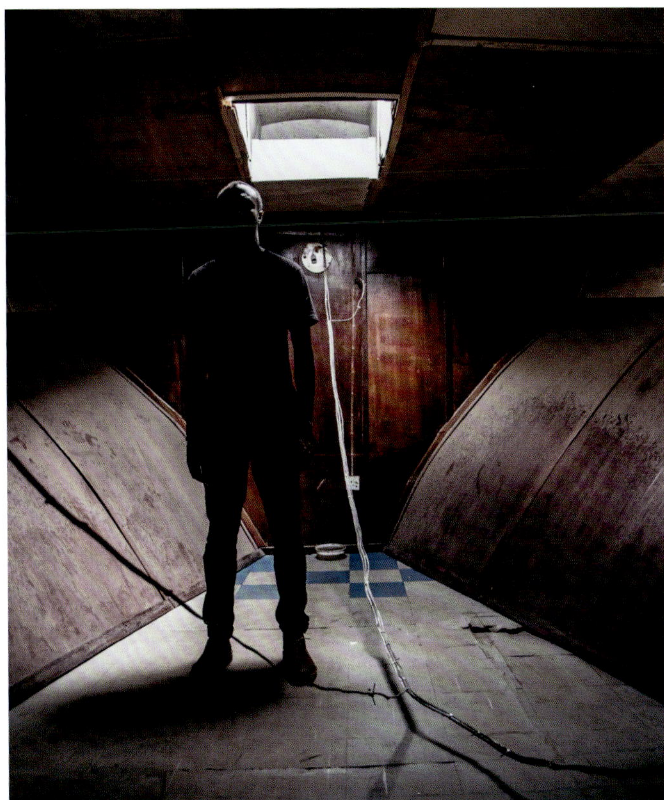

From top:
Ruptured Rupture, Hope Waddell Training
Institution (founded 1895), Calabar, 2016
Tapestry of Time (Inside NNS Bonny), War
Museum, Umuahia, Abia State, Nigeria
Both from *As We Recede*

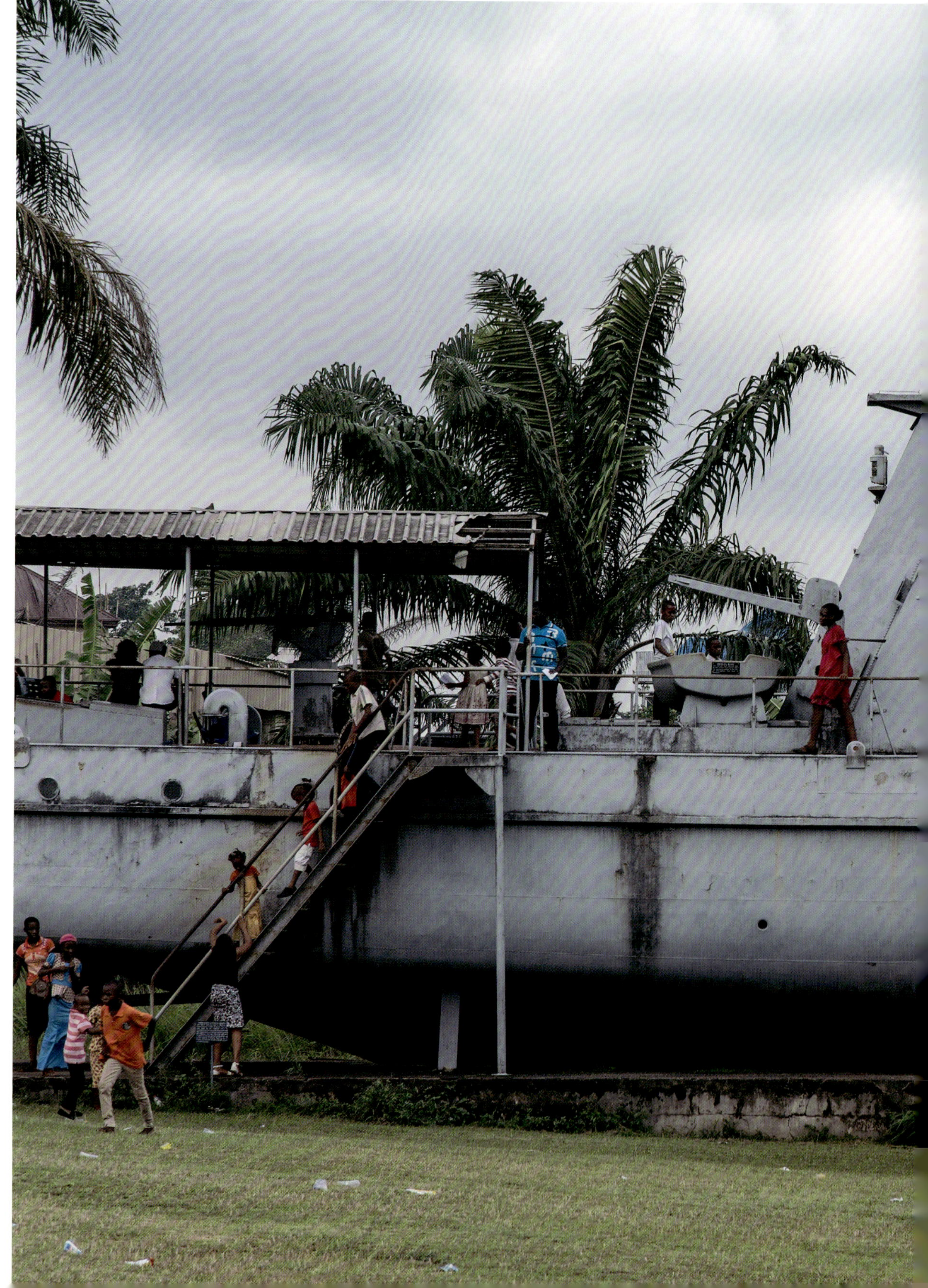

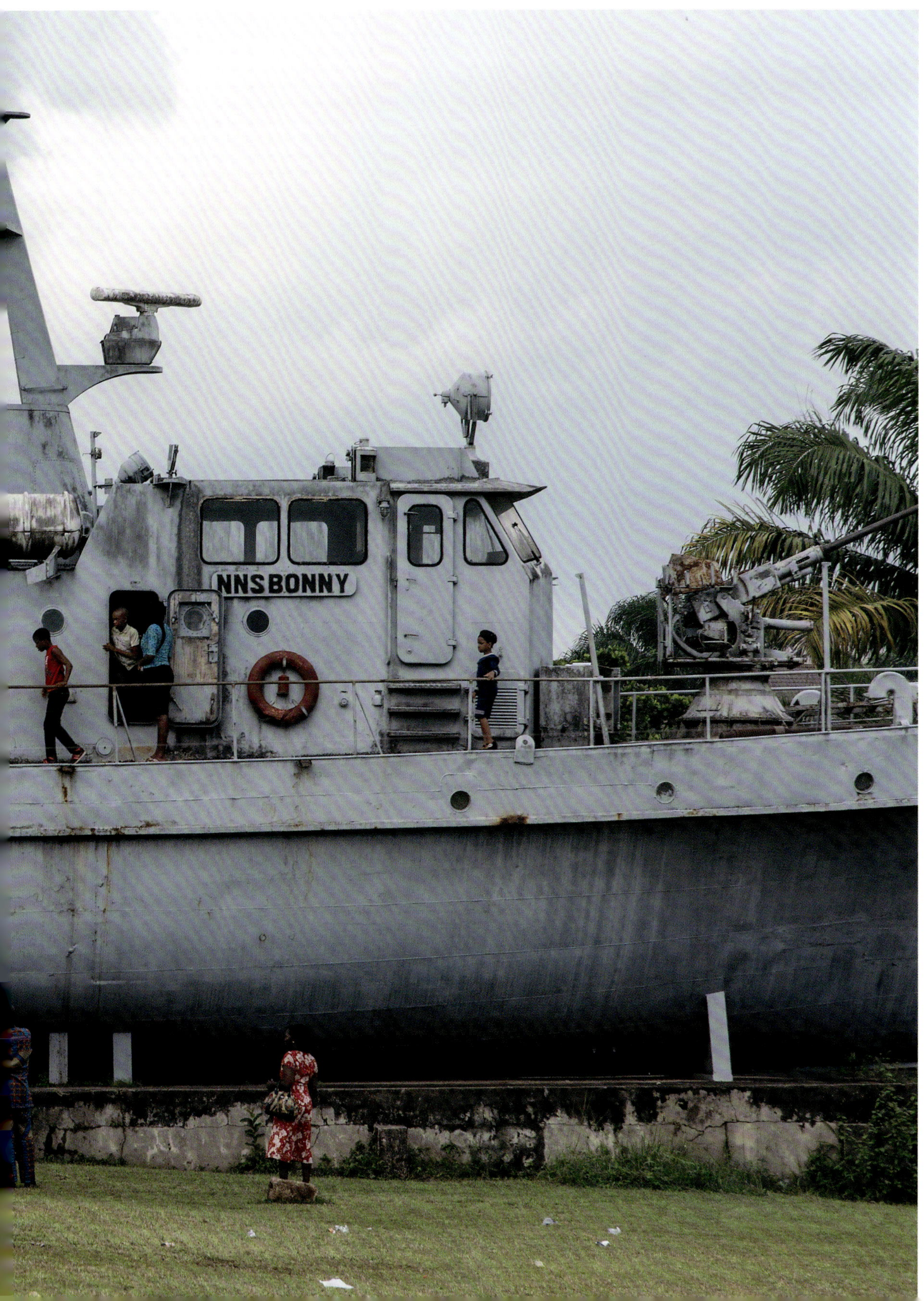

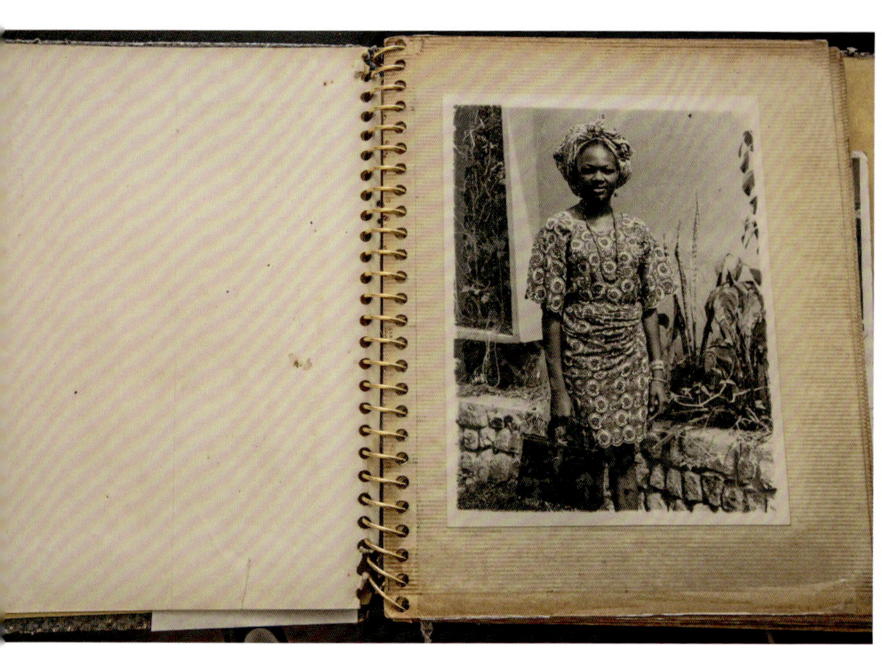

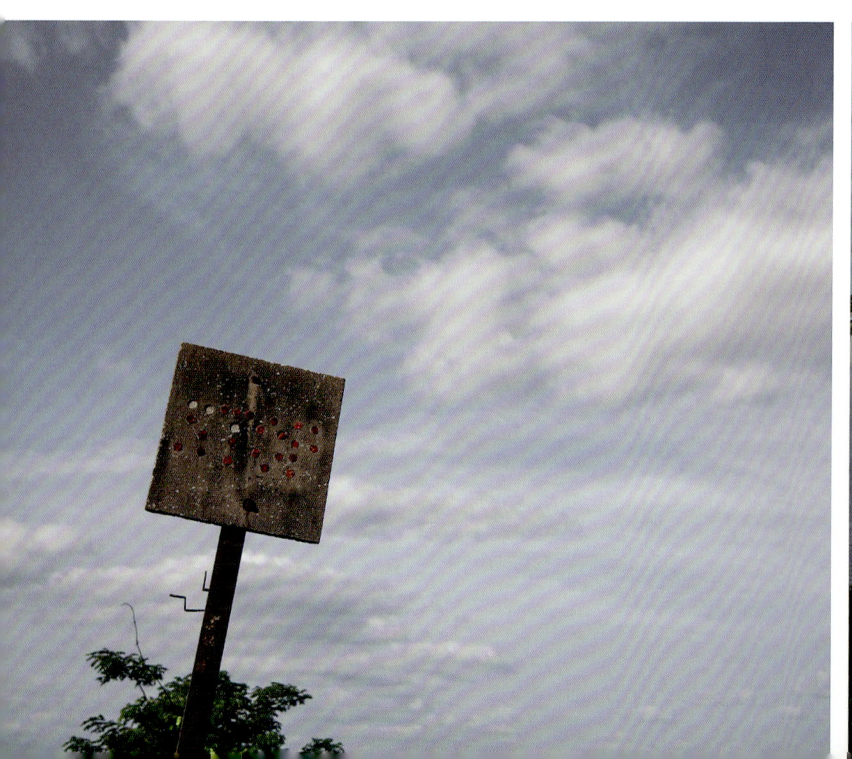

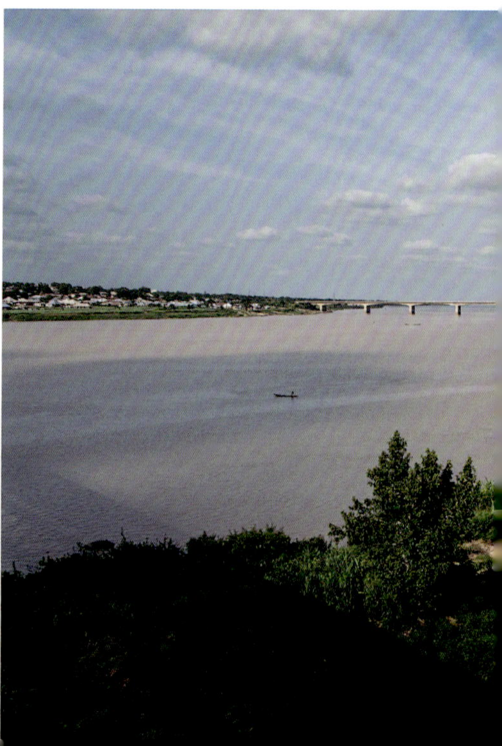

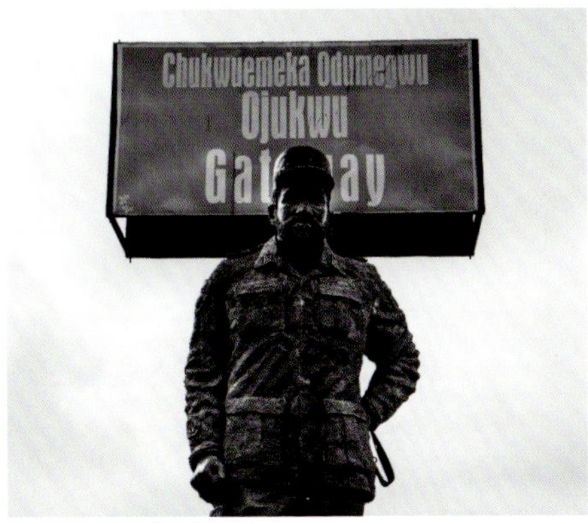

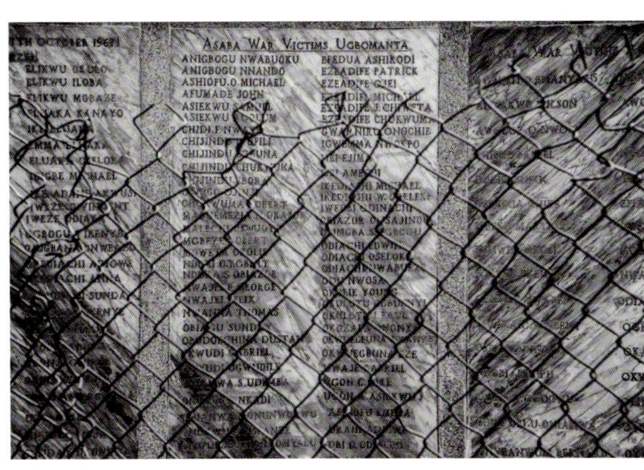

Previous spread: *Visit Time at the War Museum*
Umuahia, 2016
These pages, clockwise from left:
Mrs Effiong, Calabar, 2016
The Gateway, The Niger Bridge, Onitsha, 2016
As We Recede, 2016
Here We Think Only of the Beginning of Things, River
Benue Bridge, Makurdi, 2016
All from *As We Recede*

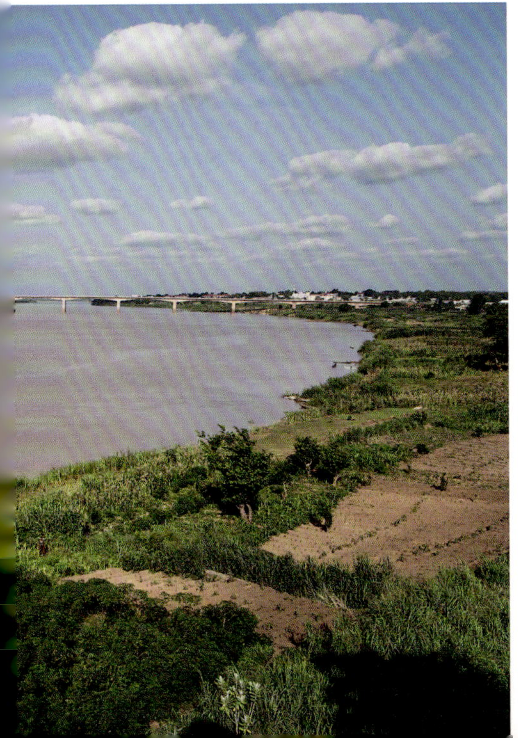

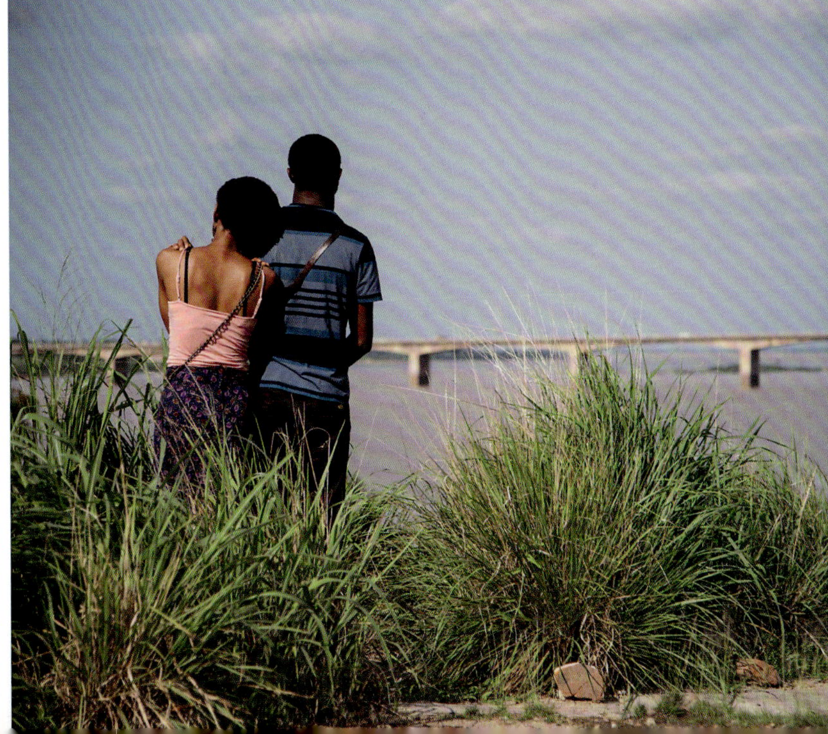

Lina Iris Viktor

Gold Is Light

Lina Iris Viktor is a British-Liberian multidisciplinary artist based in New York, who came to visual art after initially studying theatre at Sarah Lawrence College and then filmmaking and photography at the School of Visual Arts. Her paintings, which often incorporate photographic self-portraits, are known for their bold use of colour – jewel blues, bloody maroons, stark primordial blacks – and 24-carat gold leaf. They draw on mythological narratives, referring to the spiritual cultures of ancient civilizations but also colonial history with an Afro-futuristic slant. In Viktor's work, gold is light, magic, mystical. The properties that make it valuable regain their metaphorical significance in her work: its malleability, its lustre, its longevity.

In her series *A Haven, A Hell, A Dream Deferred* (2018) – a reference to the poem 'Harlem' by Langston Hughes – Viktor created 12 works exploring the "mythicized history" of Liberia, the West African nation founded in 1822 by the American Colonization Society and touted as a refuge for free Black people and the formerly enslaved. The works take aim at this idea, wanting to bring attention to the other, less-explored reasons for Liberia's founding, among which was fear of Black retaliation in America after slavery. Viktor uses the colour scheme of blue, red and gold, colours that take on heavy significance considering the history of the West Coast of Africa: blue for the ocean, red for blood and gold for the valuable resource that brought so many to its shores. In *First*, a woman sits on a stool, her partially bared back turned to us. The stool, reminiscent of those made for monarchs in the Akan culture of Ghana, confers a sense of the regal. Viktor's works are both a tribute to and a questioning of the power of iconography – the meaning of symbols across time. Which images persist and why? *Eleventh* borrows iconography from a map of Liberia, traced out in gold and overlaid with palm fronds and a patterned print. The creation of the map and the geopolitical tensions it represents are brought to the forefront despite their presence as the background of the paintings.

The self-portraits incorporated in Viktor's works are inspired by warriors, goddesses and strong female figures from ancient civilizations. In this act, she also mythologizes herself, placing herself throughout time, the past, the present and the future, blurring temporal boundaries; an act that aligns with her belief that "there is no centre" and that the tendency to group things rigidly should be resisted.

> "They draw on mythological narratives, referring to the spiritual cultures of ancient civilizations, but also colonial history with an Afro-futuristic slant"

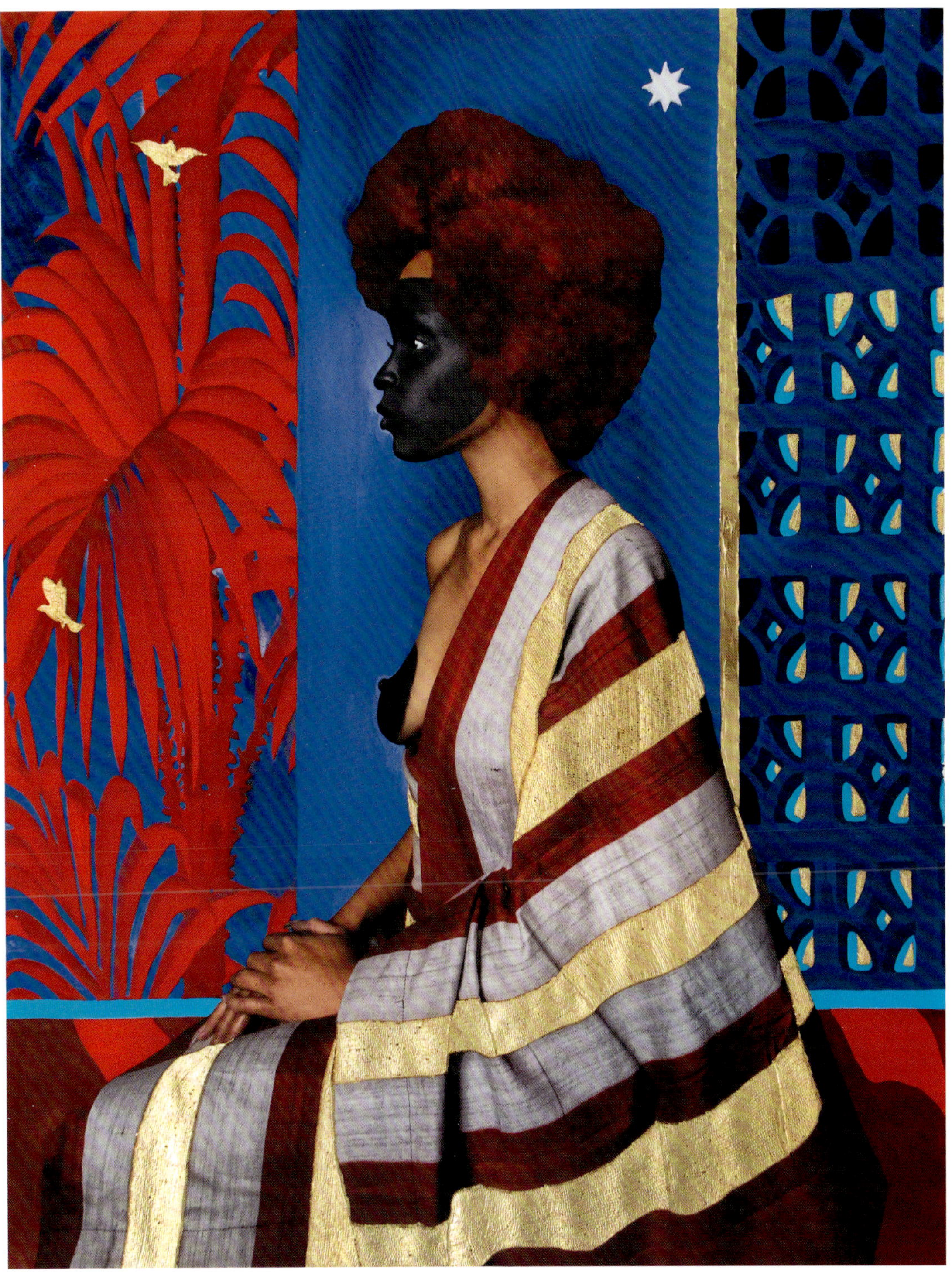

Eighth, 2018, from *A Haven, A Hell, A Dream Deferred*

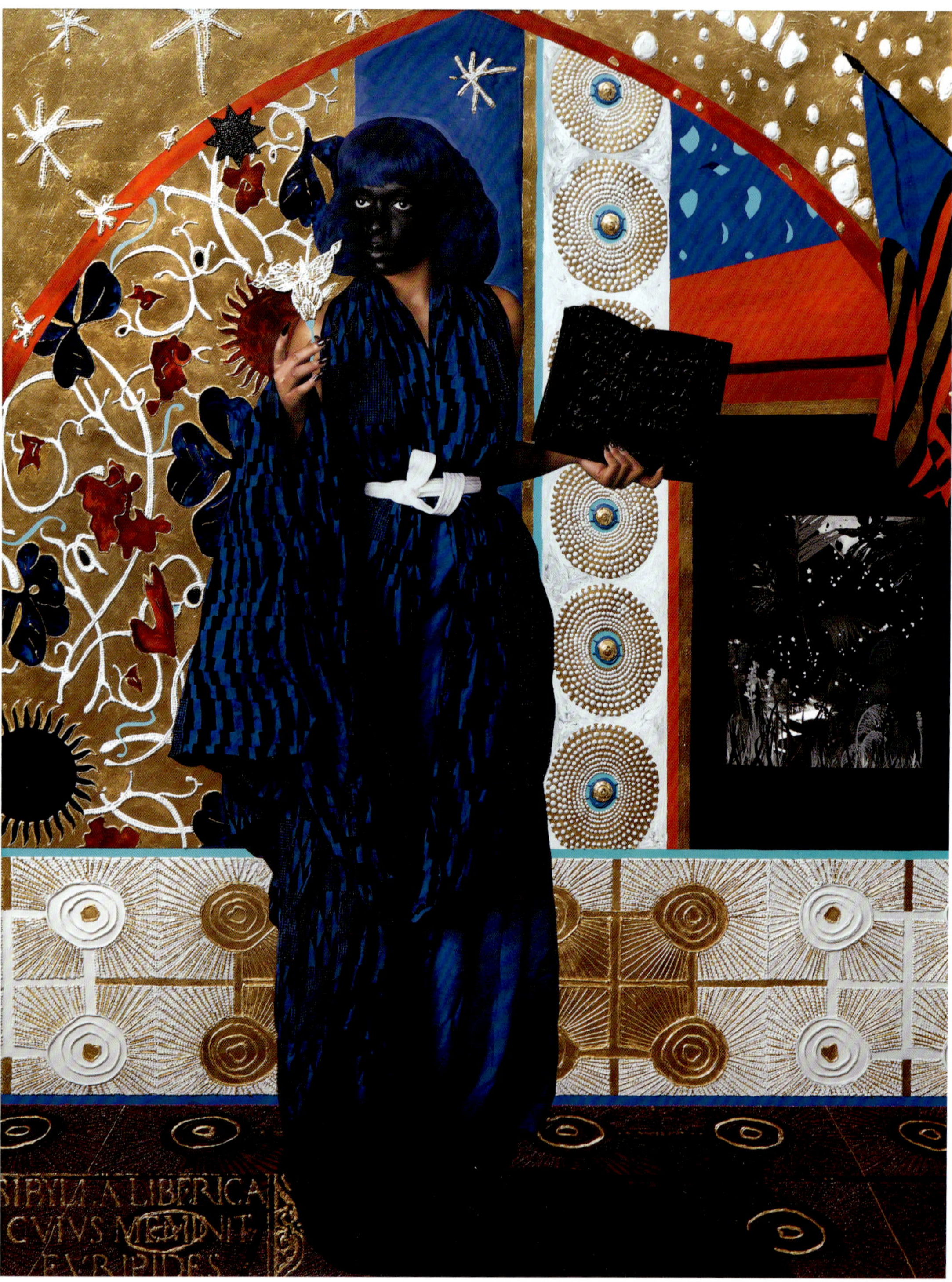

Fourth, 2017–18, from *A Haven, A Hell, A Dream Deferred*

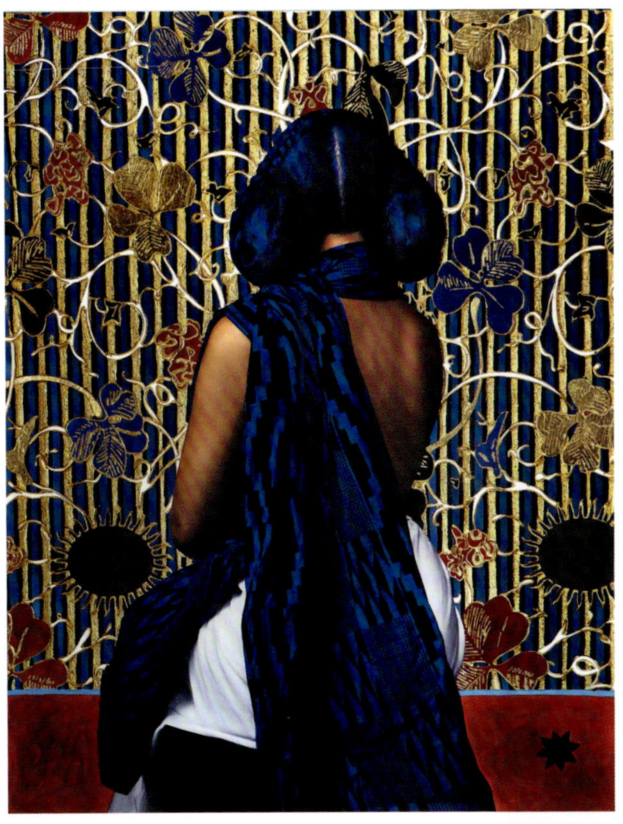

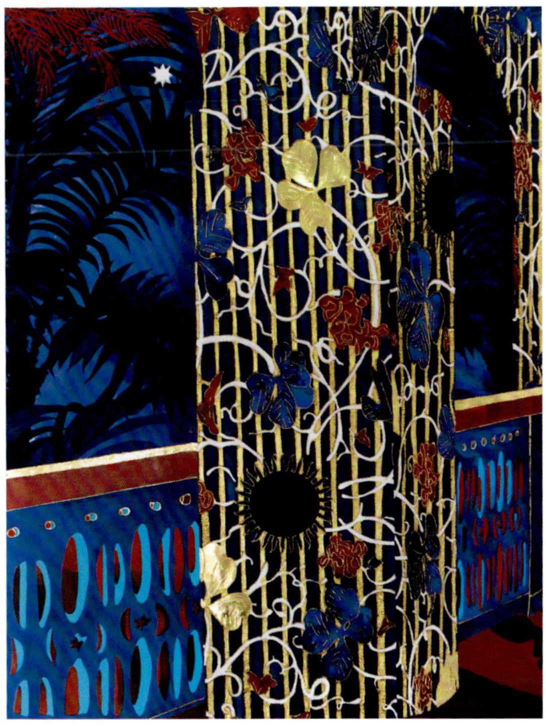

From top:
First, 2017–18
Fifth, 2018
Both from *A Haven, A Hell, A Dream Deferred*

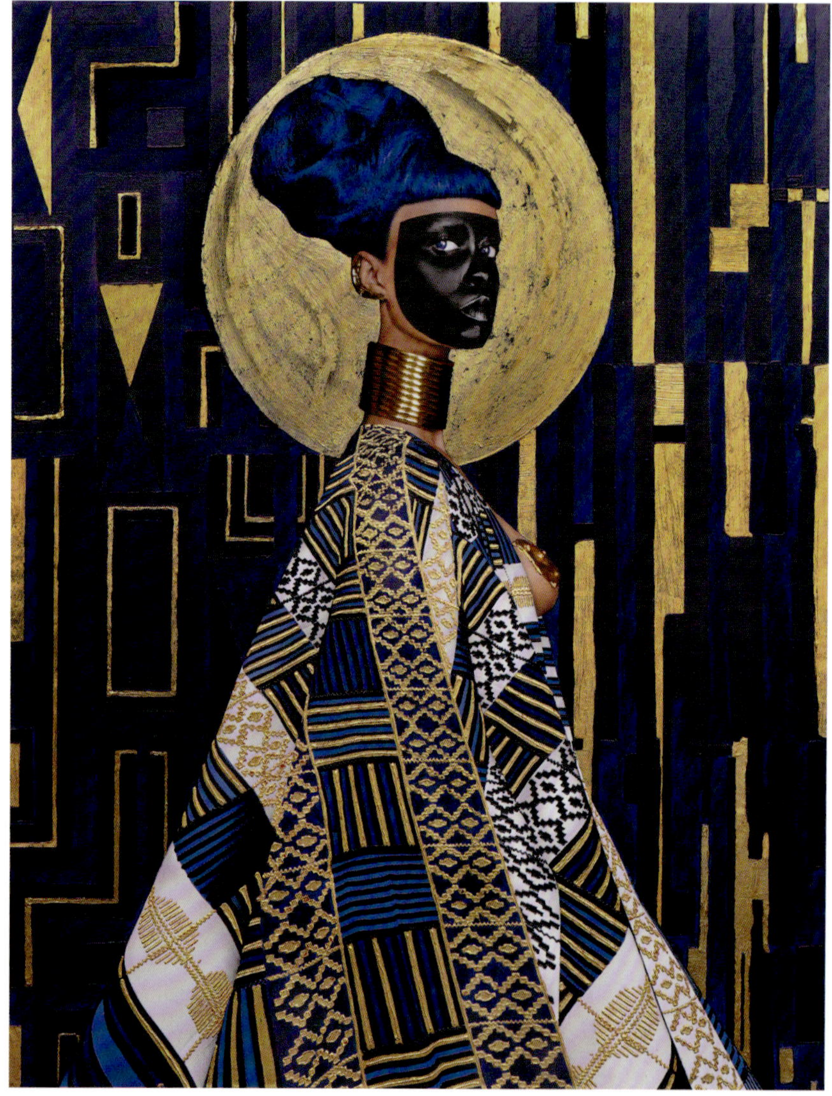

This page: *Syzygy*, 2015
Opposite: *Eleventh*, 2018, from *A Haven, A Hell, A Dream Deferred*

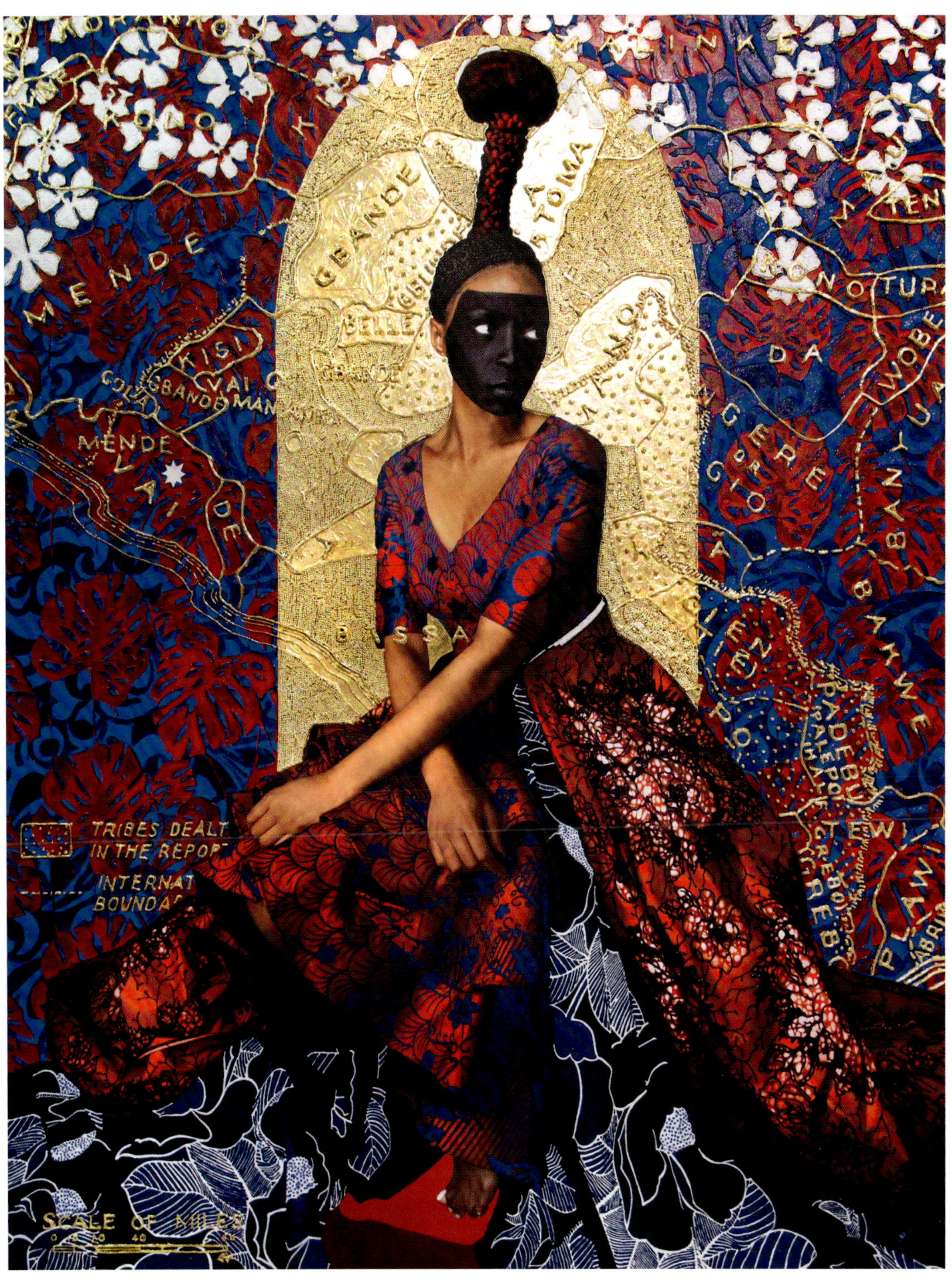

MENDE
KISI
MENDE
GBANDE
BELLE
BUSSA
TRIBES DEALT
IN THE REPORT
INTERNAT
BOUNDA
TOMA
BANWE
SCALE OF MILES

Braylen Dion

Romance and Ritual

Atlanta-based photographer and filmmaker Braylen Dion creates romantic, retro-inspired scenes and portraits with the desire to present Blackness in a "more soft or calming way", as he told *The Photographic Journal*.[10] The goal is to proliferate alternative images to the stereotypically negative representations of Blackness that revolve around aggression, exaggerated physical size and physical unattractiveness.

In his short film *complexion – being a black girl* (2018), Dion speaks to six young dark-skinned Black women about their self-perception and how others have treated them. The film's opening images include a close-up of an Afro and somebody braiding a young woman's hair. The use of slow motion allows the viewer to take in the lovingness of the act, and supposedly mundane actions are imbued with extra significance, romanticized and made almost ritualistic. The girls speak about being taunted for the darkness of their skin, being called a "roach" and being warned not to be "too dark". There is a pivot as they begin to talk about when they realized how the internalization of European beauty standards had made other Black people denigrate their darkness and even their own.

"The apotheosis of the young Black man as an angel seems to overturn that narrative of young Black men being 'no angels'"

You could say that that awareness, which seemed to bring with it a newfound and defiant pride in the face of colourism, is what photographers like Dion envision as the eventual effect of their own work.

Dion's series *Dodging the Devil* takes its title from a song by American musician Mereba, which contains the very appropriate line "No ruler can size you", which in the context of Dion's work feels like a rebuke to any attempt at reducing what Black people can be. In this series, a young Black man appears as an angel sitting by a stream, white feathered wings sprouting from his bare back. In each of the photographs, his face is either completely obscured from view or partially hidden. Coupled with the cool, blue tone to the photos, the inaccessibility of the face – and therefore the eyes – creates the distance we associate with awe and reverence. And yet the images are still casual; they're impressive without being imposing. The apotheosis of the young Black man as an angel seems to overturn that narrative of young Black men being "no angels", and a sense of elevation can also be seen in an image where a baby is literally lifted up, the tight curls of his Afro like a little halo, his arms raised to the sky, his face obscured.

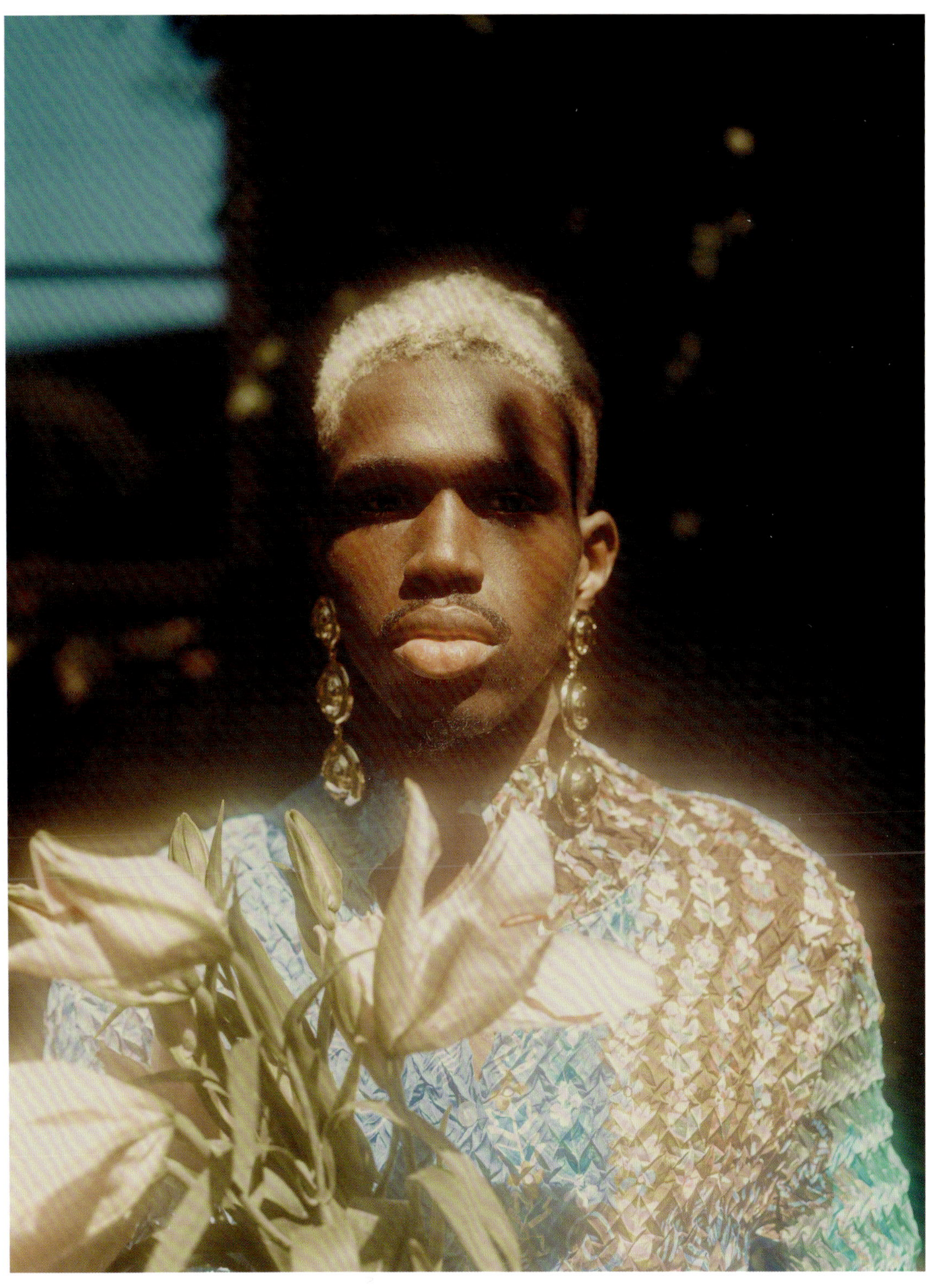

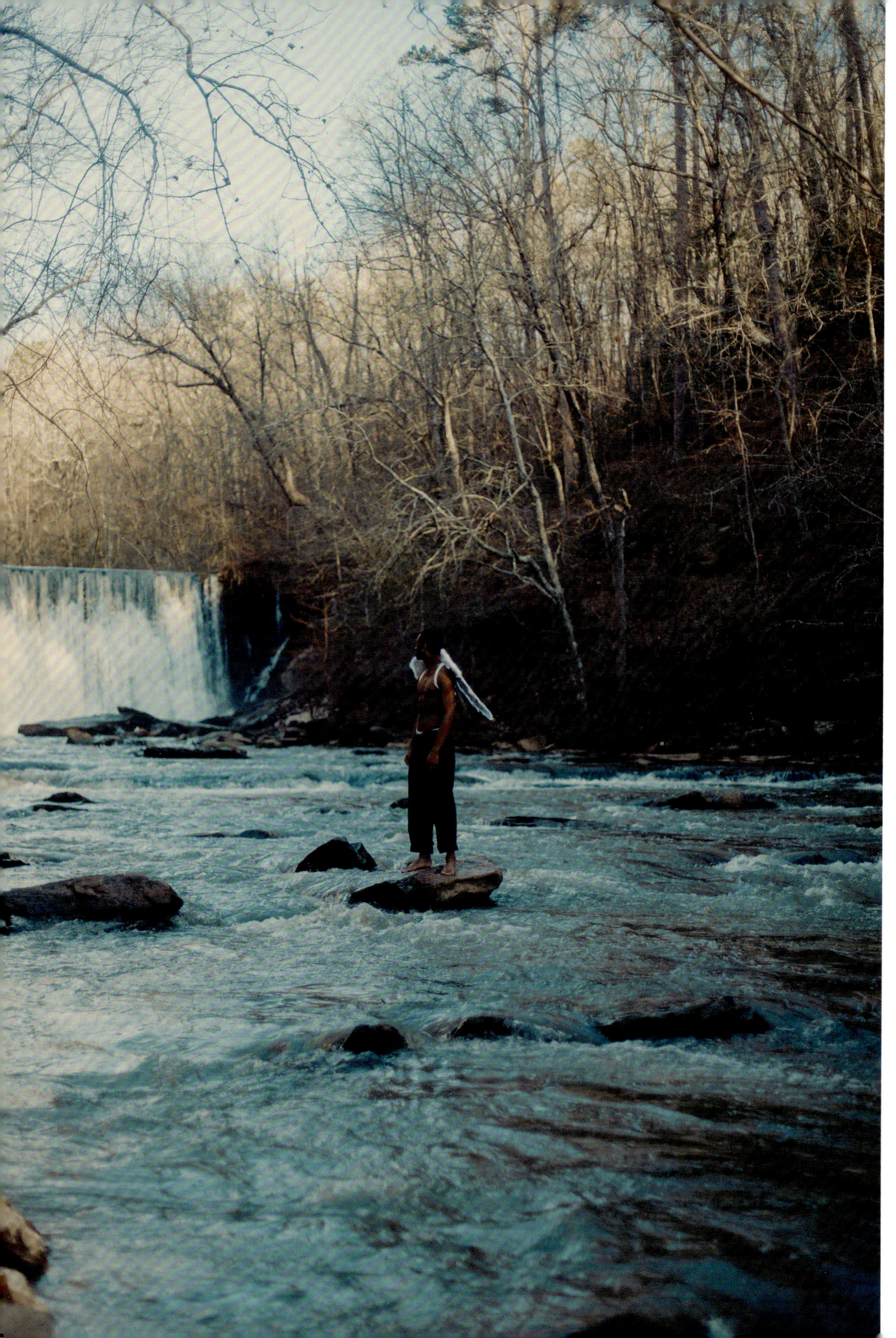

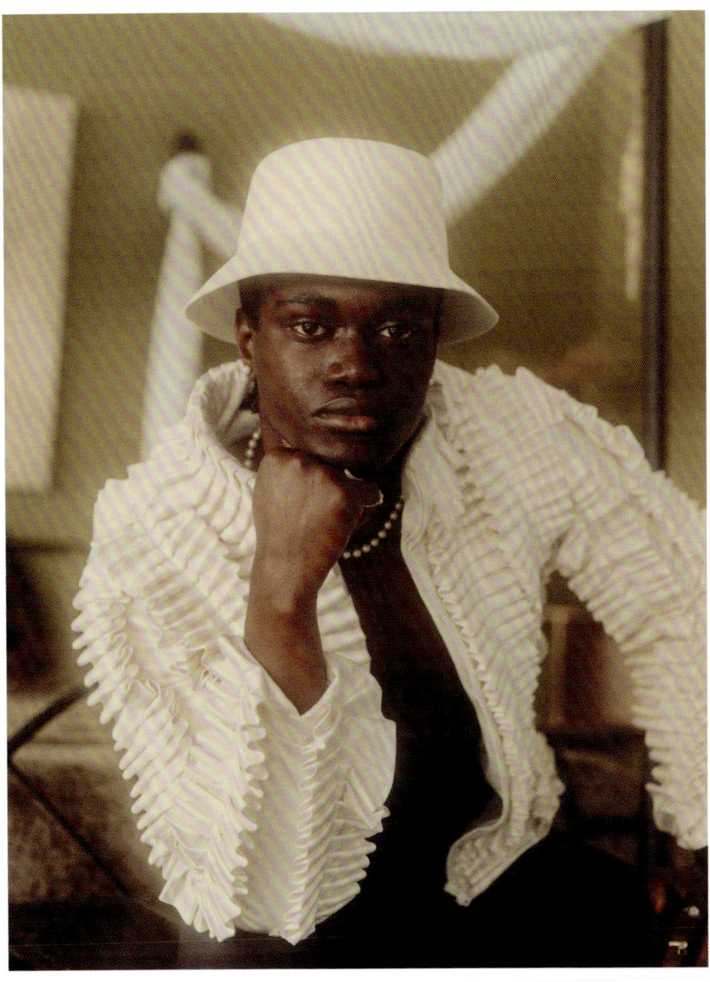

Previous spread:
Personal Work, October 2020
These pages, from left:
Personal Work, January 2020
Personal Work, April 2021
Personal Work, January 2020

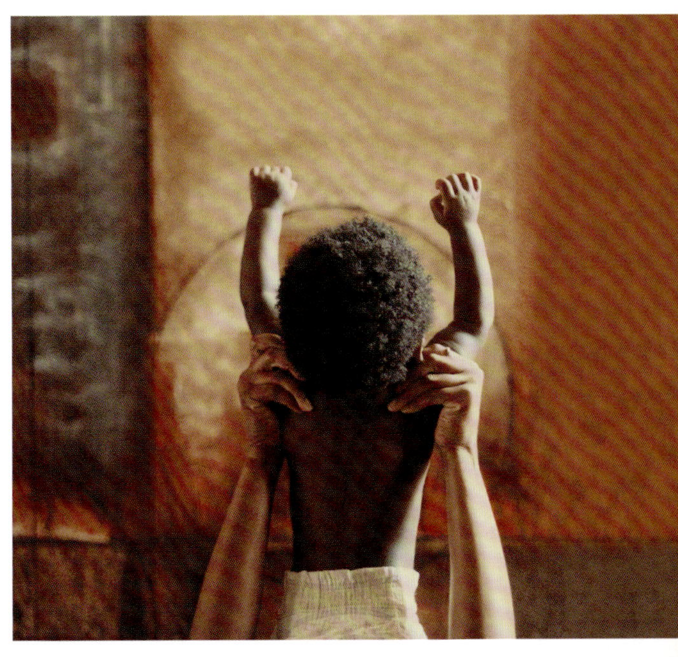

Girma Berta

The Hero's Journey

The self-taught Ethiopian artist Girma Berta is most known for his *Moving Shadows* series, in which he uses digital editing to blur street photography – taken with his iPhone – with fine art. Berta shoots the habitués of Addis Ababa going about their daily lives. His deft use of colour transforms their environments from streets and busy markets into vibrant, abstract landscapes. Rich solid hues, from lapis lazuli blue to royal purple, form the backdrops for Berta's subjects. Nothing else populates the scene save for their shadows, which cleverly create a sense of place in the void; the figures don't look as if they are floating in mid-air but are in another realm. This is also achieved through the sense of movement; his figures seem to be on the way somewhere. Some of the images have a painterly quality, while in others, the background looks like light caught on water, wisps of cloud in an otherwise clear sky or luxurious fabric. The word "authenticity" so often follows the words "street photography", often with the meaning of removing all sense of fantasy, curation and performance. Berta's photos challenge this and serve to ask us about the role of street photography in portraying the so-called "reality" of the places in which they are taken.

Berta once claimed in an interview with *Nataal* that his aim in documenting Addis Ababa and its people was to capture "the beautiful, the ugly and all that is in between".[11] But what does it mean to remove the people from the immediate context of their surroundings? What does removing his subjects from almost all sense of time and place do for them and for the viewer? What preconceptions are challenged or prevented from forming? Is universality the aim? The images do take on a grander, almost cosmic atmosphere. In the vast expanse of colour, many of the subjects' faces are fully or partially obscured, and the figures come to represent the human experience as we trudge along, carrying our loads to who knows where. There's a sense of an epic tale, a hero's journey. But Berta also demonstrates that, for him, an appeal to what is universal in the human experience doesn't require the generic. There is no denial of the Ethiopianness of his subjects; it is that Berta's treatment of them discourages an orientalist gaze determined to keep them as an Other for consumption instead of empathetic connection.

> "Berta's photos challenge this and serve to ask us about the role of street photography in portraying the so-called 'reality' of the places in which they are taken"

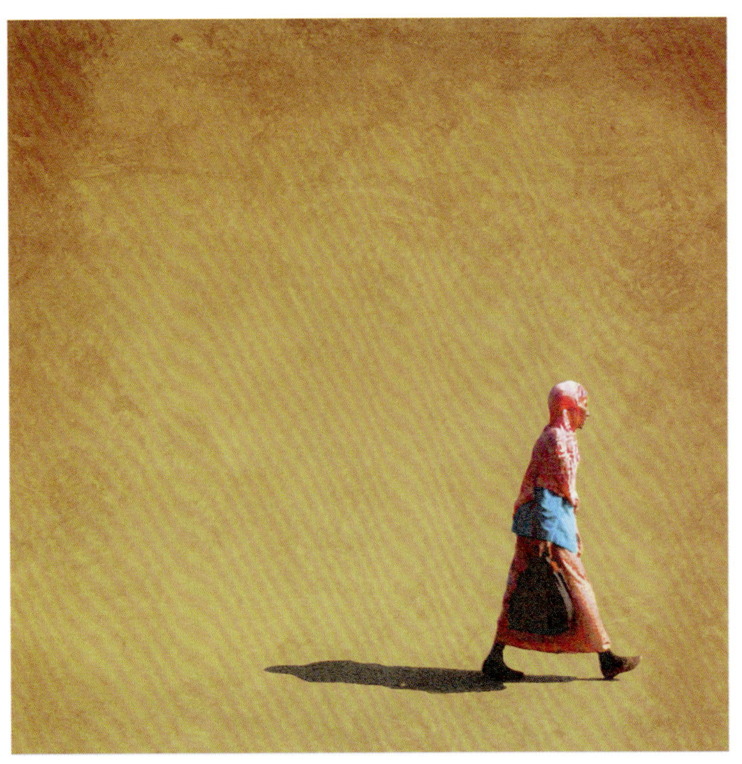

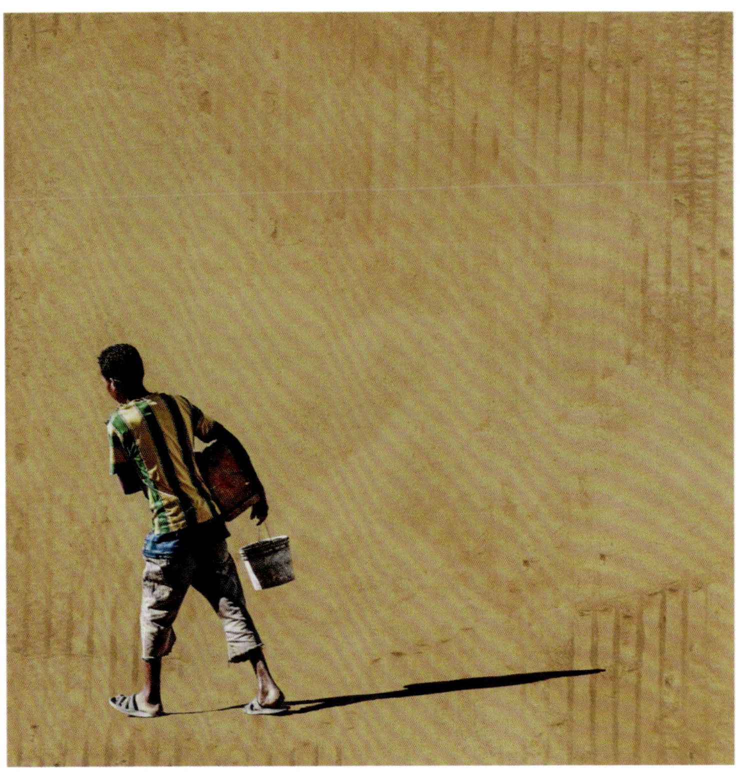

From top:
Moving Shadows I, XI, 2016
Moving Shadows II, V, 2017

As We See It

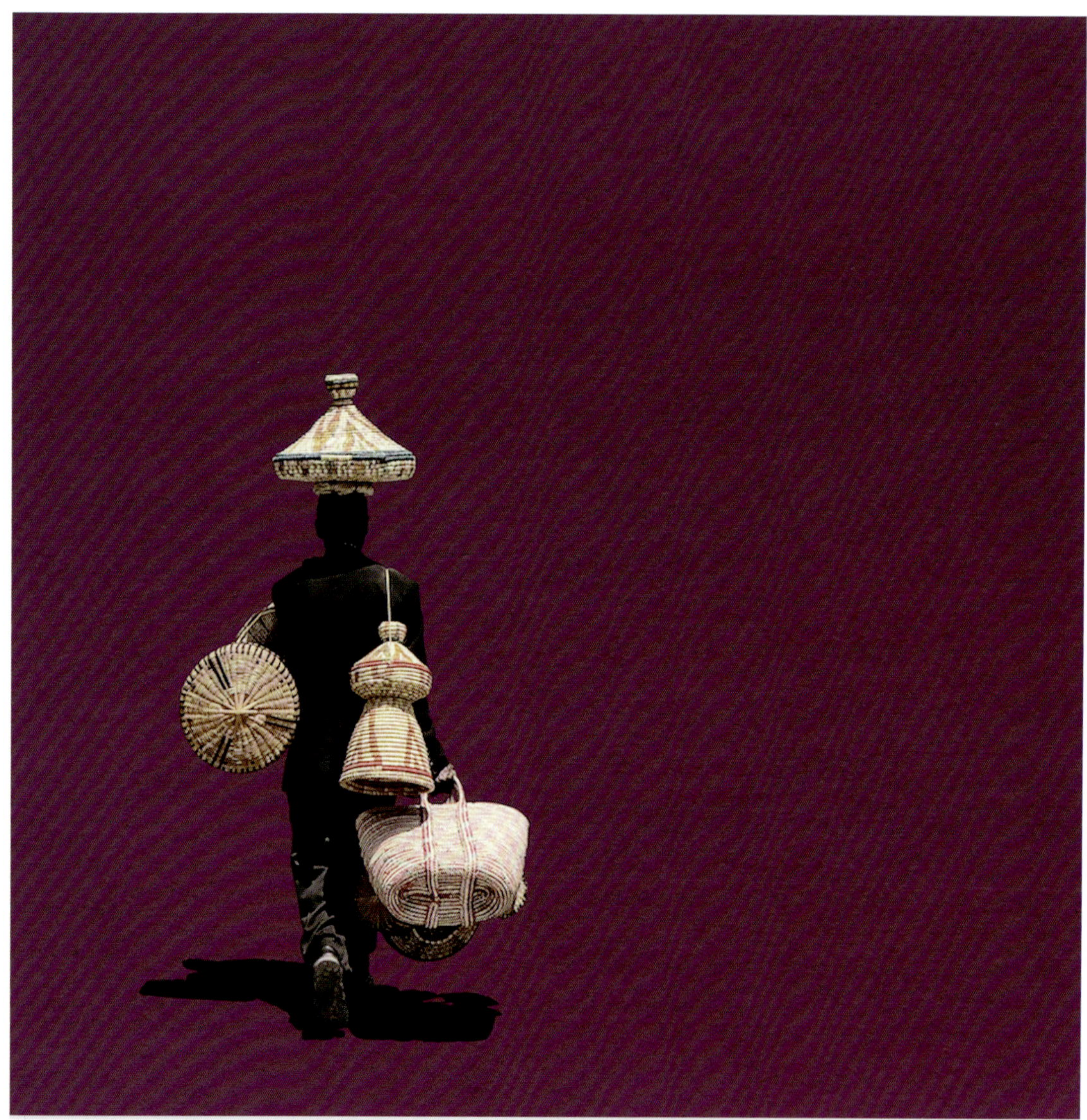

Moving Shadows II, XII, 2017

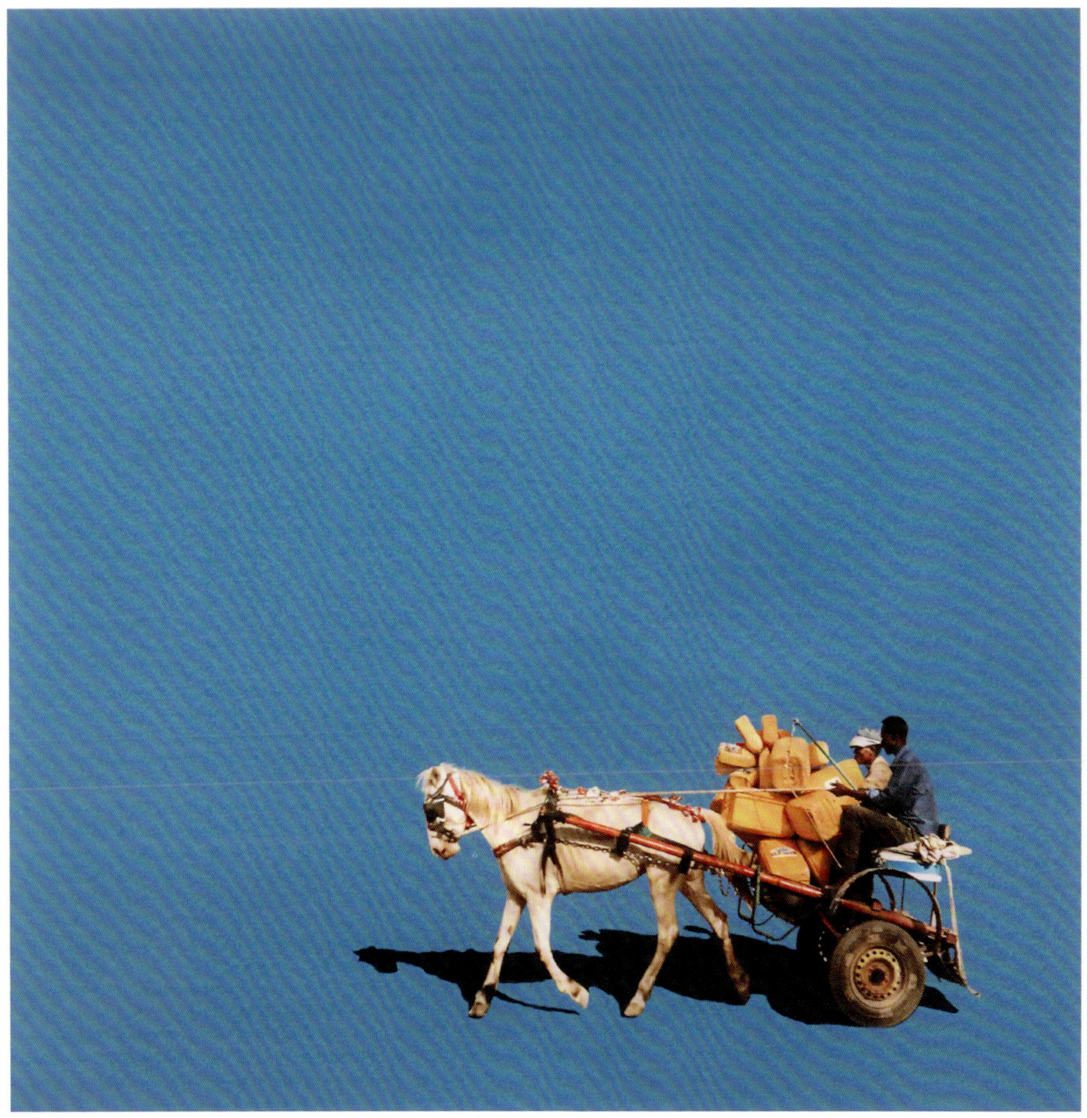

Moving Shadows II, VIII, 2017

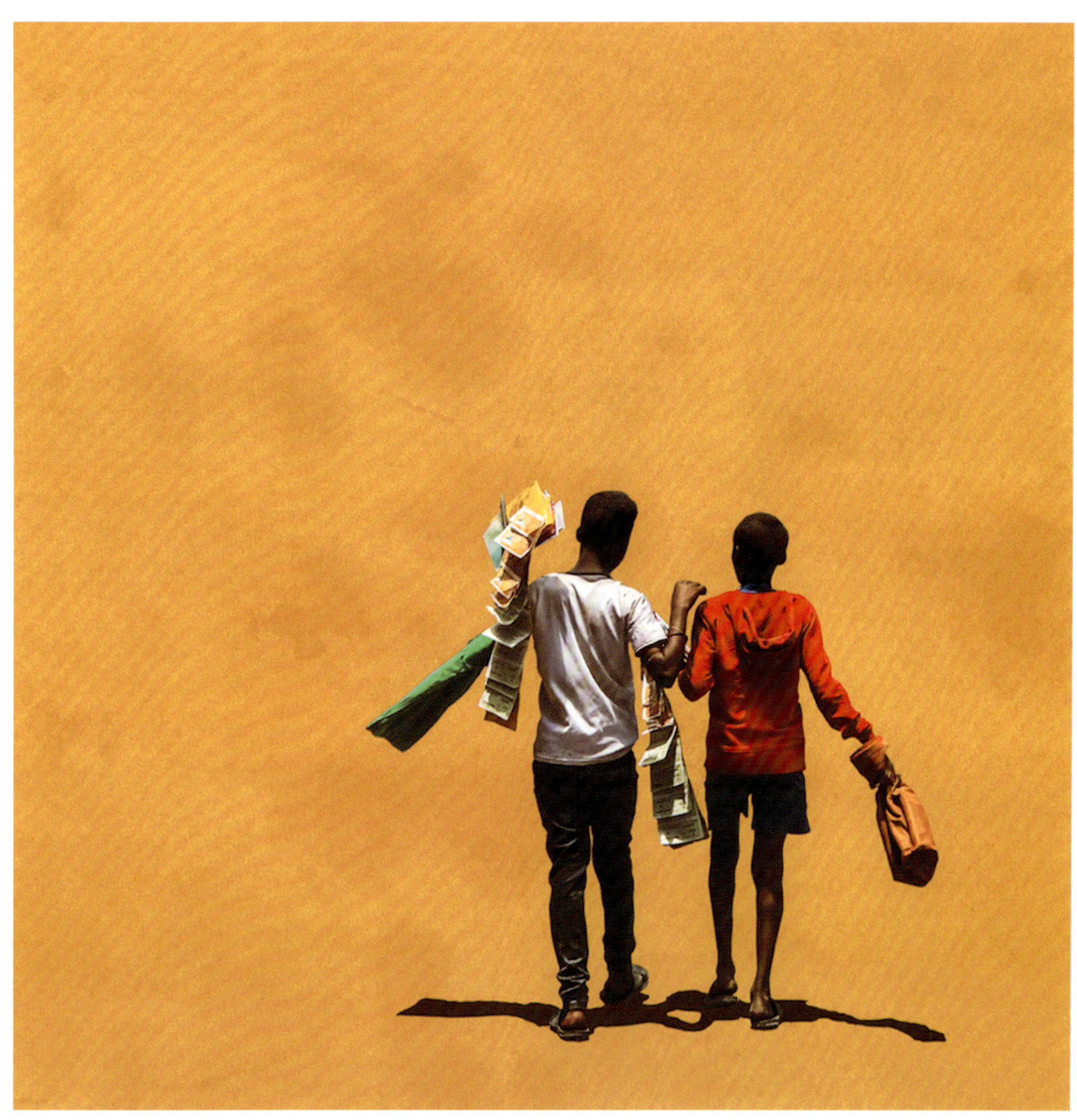

Moving Shadows II, X, 2017

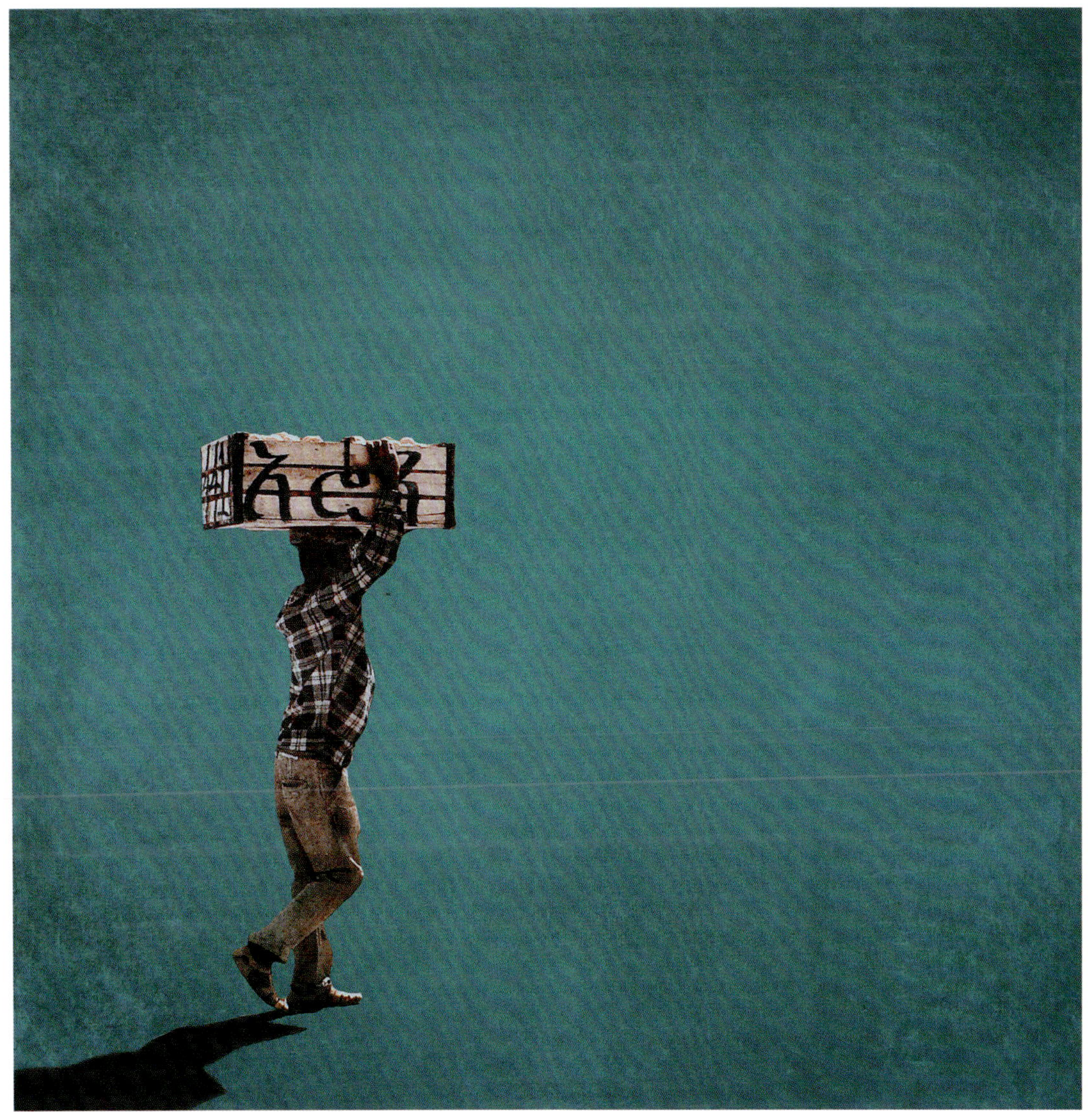

Moving Shadows I, XVII, 2016

Kenny Germé

Subversive Fantasies

In Paris-based photographer and stylist Kenny Germé's work, mainstays of popular culture, historical icons and mythic tropes are refreshed. In an editorial for *Interview* magazine, Germé worked with his friend and frequent collaborator, stylist Edem Dossou, to create a Black Marie Antoinette. In one image, the model poses with the trademark towering hair adorned with the outrageous accessory of a model ship. All the images are characteristically bold and imbued with fantasy, but there is also a knowing wink not just to the cultural reference but to the subversive act of its reinterpretation here. In another image, the model holds cotton stems like a bouquet of flowers. In yet another, she wields a scythe.

This sense of knowing quirkiness is also embodied in another *Interview* editorial in which Germé looks to our friends beyond the stars. Black models are transformed into extraterrestrial beings with huge, shiny black pupils, asymmetric hair, Maison Margiela masks and du-rags. It connects Blackness and alienness in a way that doesn't denigrate but takes a certain pride in that otherness; it almost seems to laugh at the norm. It is a reflection of an ethos that has led Germé not just to reinterpret old ideas but also, in the case of negative images surrounding Blackness, to challenge and subvert them.

Germé grew up in Drancy, a northeastern Paris suburb often demonized in French mainstream media, so he is no stranger to negative media narratives. During the lockdowns triggered by the COVID-19 pandemic, he came up with his *Godfather* series, inventing a nurturing character through which to examine aspects of Black masculinity. He utilizes neutral backgrounds and a minimalistic set-up. A little boy wears the blazer of the young man, the jacket dwarfing him. Germé uses fashion to explore status, the passage of time and the relationship between role model and mentee. The jacket fits the young man perfectly but hangs off the little boy. There is no attempt to present the child as a "mini-adult" but instead to emphasize the youth, innocence and potential to grow that must be protected. The image responds to the prevalent perception of young Black boys as much older than they are, to the point where boys not even in their teens are referred to as men, as we have seen in police brutality cases. "Male Black bodies have become a site for fantasy which diminishes them," Germé said to *Nataal*.[12] He doesn't baulk at fantasy but instead uses it as a tool to expand the ways in which Black men in particular are seen. For Germé, clothing, cultural references and a subtle nod to the expectations of the viewer combine to create compelling images that invite spectators to share his world.

> "In one image, the model poses with the trademark towering hair adorned with the outrageous accessory of a model ship"

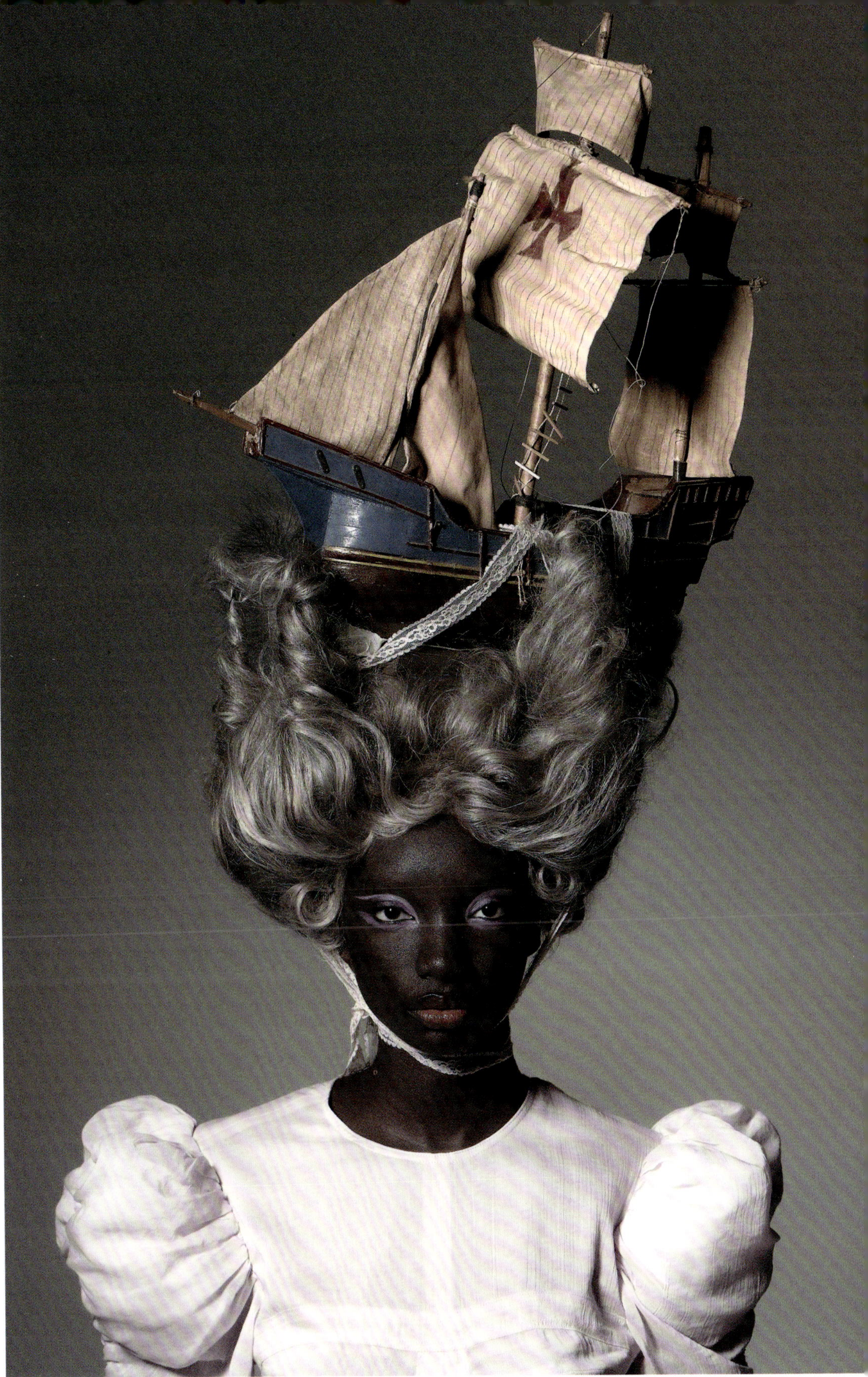

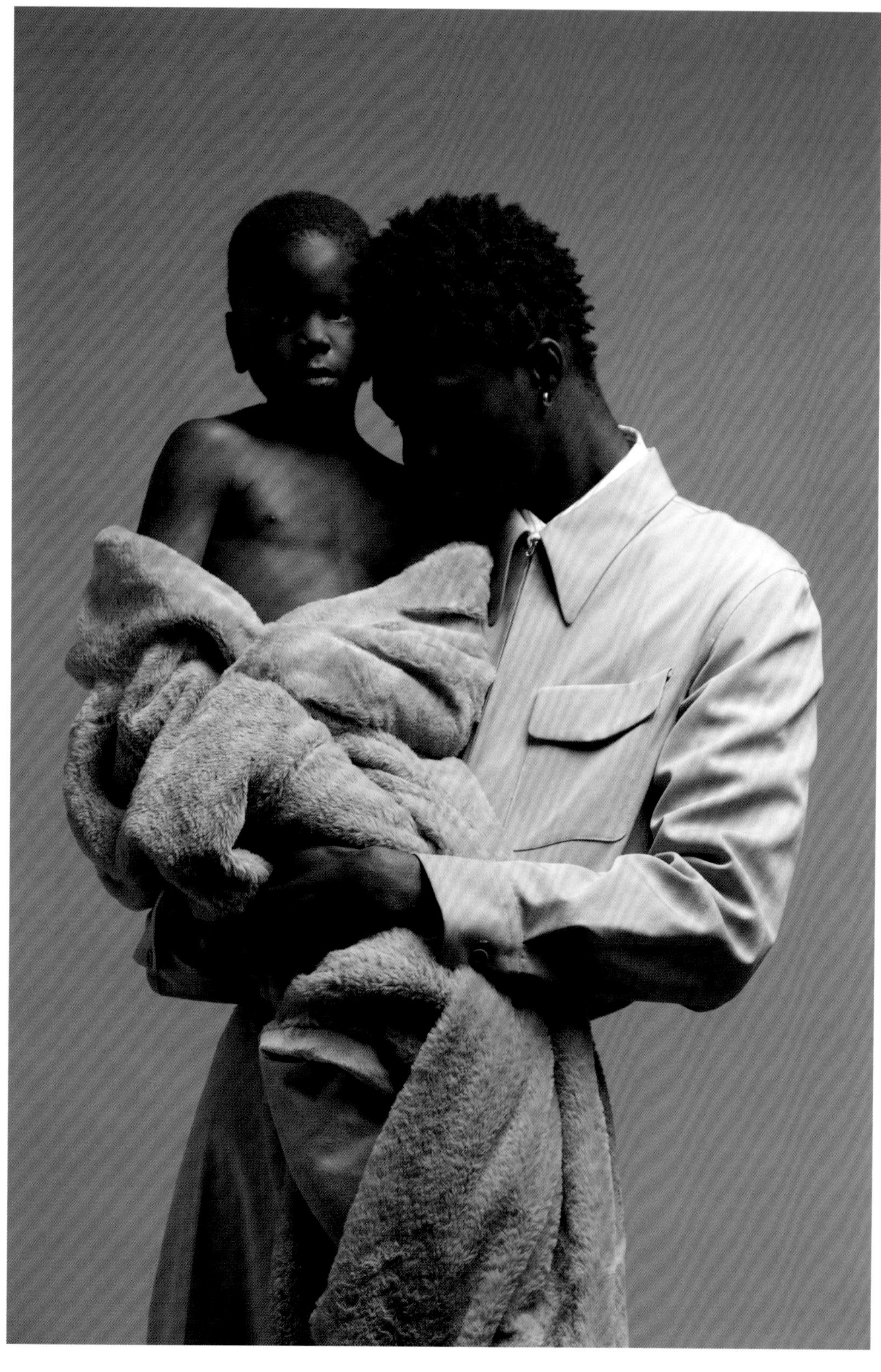

Previous spread: *Marie the Farmer*, 2021, *Interview* magazine
These pages: *The Godfather*, 2020, Highsnobiety

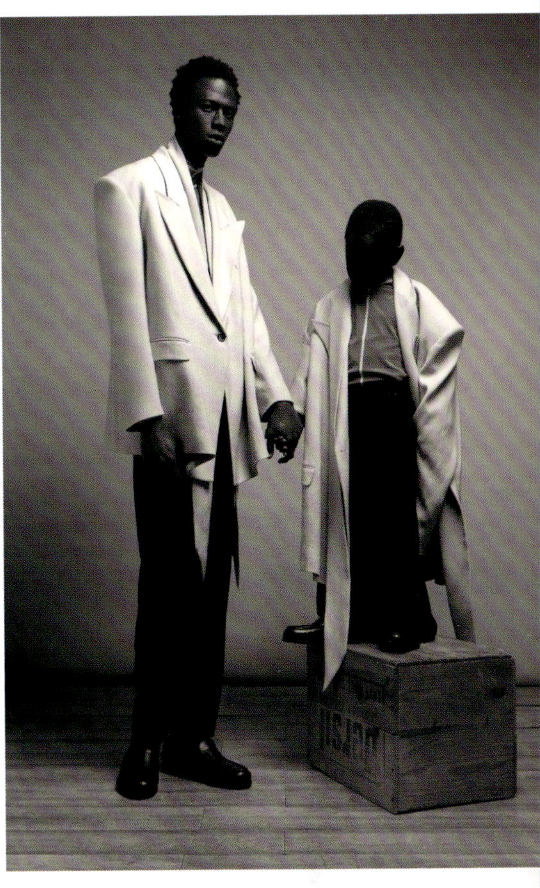

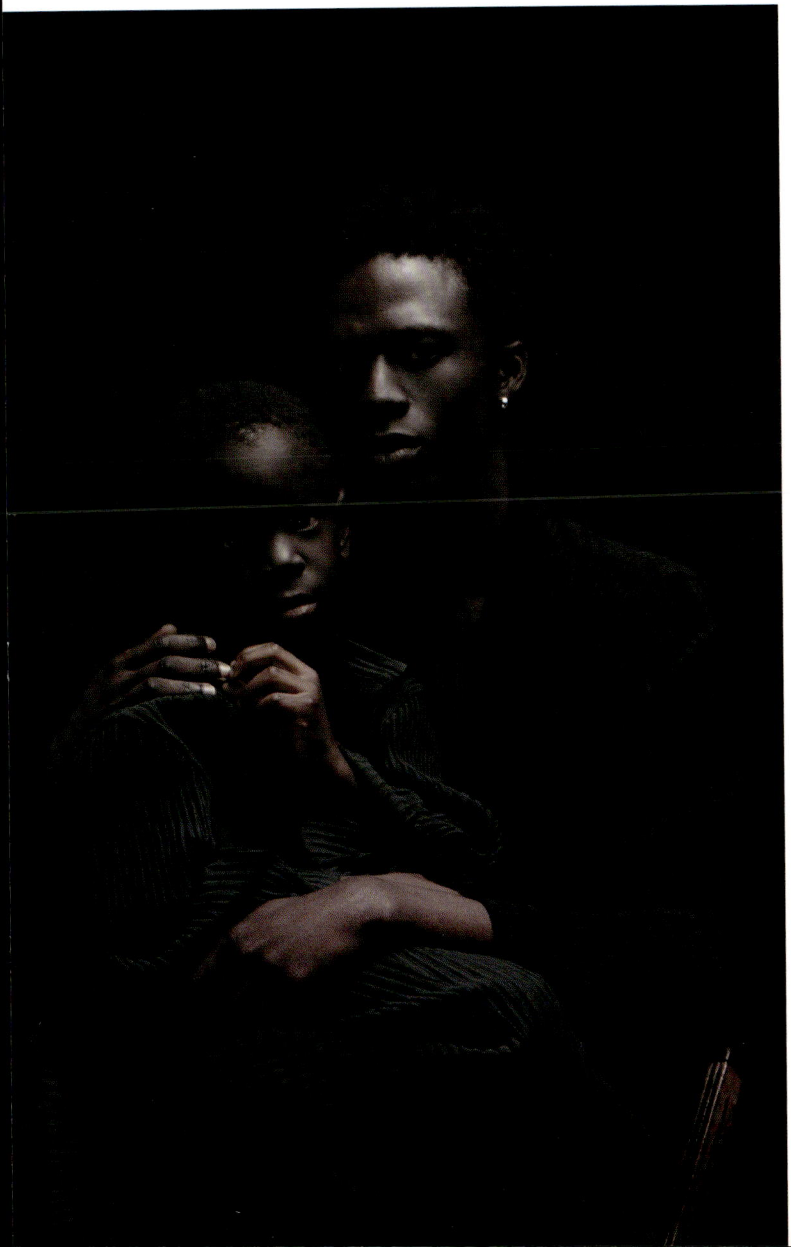

As We See It

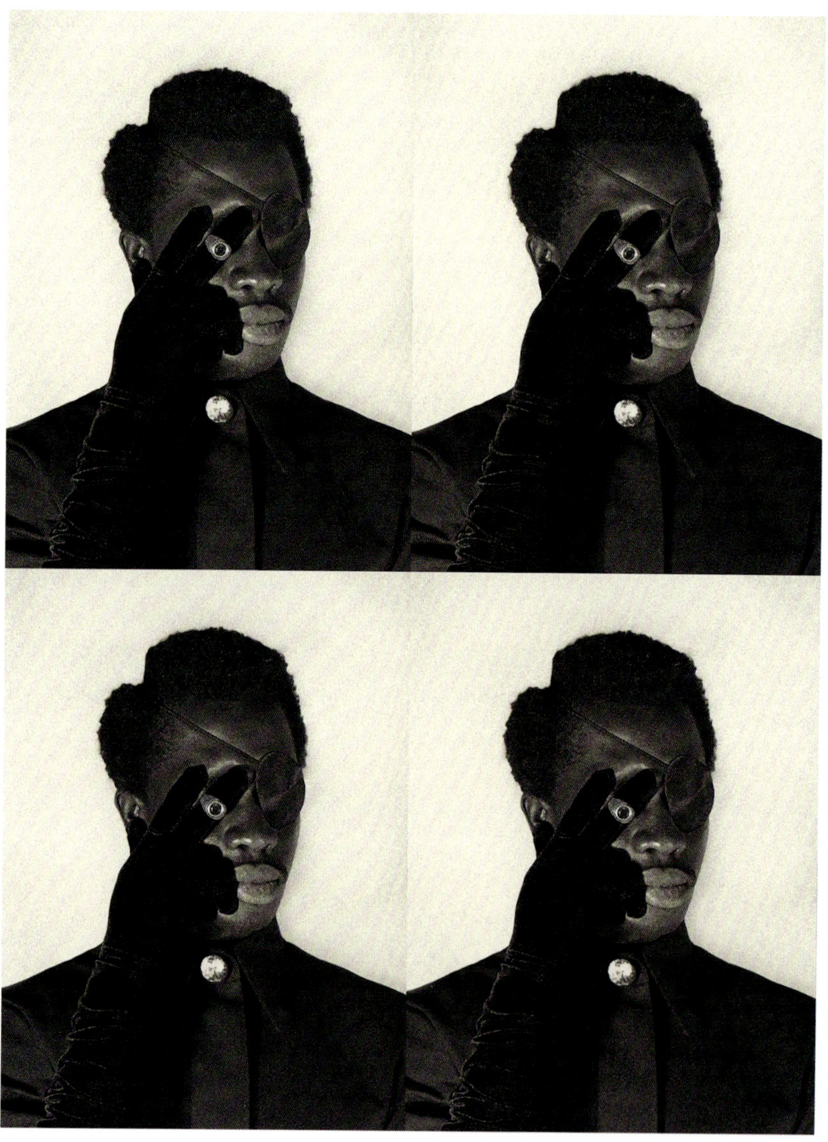

These pages: *010C6C*, 2018, *Dedicate* magazine

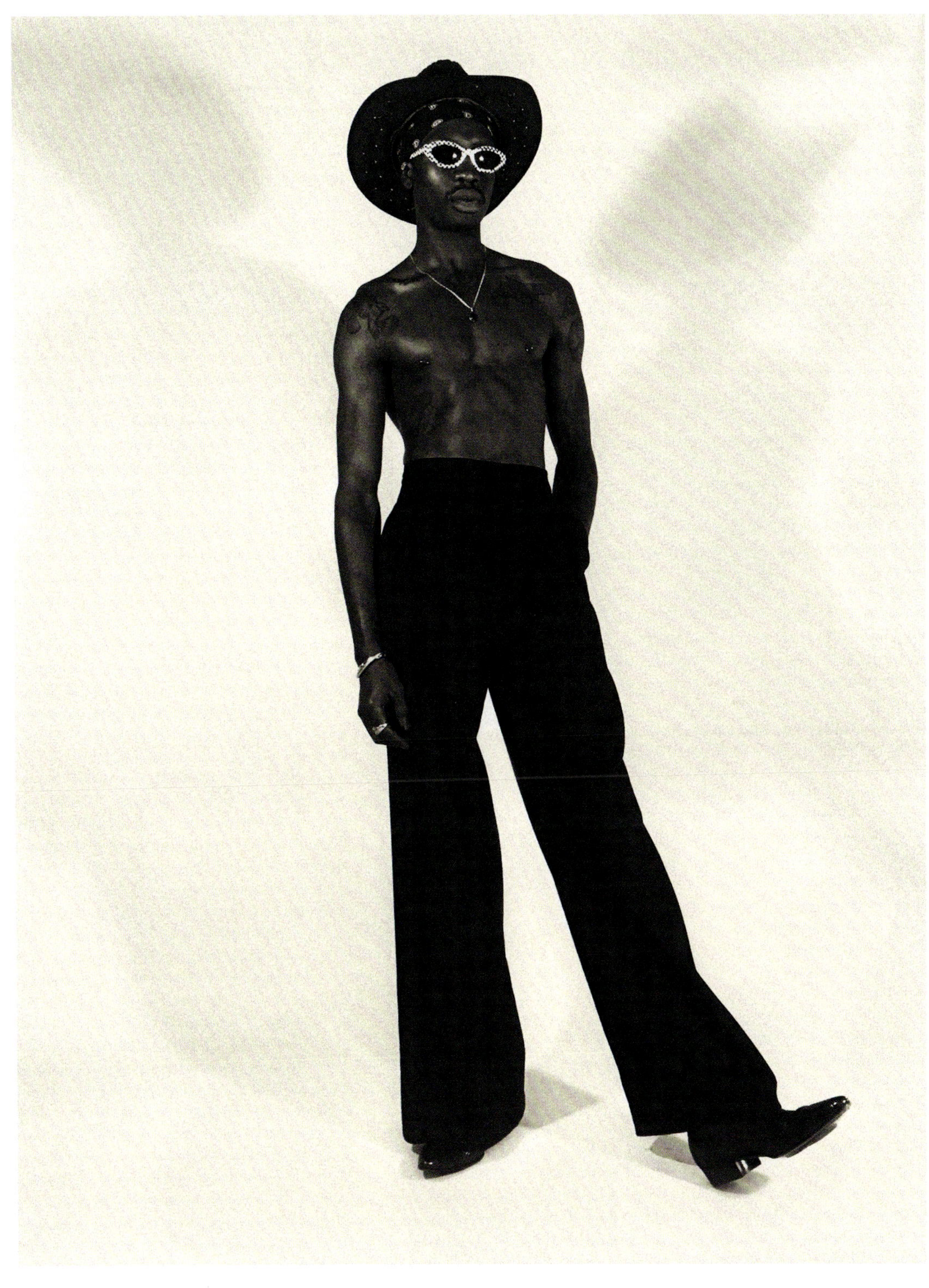

Naima Green

Dealing Us In

Artist and photographer Naima Green shoots both studio portraiture and street photography. The former includes what is perhaps her most well-known project: *Pur·suit*, a deck of 54 playing cards featuring photographs of queer, transgender, nonbinary and gender nonconforming people. Originally launched during Pride in 2019, Green's cards, which feature vibrant portraits of her friends and acquaintances, were inspired by artist Catherine Opie's *Dyke Deck* (*c.*1995). The cards, ordinary objects at first glance, take on a new significance as these photographs replace the traditional French suit illustrations. *Pur·suit* isn't a novelty item, it is a mini-archive; a tangible one too. With it, Green honours and cements in art history the queer communities she has photographed: a record to say "yes, we were here". The use of a card deck also speaks to that desire for inclusion. Just as a deck would be incomplete without one card, so, without the inclusion of the narratives of queer people, art and cultural history would be lacking. "I looked around at the queer communities I'm a part of and those I'm not and wanted to hold and interrogate our joys and challenges," Green told *Office* magazine.[13]

There is an ease in the poses of her sitters. Green doesn't just take photos of them but also asks her subjects if there is a way that they would like to be portrayed, inviting them to be part of the process of image-making. Portraits from this series became part of her solo exhibition *Brief & Drenching* (2020), transformed from the small format of the cards to larger portraits in the gallery space to give the images their full due. *Pur·suit* was an exercise in reimagining, which is also the case with the critically acclaimed *Jewels from the Hinterland* (2013–present), for which Green photographs Black creatives in urban green spaces. Green studied urban studies and sociology at Barnard College, Columbia University, and with this series wanted to, as she told the *New York Times*, "interrupt the predominant narratives about people of colour surrounded by urban decay".[14] *Jewels from the Hinterland* depicts a more harmonious relationship between Black and Brown people and nature than has been portrayed in the mainstream. Taken in spaces across New York such as Prospect Heights Community Farm in Brooklyn and Morningside Park in Manhattan, the images demonstrate the importance of place not in an inherently geographical sense but in terms of the emotional connections we make.

> "With this archive, Green honours and cements in art history the queer communities she has photographed: a record to say 'yes, we were here'"

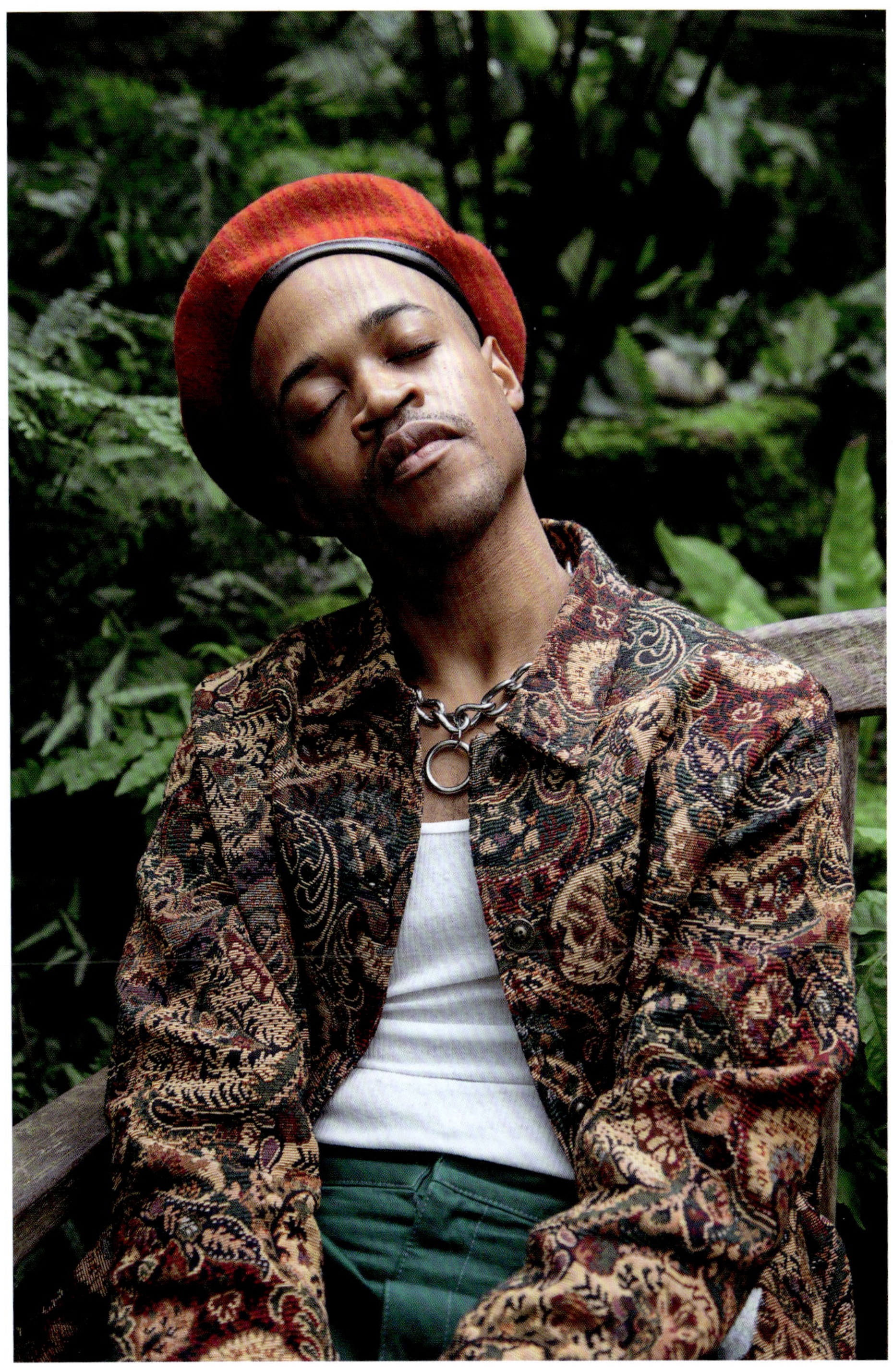

Vincent Martell, Garfield Park Conservatory, 2019, from *Jewels from the Hinterland*

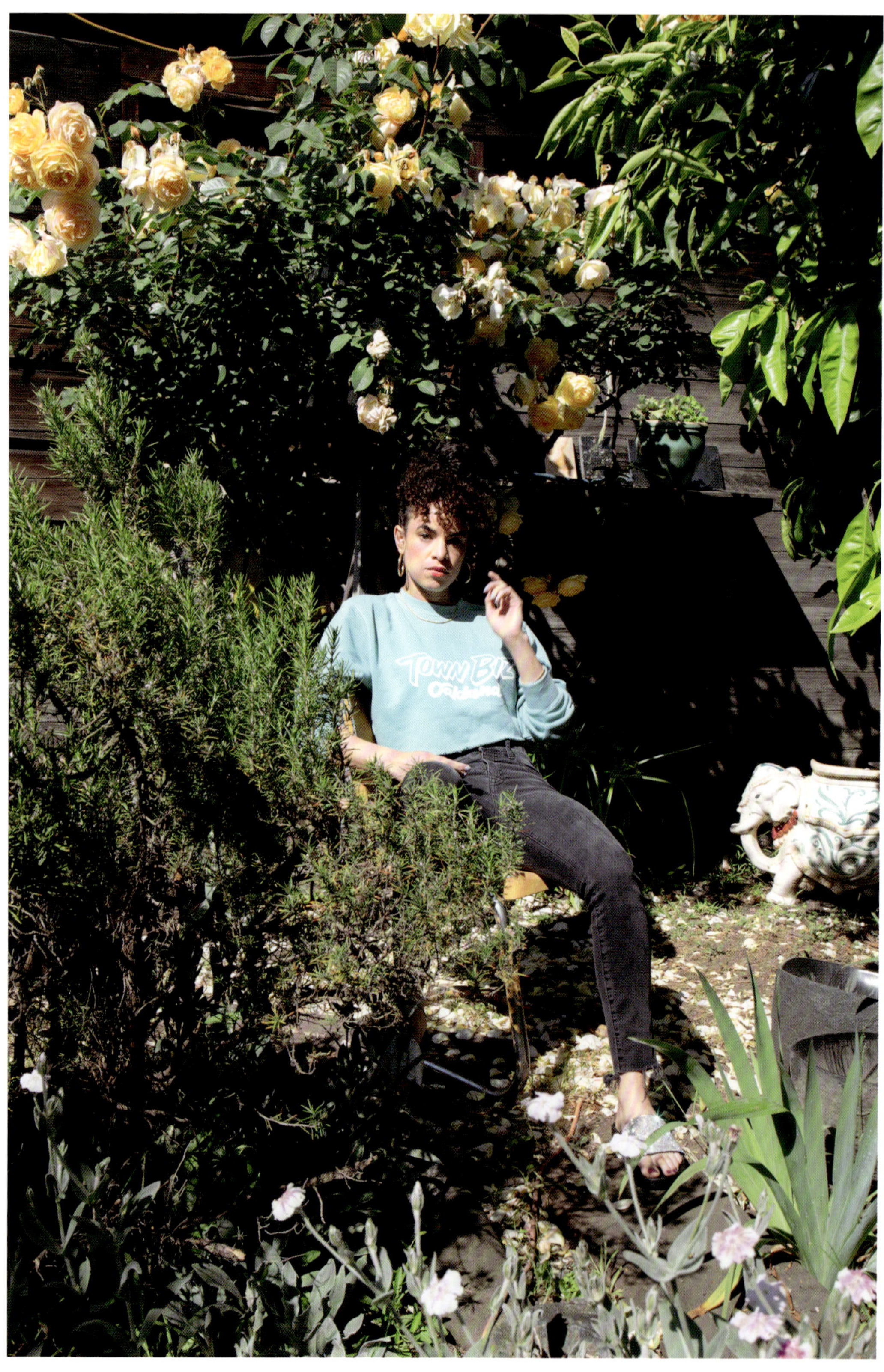

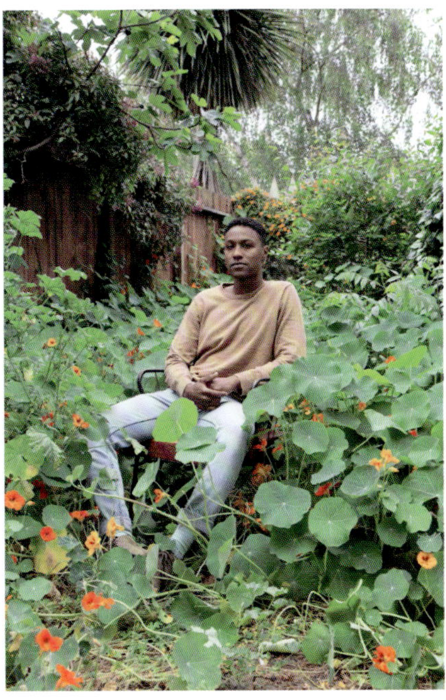

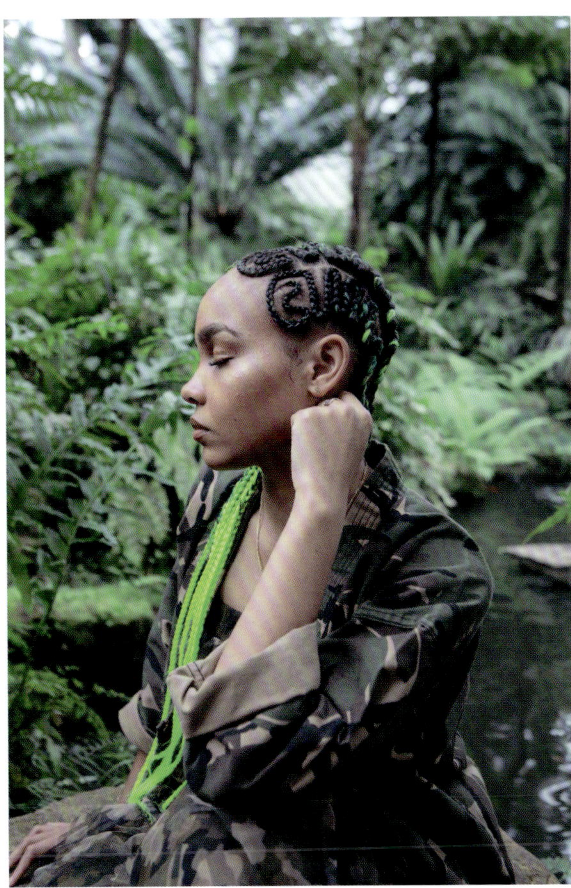

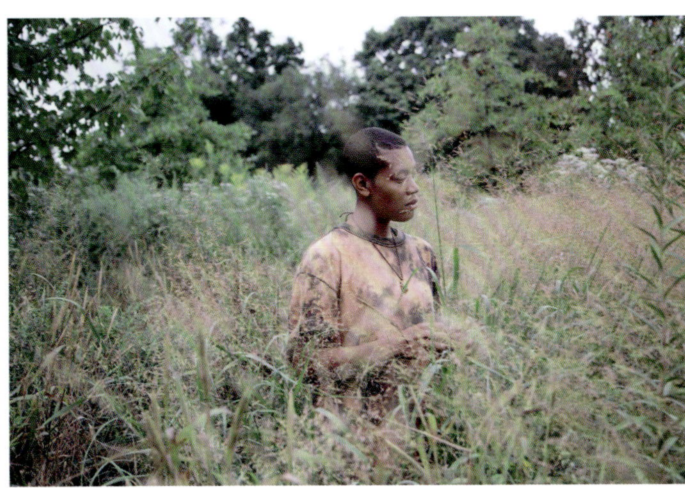

Opposite: *Sadie Barnette,
West Oakland*, 2018
This page, clockwise from above:
*Shani Crowe, Garfield Park
Conservatory*, 2019
Jay Wilson, Oakland, 2018
Naeem, Brooklyn Botanic Garden, 2016
All from *Jewels from the Hinterland*

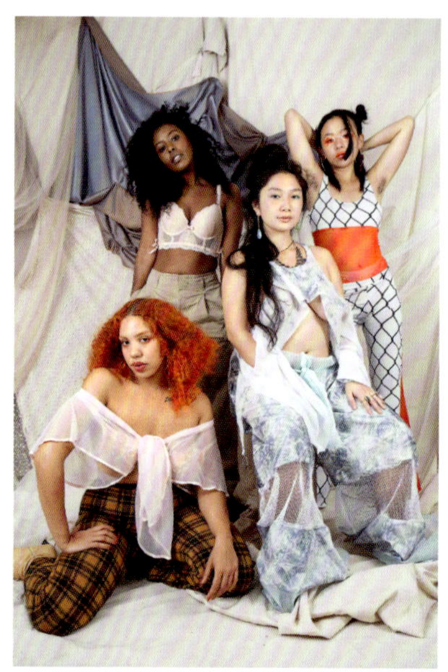

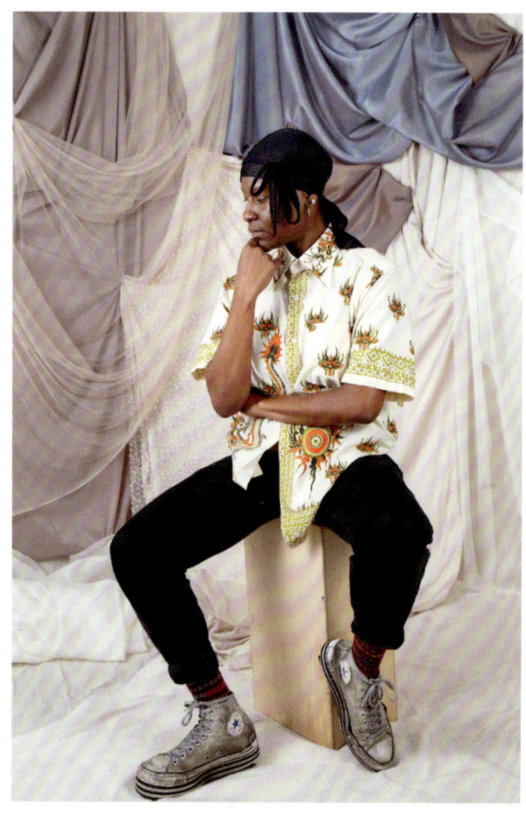

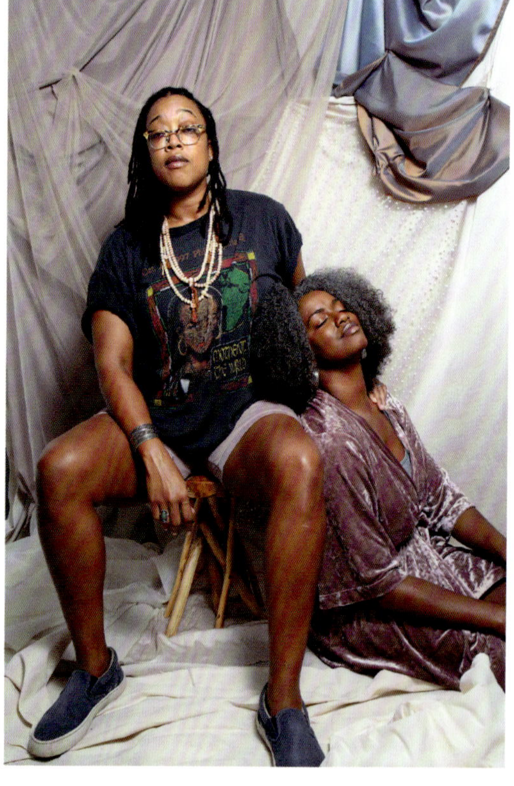

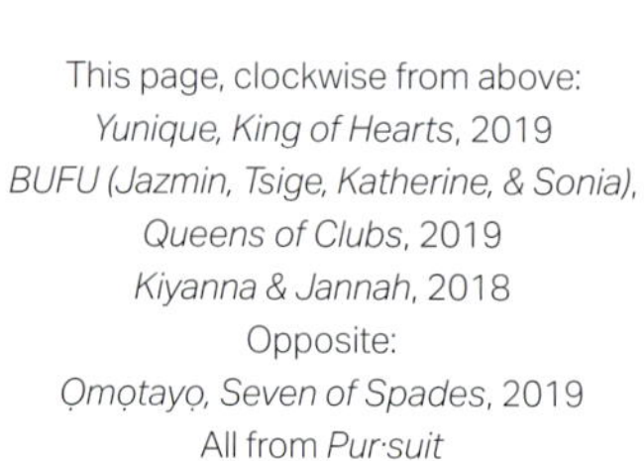

This page, clockwise from above:
Yunique, King of Hearts, 2019
BUFU (Jazmin, Tsige, Katherine, & Sonia),
Queens of Clubs, 2019
Kiyanna & Jannah, 2018
Opposite:
Ọmọtayọ, Seven of Spades, 2019
All from *Pur·suit*

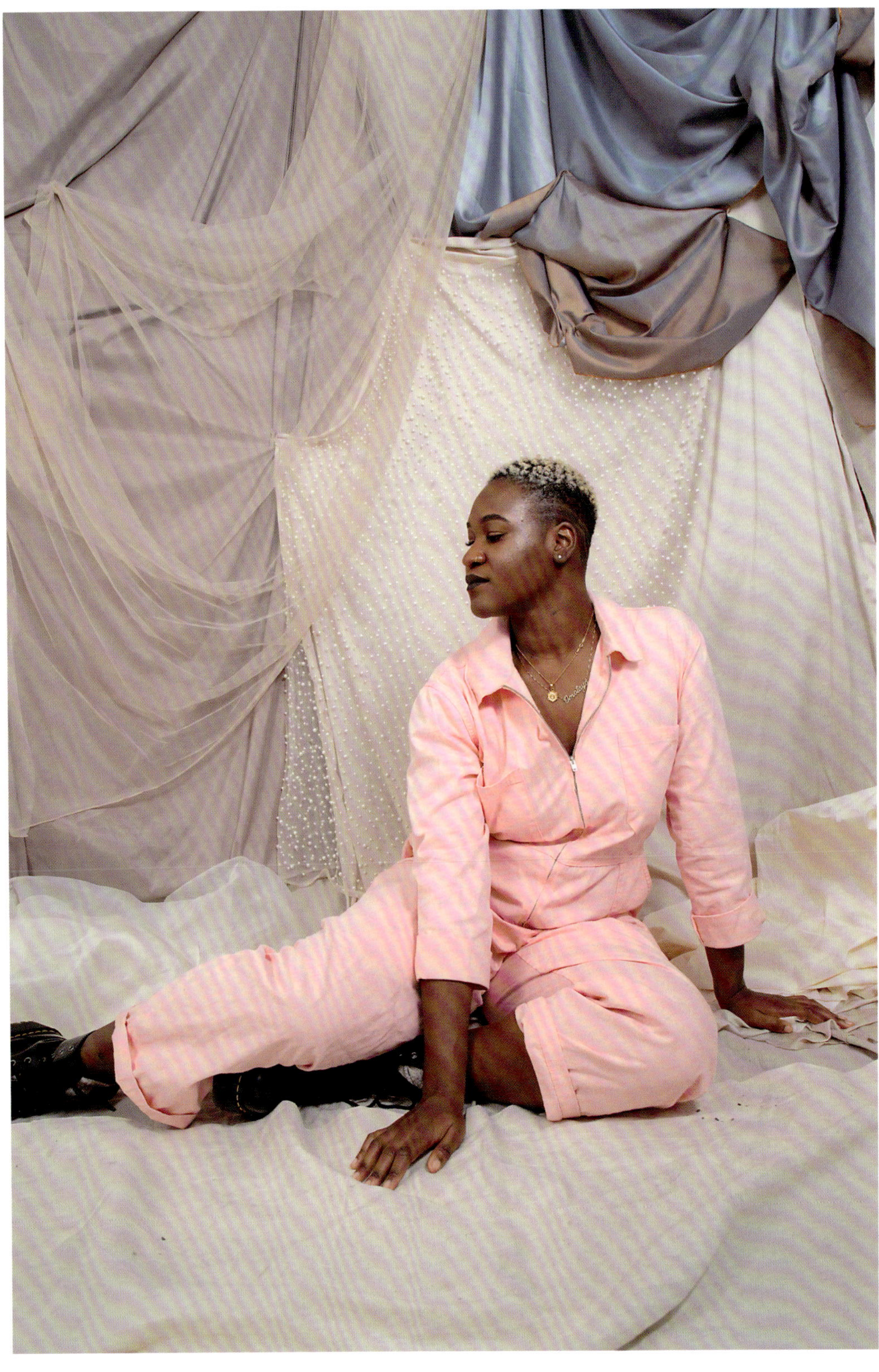

Mikael Owunna

Infinite Potential

Pittsburgh-based multidisciplinary artist Mikael Owunna created his series *Infinite Essence* (2019) in response to the plethora of images in the American media of Black people being shot and killed by the police. *Infinite Essence* is instead about life and potential. Black, here, is the colour of creation, of beginning, not ending. The limbs of his models are unrestricted, unbounded by gravity. They look as though they are floating in space, their bodies speckled with fluorescent UV paint. They look like the source of all the galaxies in the universe, the initial singularity from which everything will burst forth. In one image, a figure poses like a dancer, streaks of blue at his feet that look like water or cosmic dust. He seems like a prelapsarian creature, a giant. In another, a male figure lies naked in the foetal position. An adult man is born again: new life, new potential. Owunna's use of light and dark emphasizes the idea that there is always more than one can see; there is always and will always be more behind every image than what is depicted. The name for the series came from writer Chinua Achebe's discussion of Odinani, a concept in Igbo Nigerian spirituality surrounding the idea of "chi" – the manifestation of the Igbo deity Chukwu in every human: an infinite essence.

In his documentary photography series *Limitless Africans*, Owunna continues this thread on infinity. He travelled across ten countries between 2013 and 2017, taking photographs of LGBTQ+ African immigrants, refugees and asylum seekers. The motivation was partially autobiographical. Owunna, himself a queer man, was subjected to a so-called exorcism when he was 18 with the rebuke that homosexuality was not a part of his "culture". In his travels and interactions with his subjects, he encountered similar experiences of rejection, fear, guilt and confusion about a perceived incongruence between being African and having a non-heterosexual sexual identity. An Nsibidi character – an early pictographic writing system – features on the cover of the series book, representing two women in bed together, affirming the existence of same-sex affection in precolonial southern Nigerian culture. The images evoke a strong sense of community united across thousands of miles, but what they also do is shake the dichotomy of a hostile and "backwards" Africa and a completely tolerant West, as Owunna documents the struggles of Black LGBTQ+ people in Western countries. The series was originally called *Limit(less)*, but when the book was due to be published (it was eventually published on 11 October 2019, National Coming Out Day), the parentheses were dropped to make a more confident assertion: Black people are limitless, full stop.

> "They look like the source of all the galaxies in the universe, the initial singularity from which everything will burst forth"

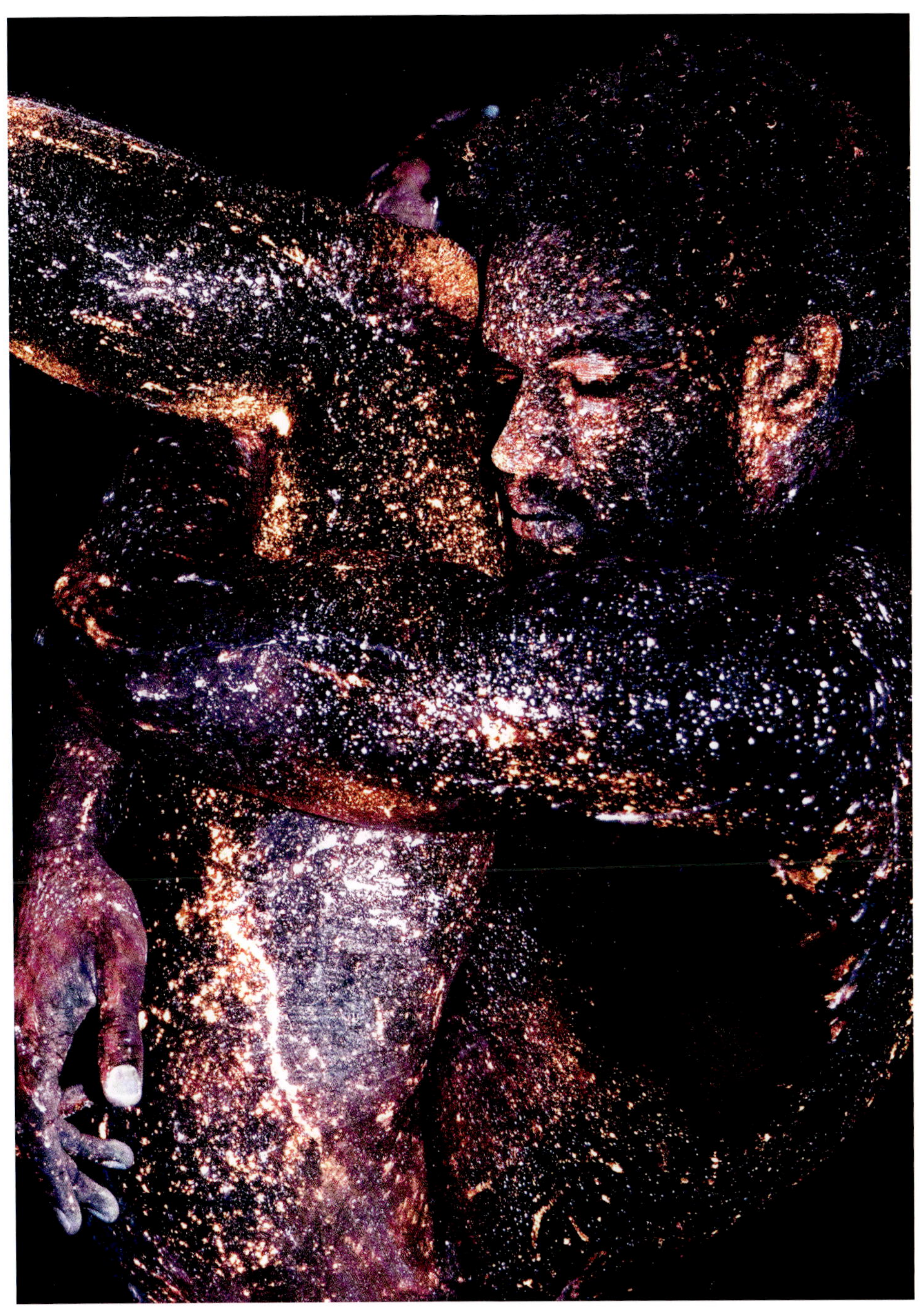

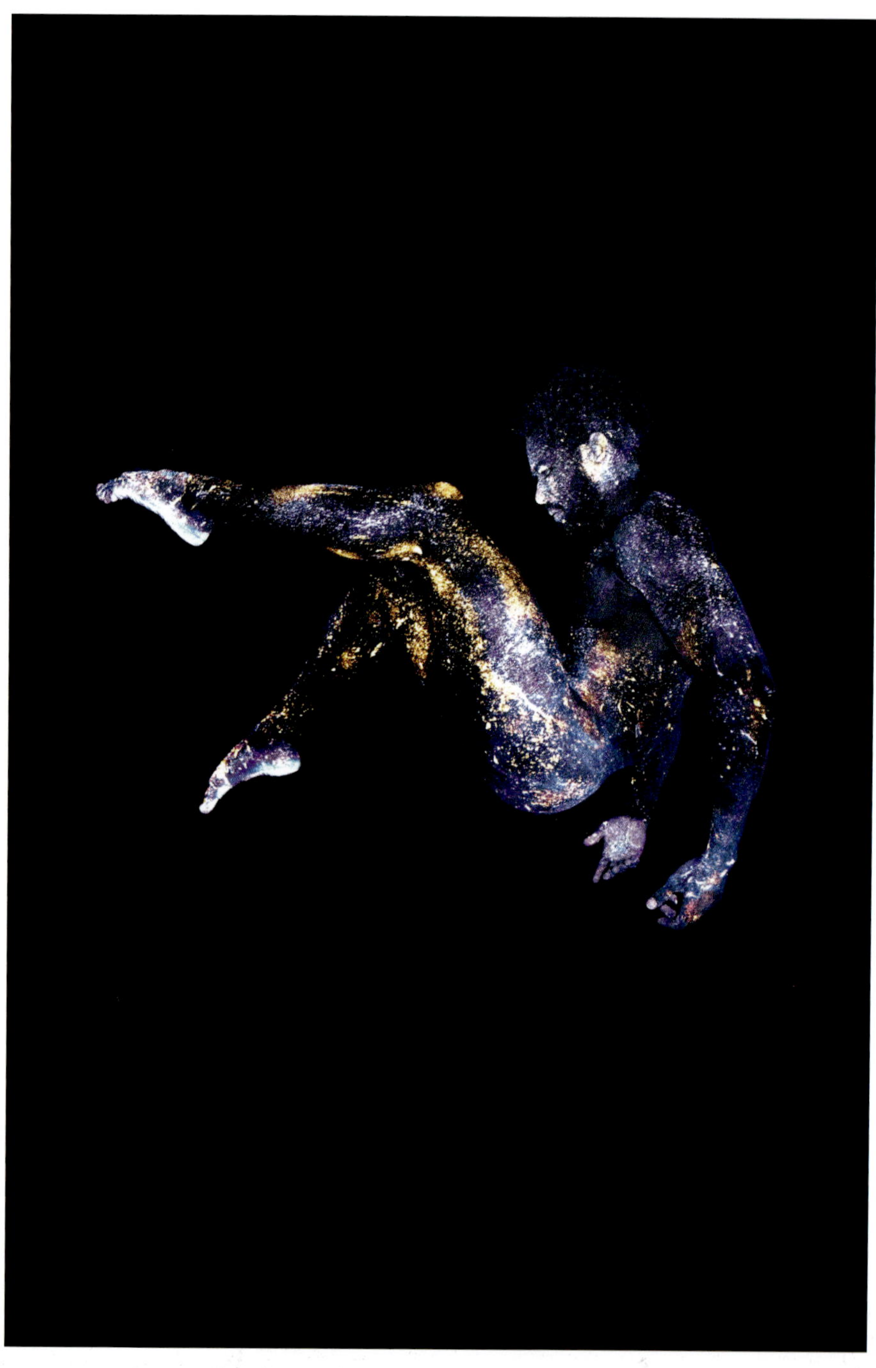

Previous spread: *Amma's Womb*, 2018
Above: *Amma Emerges from their Womb*, 2018
Opposite, clockwise from top left: *The Flying African*, 2018
Lébé and his Articulations, 2019
Oku na Mmiri (Fire and Water), 2018

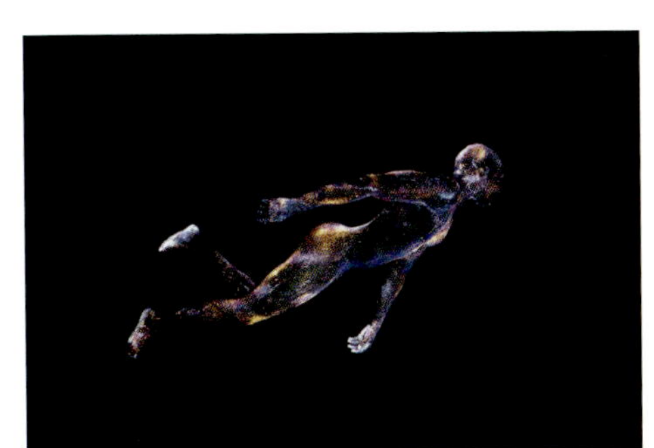

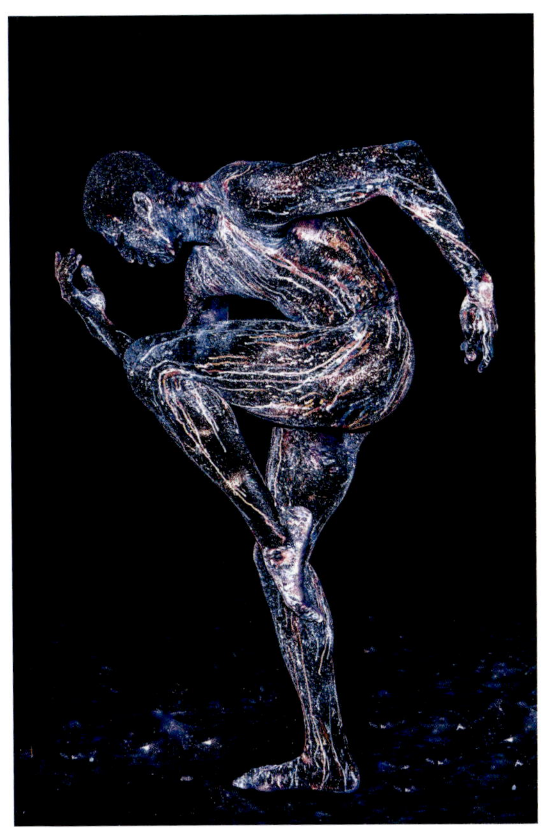

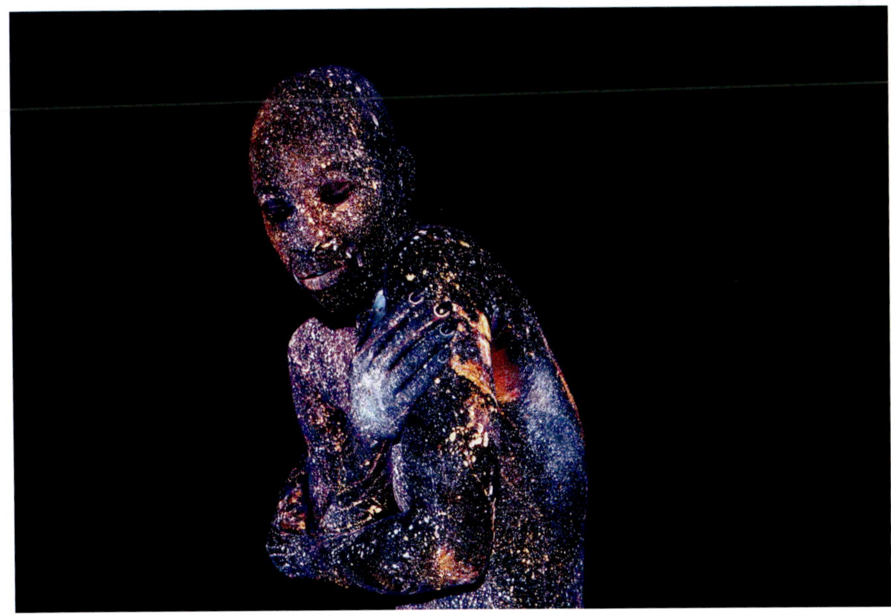

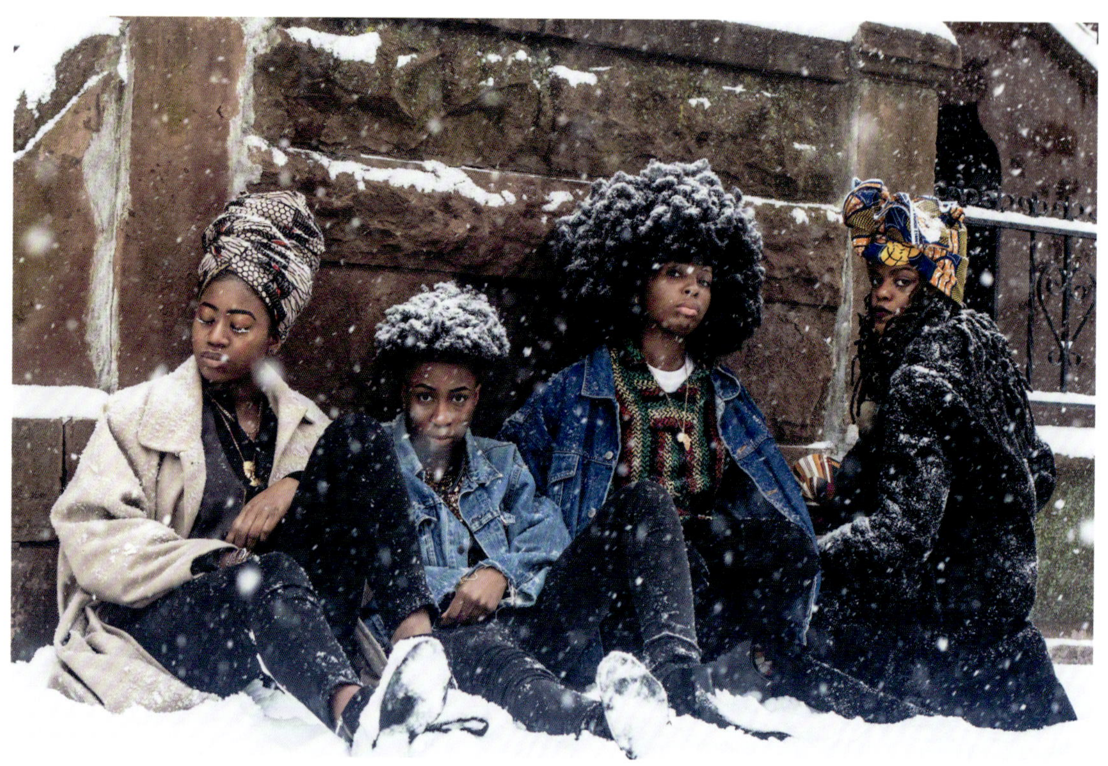

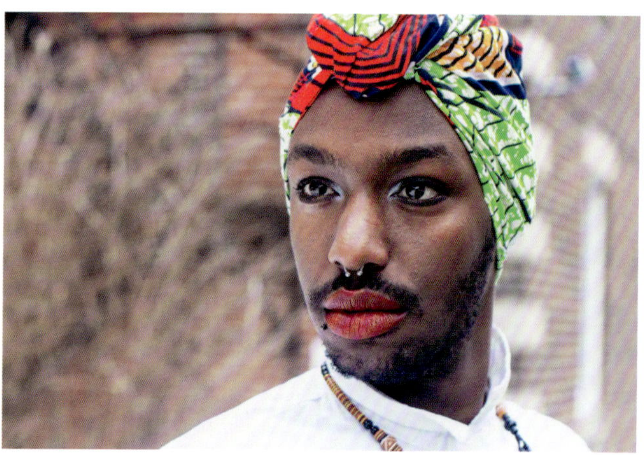

From top: *Four Women in the Snow*, 2017
Brian – Queer Rwandan, 2017
Both from *Limitless Africans*

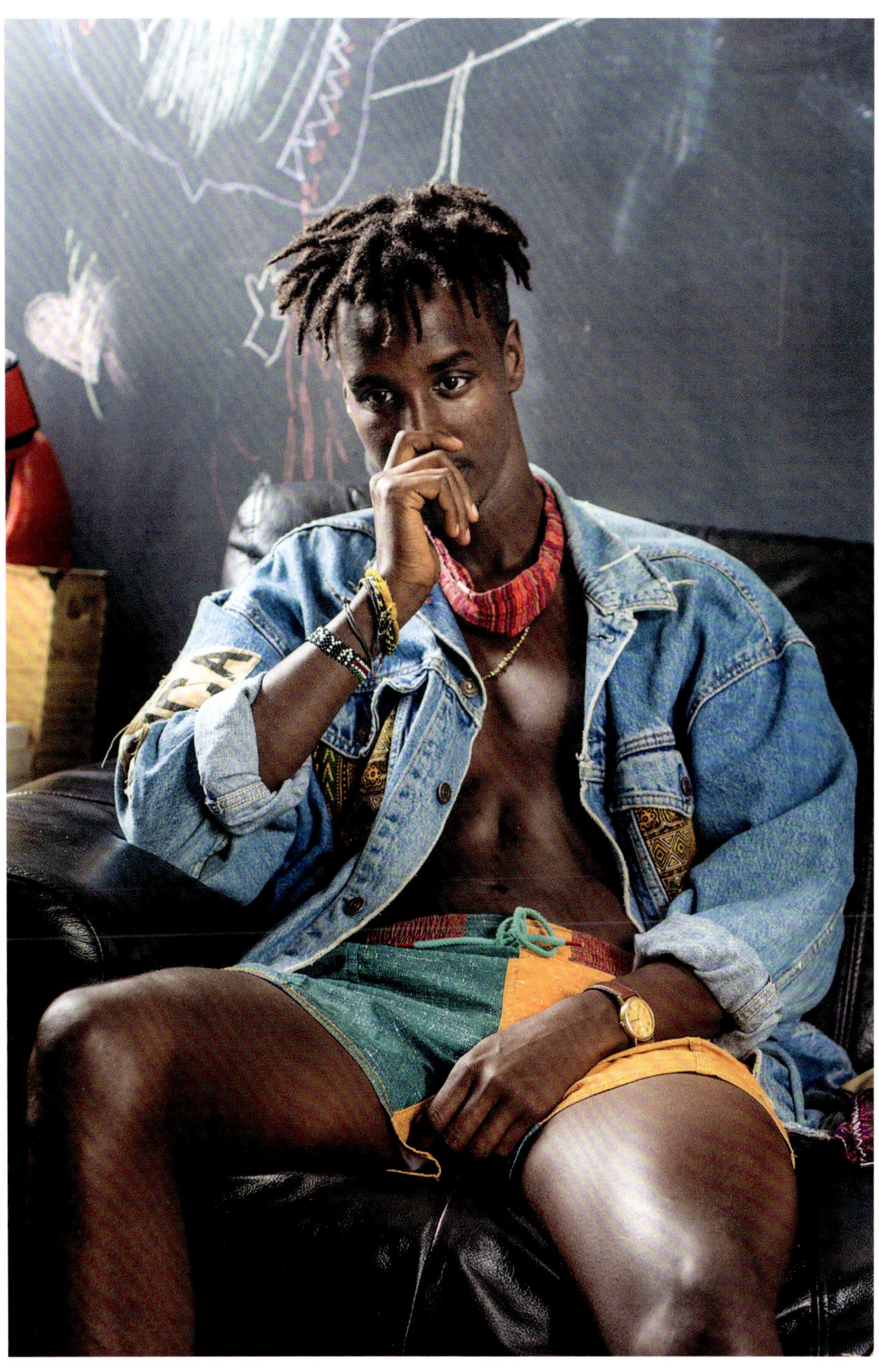

Tyler – Queer Kenyan-Somali, 2017, from *Limitless Africans*

David Nana Opoku Ansah

A New Black Aesthetic

Inspired by photographers such as fellow Ghanaian James Barnor, Accra-based photographer David Nana Opoku Ansah's documenting and storytelling work zeroes in on the everyday to create what he called in an interview with *It's Nice That* "a new aesthetic of Blackness".[15] For Ansah, this involves contributing a different vision of his Accra to the stock of images of Ghana's capital, wanting, like other photographers in this volume, to portray an image that looks and feels more authentic to those who live in the city. Ansah looks to Accra's youth culture, characterized by increasing freedom and a strong, intimate sense of community. "I feel there is more to achieve if we believe in moving together collectively and as a family – it can make so much [more] happen than individualism," he told British *Vogue*.[16] He photographs young people in their own clothes, showing them in their joy and at leisure, a rebuke to what he sees as a "glorification of suffering" in Ghanaian cultures. He originally began shooting using an iPhone 5C, manipulating the photos to create more conceptual images. His images are soft, slightly hazy, not with nostalgia per se but with a quality that looks as though the subjects are aware they are making

> "He photographs them in their own clothes, showing them in their joy and at leisure, a rebuke to what he sees as a 'glorification of suffering' in Ghanaian cultures"

memories in those moments. His photos of young men in *We Are They* (2020) – which takes its title from the gender neutrality of pronouns in the Twi language – convey Ansah's personal view of African masculinity. A collaboration between Manju Journal, an international arts and culture platform for young African creatives, and the luxury brand Gucci, *We Are They* aims to bring to light underappreciated stories about gender nonconformity in Ghana.

Ansah is interested in getting into filmmaking, and many of his photographs have a cinematic quality, his subjects sometimes feeling like the protagonists of a fun and stylized film. Ansah incorporates the small screen into his series of photographs entitled *Family Property* in which a young man, dressed in a white shirt, with off-white clothes draped behind him, alternately sits and stands barefoot on an old analogue television that fizzes with noise. The young man towers over the small box, dominating this device that disseminates powerful images that shape the consciousness and collective imaginations of those who receive them. Here, those messages are disrupted, replaced with the intense and intent focus, personality and style of Ansah's subject. His vision replaces the old.

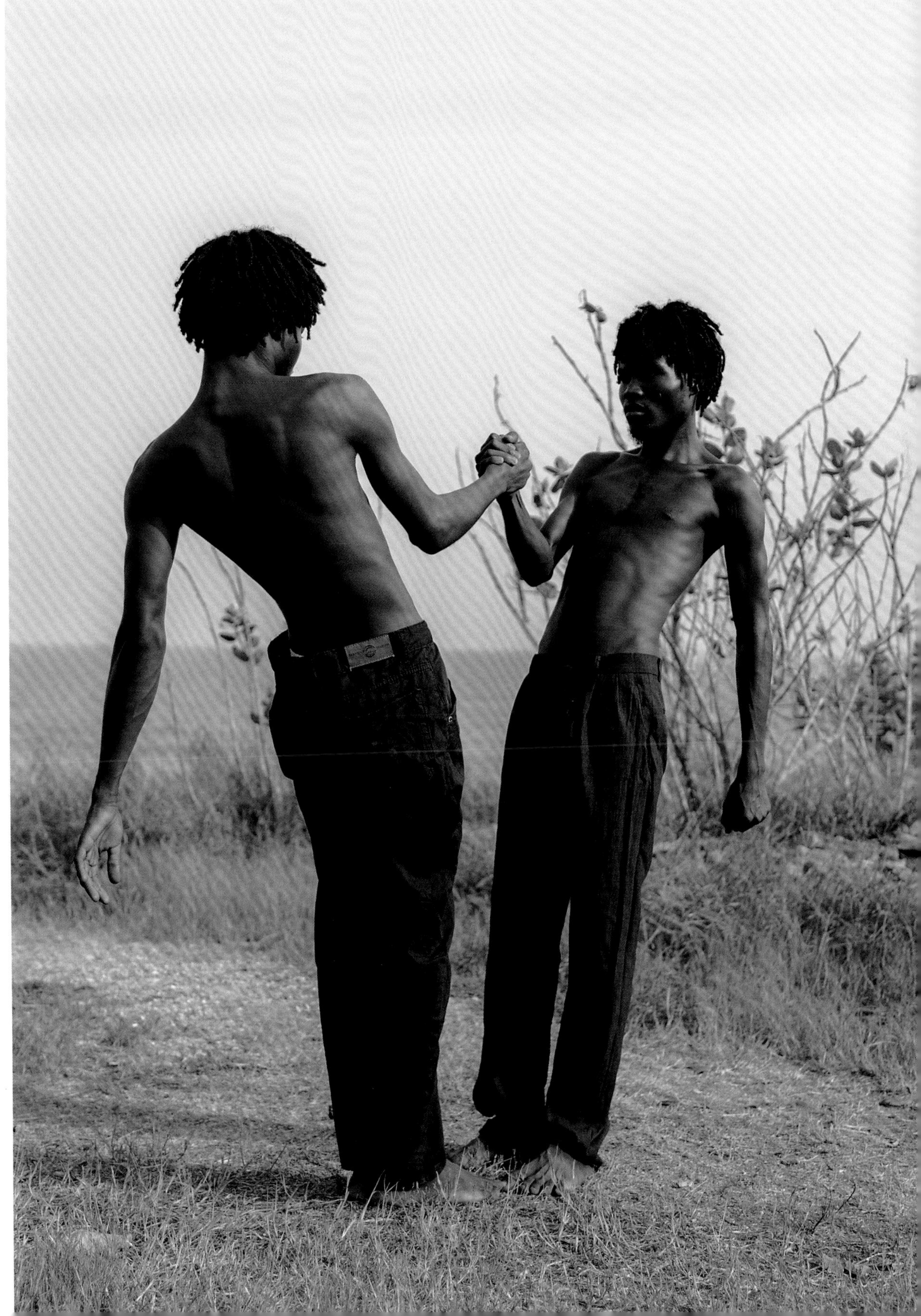

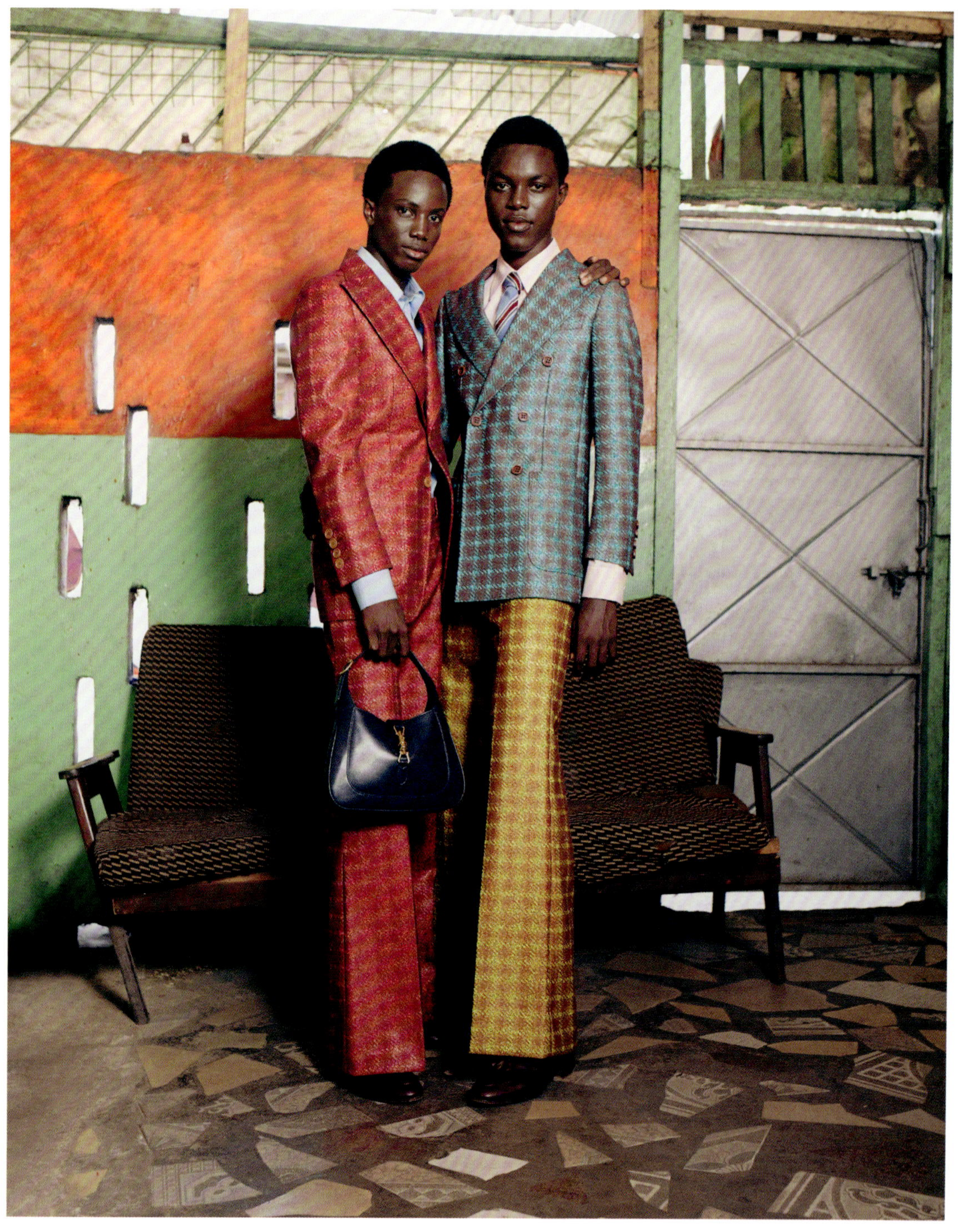

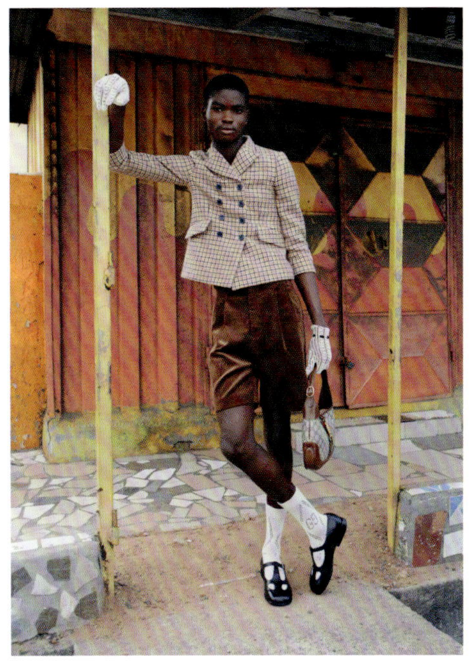

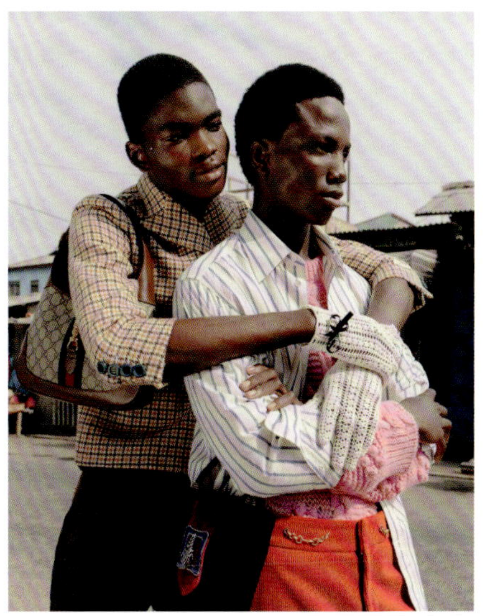

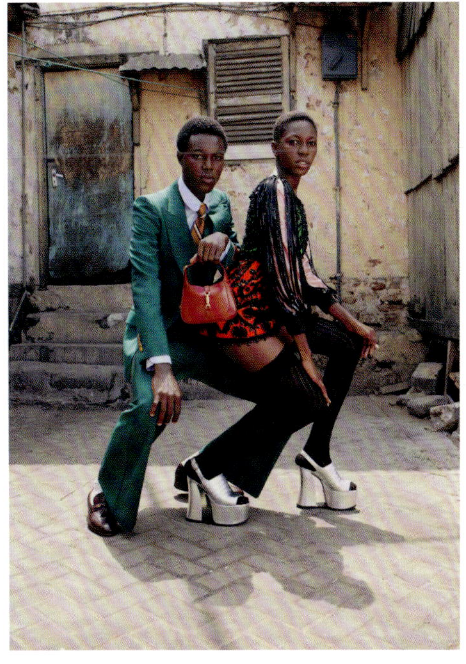

Previous spread: *Brother's Keeper*, from
Area Boys, 2019
These pages: from *We Are They*, 2020

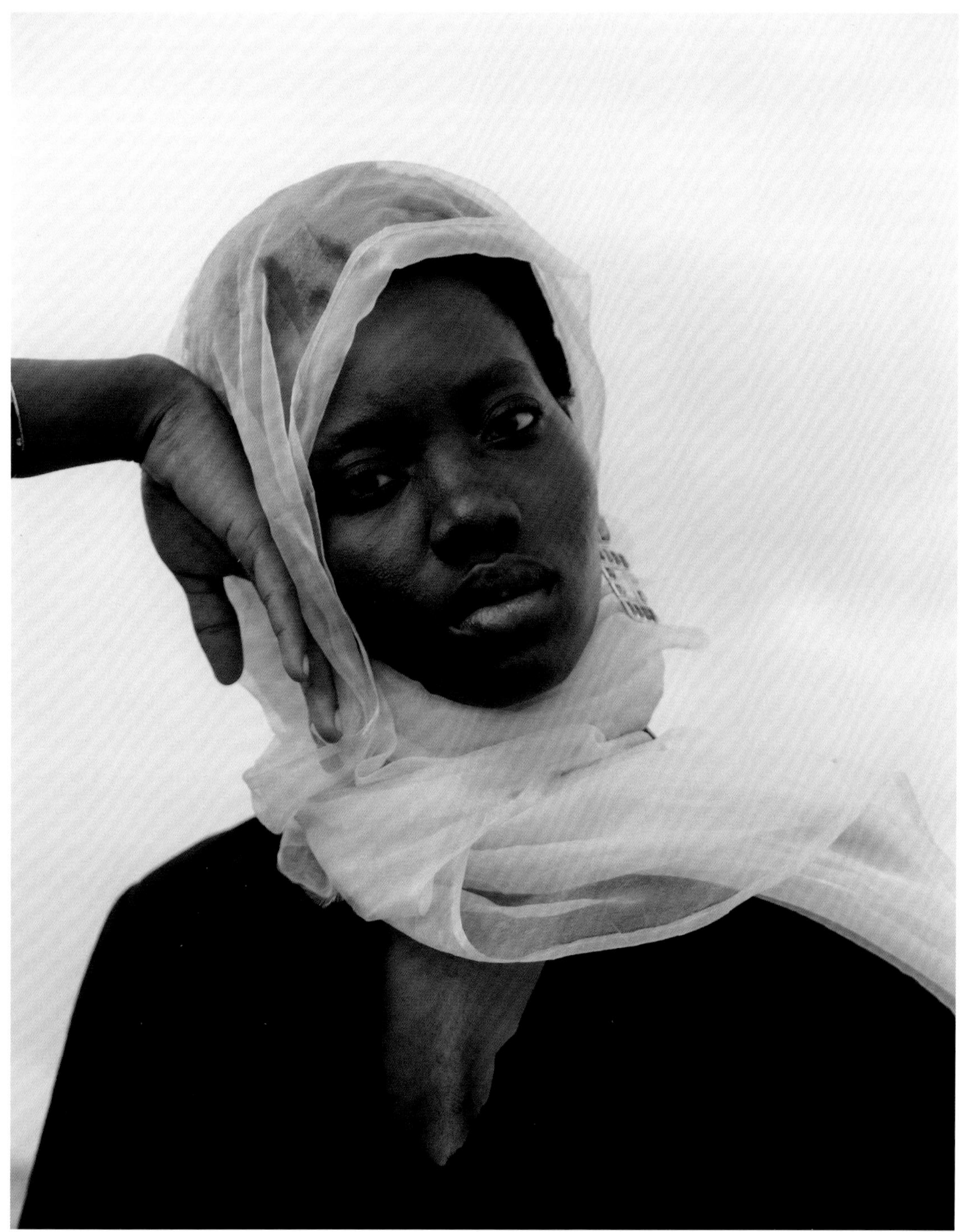

These pages: *Stillness*, from *Untitled*, 2020

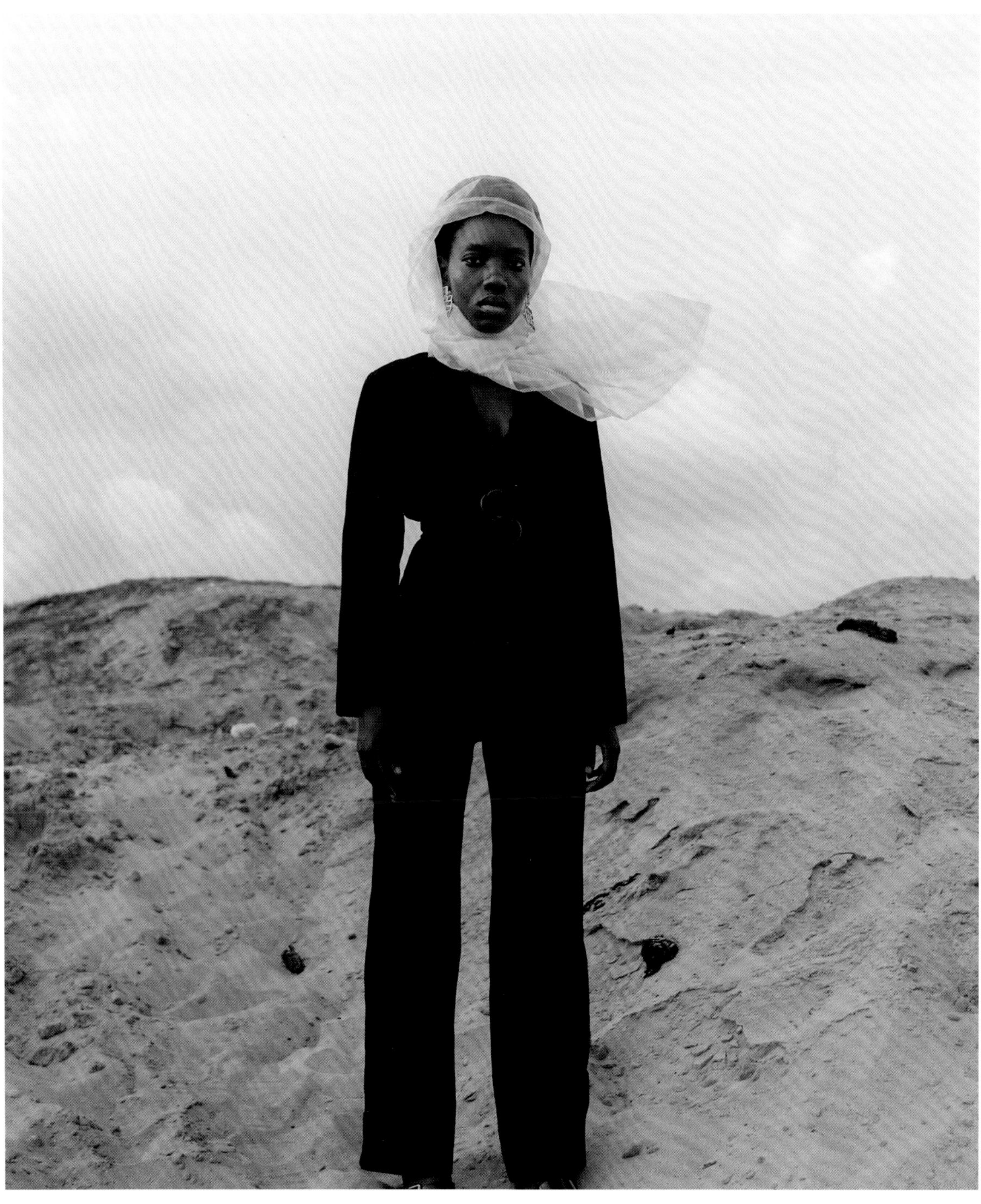

Lebohang Kganye

Insurmountable Gaps

Lebohang Kganye is an artist from Johannesburg, South Africa, who uses photography, performance and sculpture to explore themes of memory, personal and cultural history, and fantasy. In 2010, Kganye's mother died; the artist explored her grief in *Ke Lefa Laka: Her-story*, in which she superimposed herself dressed in her mother's clothes and striking similar poses onto old film photos of her mother as a young woman. Kganye turns her own image into an echo of somebody who is no longer there; the series is a compelling and moving attempt to close an insurmountable gap between past and present, life and afterlife. In the artist's hands, a photograph does not just represent the past, it is also transformed into a visual representation of how *memories* of the deceased persist. Completed between 2012 and 2013, *Ke Lefa Laka: Her-story* is also a memento mori of sorts, the layering of Kganye's ghostly self-portrait with the image of her late mother being a poignant reminder of the inevitability of death and the rituals of remembrance.

For her 2018 piece *Mohlokomedi wa Tora*, photographs are transformed into 3D cut-outs so that the installation resembles both a children's sticker book and a theatre set. The placement of the standees evokes what we traditionally see as the fixedness of a photograph, time frozen in an object, a vessel of memory and an archival object. The presence of Kganye, who inserts herself into the scenes like a pantomime actor, provides a juxtaposition to the black-and-white photography of the cut-outs, which not only emphasizes her presence in the present but also how we still associate black and white with the past. In Kganye's work, the dichotomy of past and present becomes blurry, and we are invited to consider the roles both memory and photography play in this. History is pushed into flux once more. The artist once noted in an interview with *Design Indaba* that "a large part of history and memory is in fact fantasy". This idea is embodied in 2011's *B(l)ack to Fairy Tales*, a series of 15 images for which she created staged scenes and self-portraits inspired by the Brothers Grimm and Disney, two sources through which so much folklore and mythology – predominantly European folklore and mythology – has not only survived but also remained a powerful force in the contemporary collective cultural imagination thanks to its constant reinterpretation in popular culture and art. Kganye's own reinterpretation of those stories highlights the influence of that powerful force, particularly the association of "fairness" with goodness and "darkness" with evil, and the correlation of "white" with goodness and beauty and "Black" with evil and ugliness.

> "In the artist's hands, a photograph does not just represent the past, it is also transformed into a visual representation of how *memories* of the deceased persist"

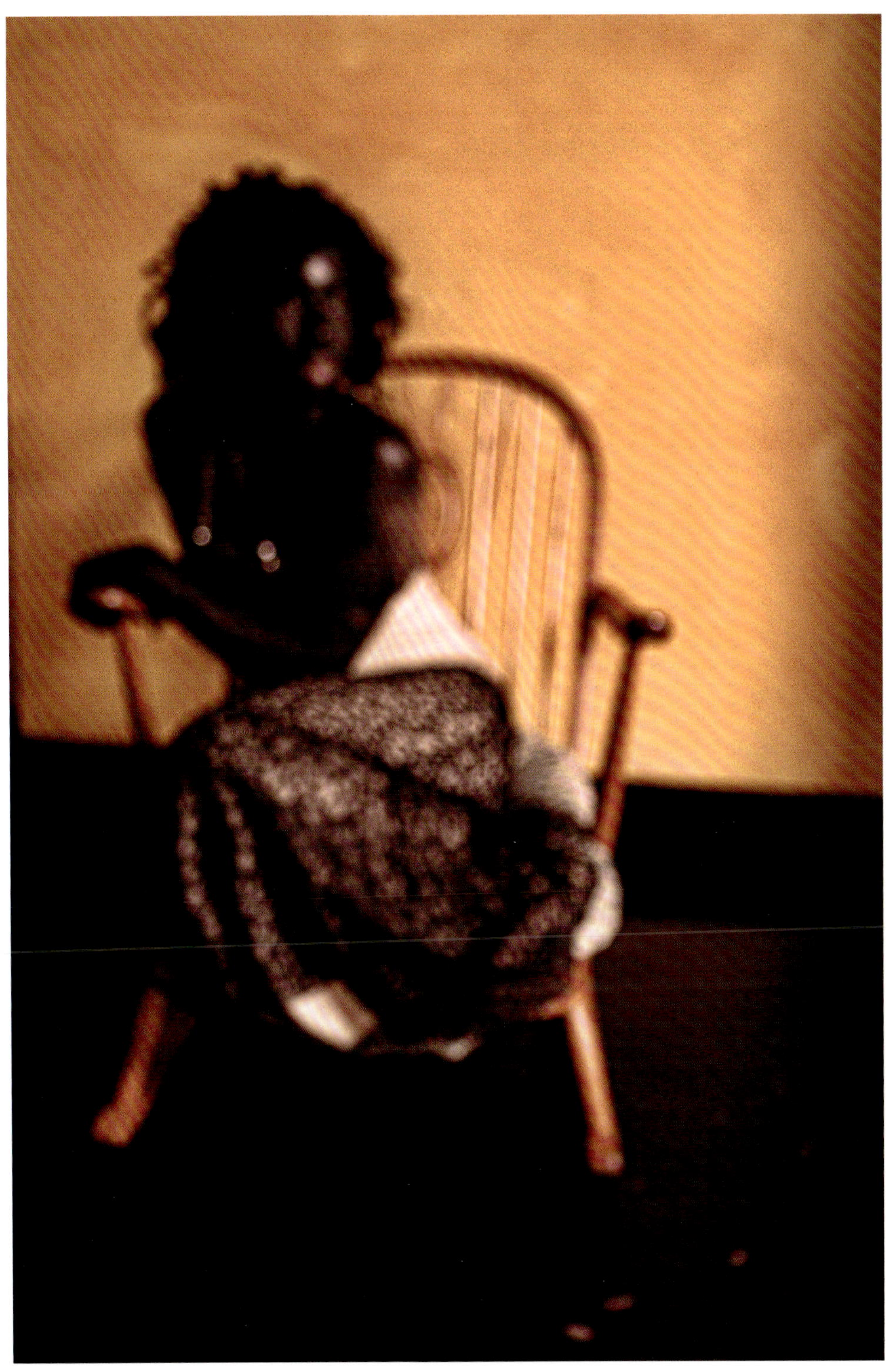

Untitled 07, 2011, from *B(l)ack to Fairy Tales*

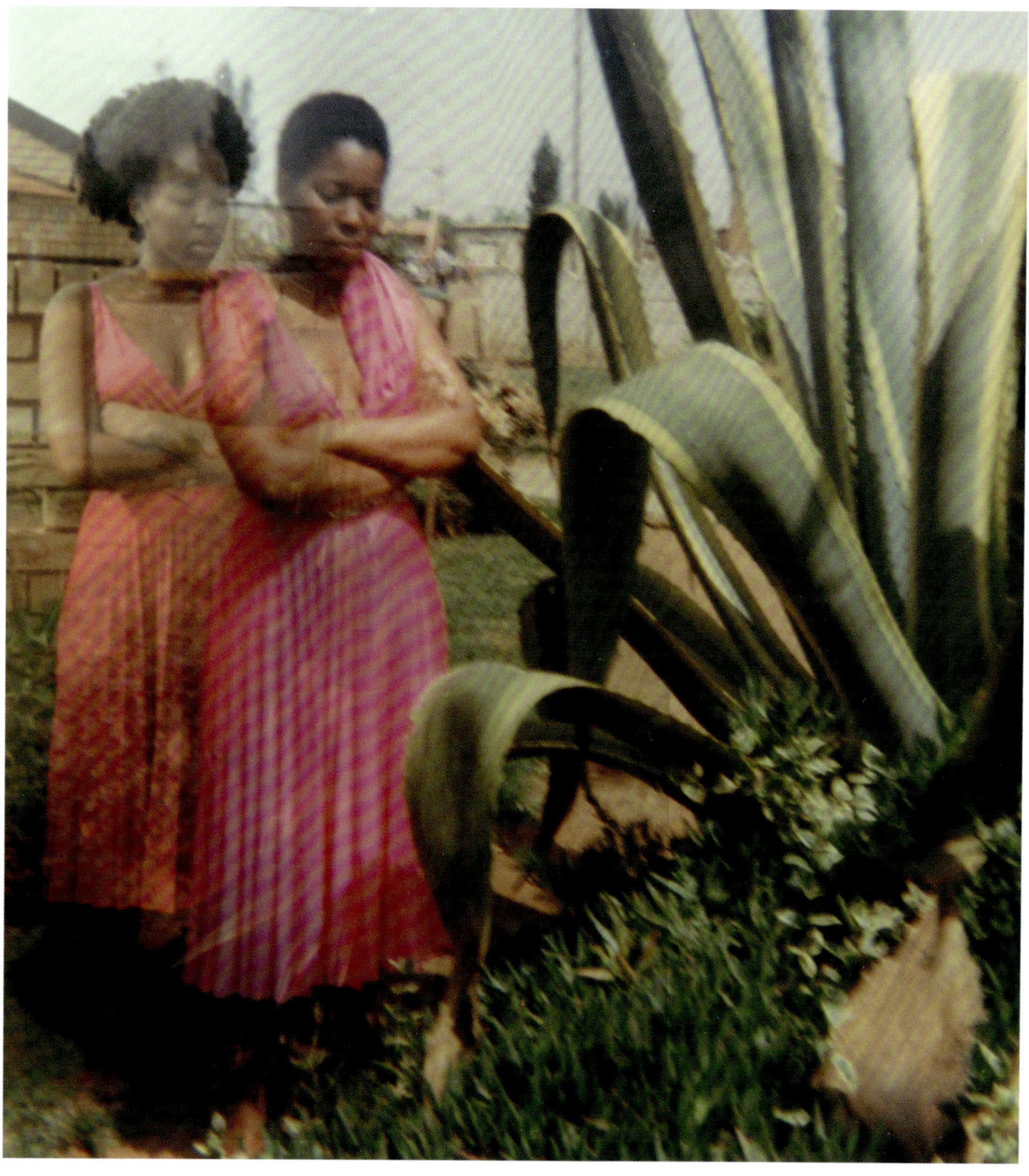

Ka 2-phisi yaka e pinky II, 2013, from *Ke Lefa Laka: Her-story*, 2013

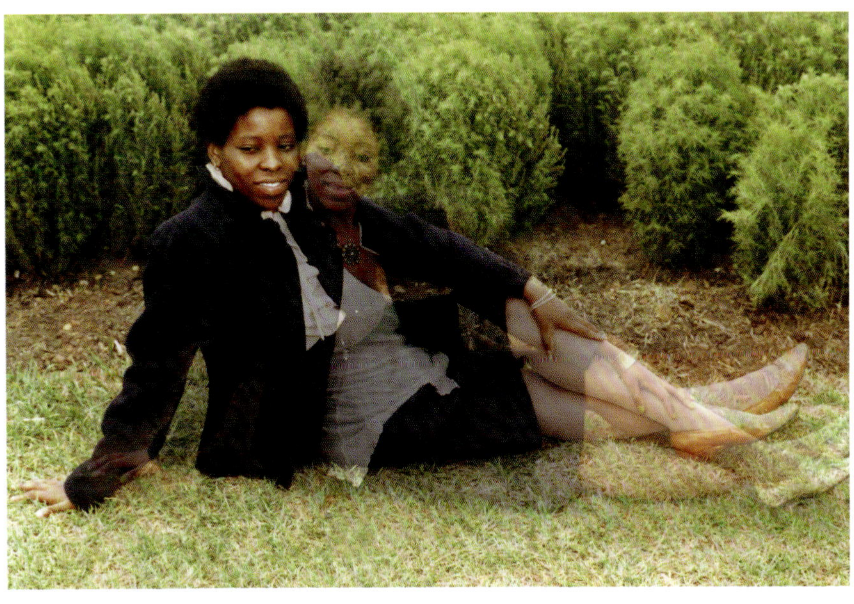

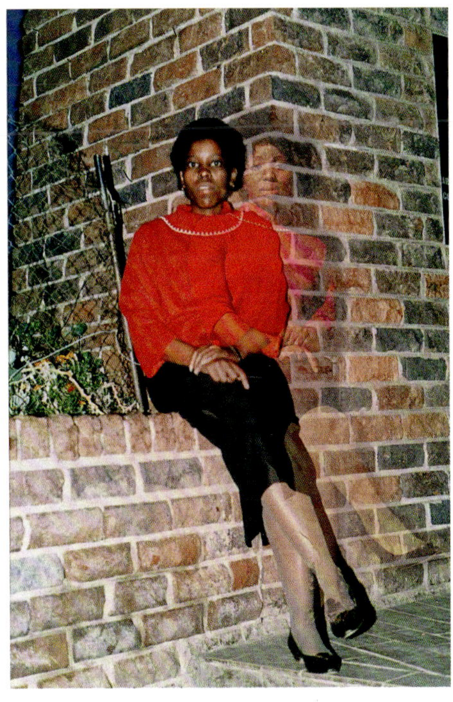

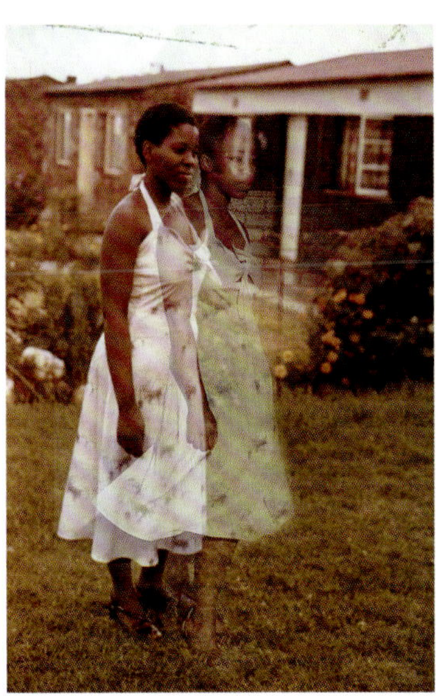

Clockwise from top: *Tshimong ka hare toropo II*
Ka mose wa malomo kwana 44 II
Kwana Germiston bosiu II
All from *Ke Lefa Laka: Her-story*, 2013

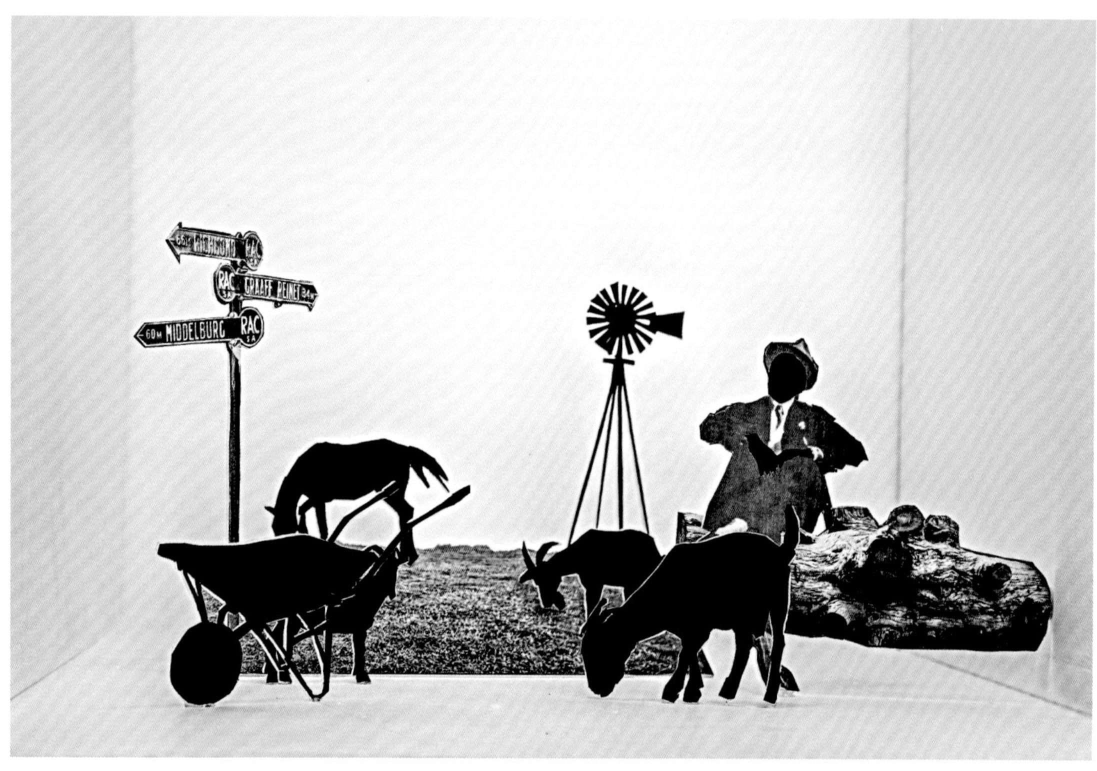

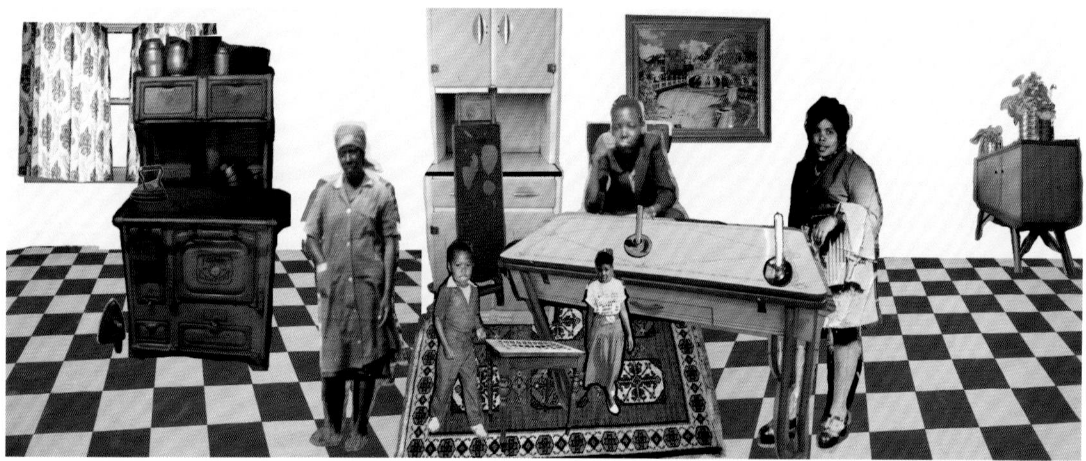

This page, from top: *Helen's Father Grazing his Goats*, 2018, from *Tell Tale*, 2018
Mohlokomedi wa tora, 2018, Scene 4
Opposite: *Untitled 03*, 2011, from *B(l)ack to Fairy Tales*

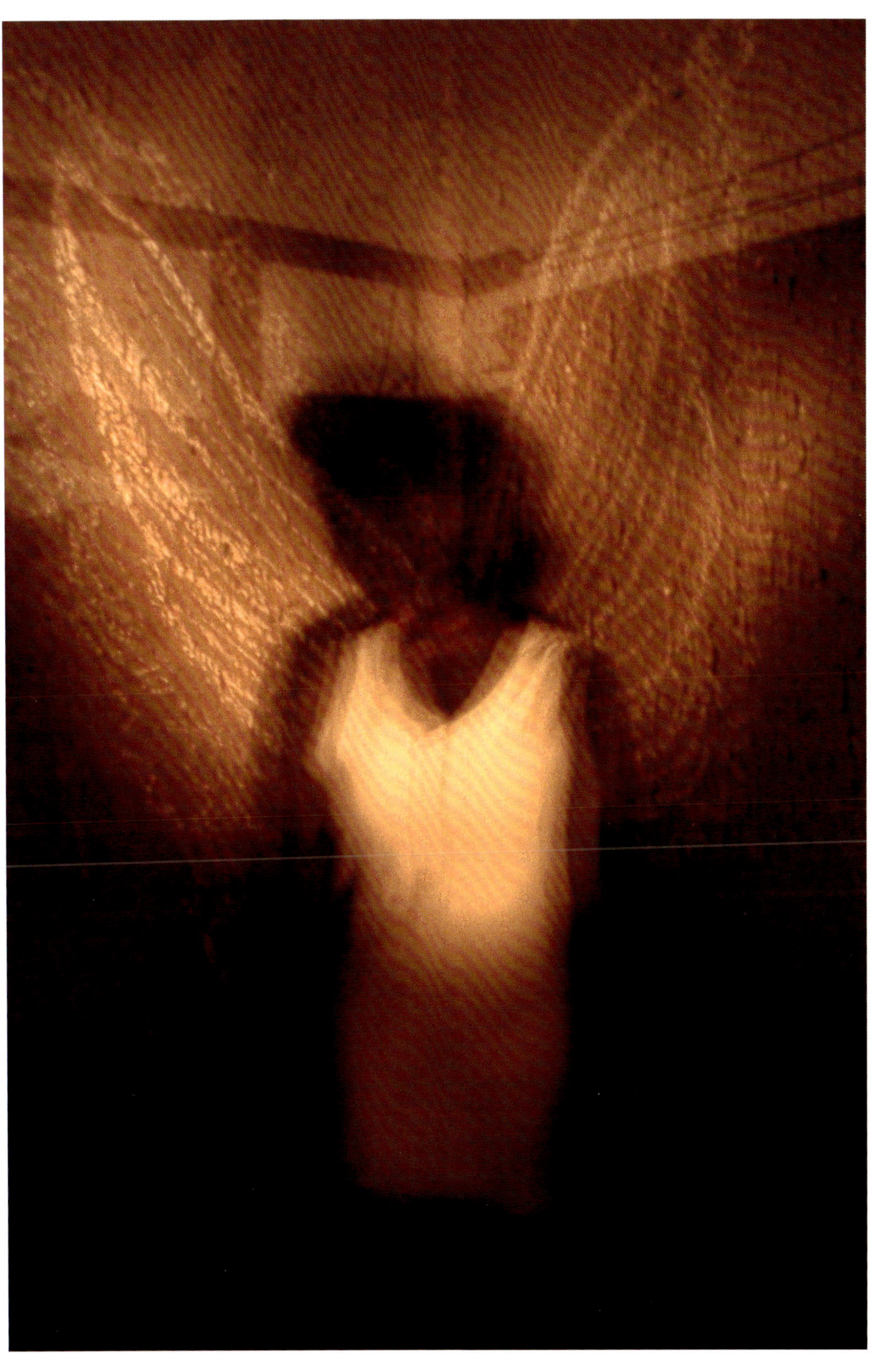

Dario Calmese

Writing Love Letters

In 2020, New York-based photographer, curator and writer Dario Calmese became the first Black cover photographer for *Vanity Fair* in the magazine's 163-year history. The striking image depicts the Oscar-winning actor Viola Davis, dressed in a blue gown with her exposed back to the camera, illuminated, her face in profile, slightly in shadow, her hair in a large Afro. In the *Guardian*, Calmese described the shoot as a "love letter to Black women".[17] His selection as photographer was historic, but the event was not without controversy. Calmese stated that he had been partly inspired by a harrowing photograph of the keloid-scarred back of an enslaved man known as Gordon or "Whipped Peter" which had been disseminated as abolitionist material in the 1800s. Was it appropriate for a cover shot supposedly evoking glamour to invoke an image of such suffering? For Calmese, it was about rewriting a centuries-old narrative about the white gaze and transforming it into something of elegance and glamour. He has also referred to the cover as his protest, his way of replacing the kind of narratives about Black bodies he feels have the power to shape people's self-image with more positive ones. This idea of alternative image-making is one that is also expressed in his series *Amongst Friends*, for which he photographed Black churchgoer and vintage clothes collector Lana Turner for five years. Evoking the mid-twentieth century, Dior's New Look and golden-age Hollywood glamour, the black-and-white photos of Turner exude the elegance Calmese speaks of regarding Davis. The series is like a poetic blazon: shots focus on Turner's glove-covered hands and her high-heeled feet; they admire the cut of her trousers, the exquisite hats on her head. The camera is presented as an apparatus that can desire, and it seems to both flirt with and honour Ms Turner. The photographs also reveal the aesthetic imagination not just of Calmese but of Turner too. There is a sense of play, a sense that this is fully a collaboration between photographer and subject. The images feel like an exercise in intentional image-making; there is a subtle, cheeky awareness of the fun of performance. Turner, who had previously been photographed by famed street fashion photographer Bill Cunningham, exudes self-confidence and self-knowledge in line with Calmese's desire to "repopulate the landscape of Black imagery and understanding that's been told to us".

> "He has referred to the cover as his protest, his way of replacing the kind of narratives about Black bodies he feels have the power to shape people's self-image with more positive ones"

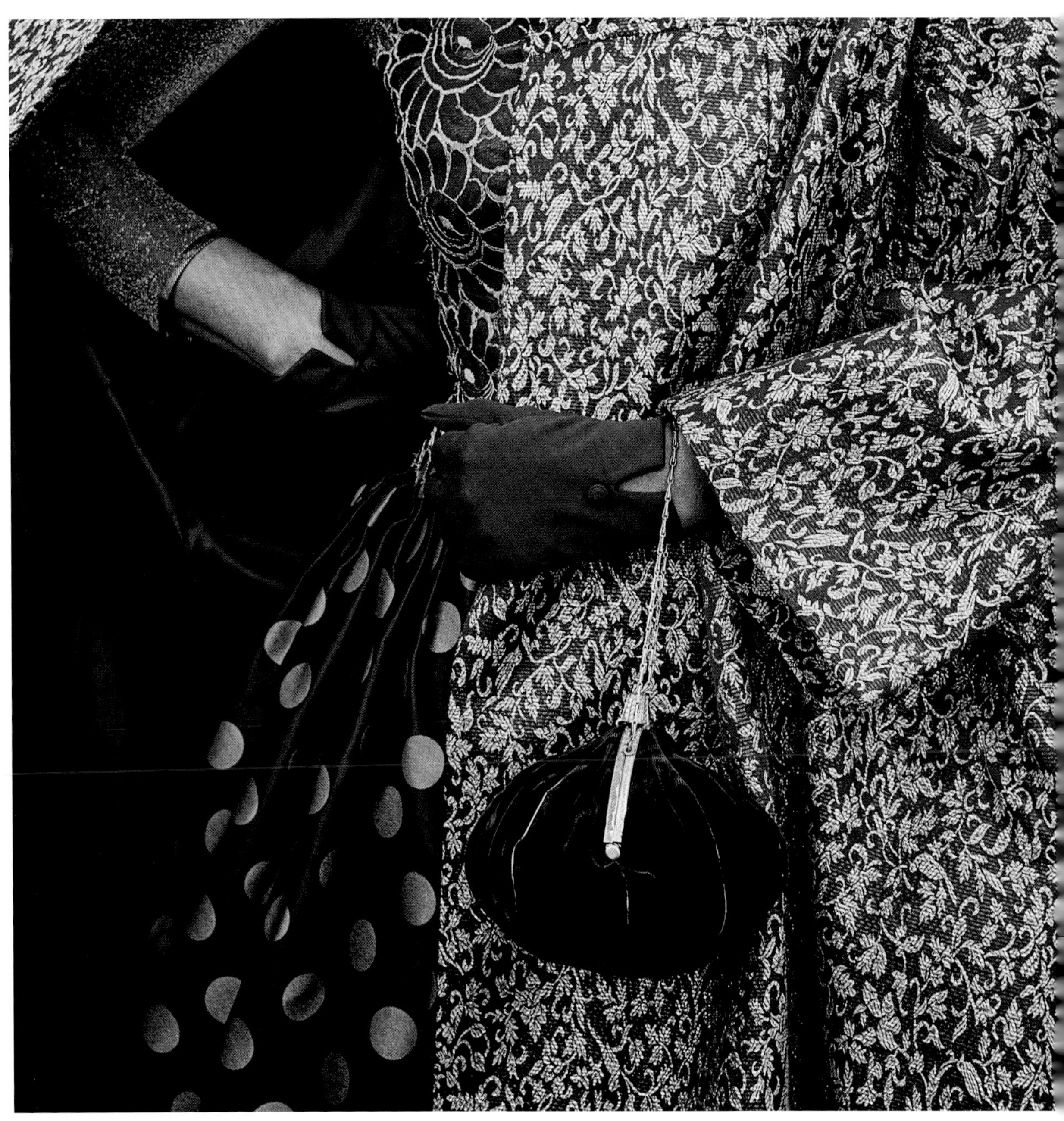

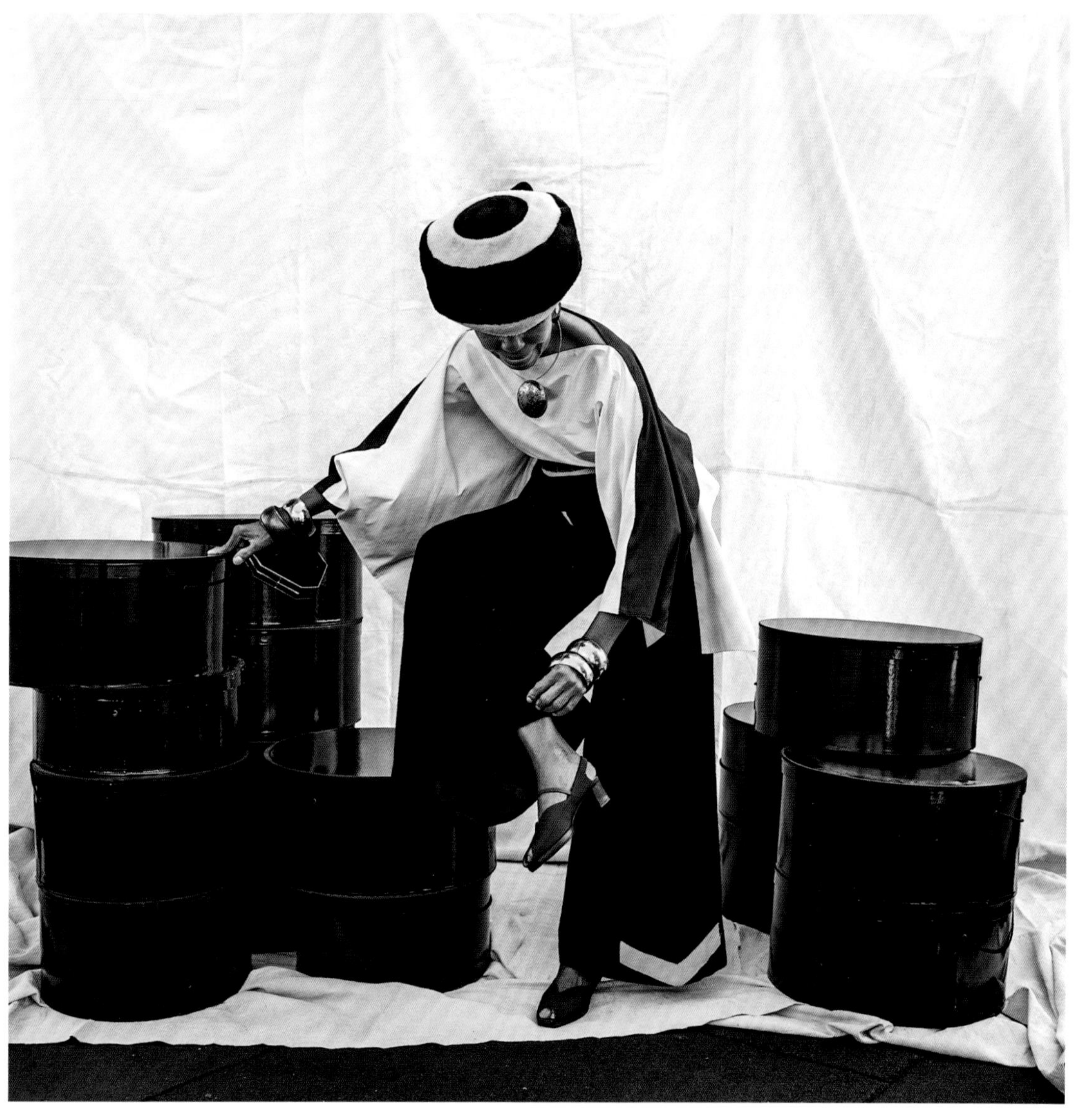

Previous spread: *Amongst Friends, No. 90*, 2012
These pages, clockwise from above:
Amongst Friends, No. 115, 2014
Amongst Friends, No. 29, 2012
Amongst Friends, No. 79, 2012

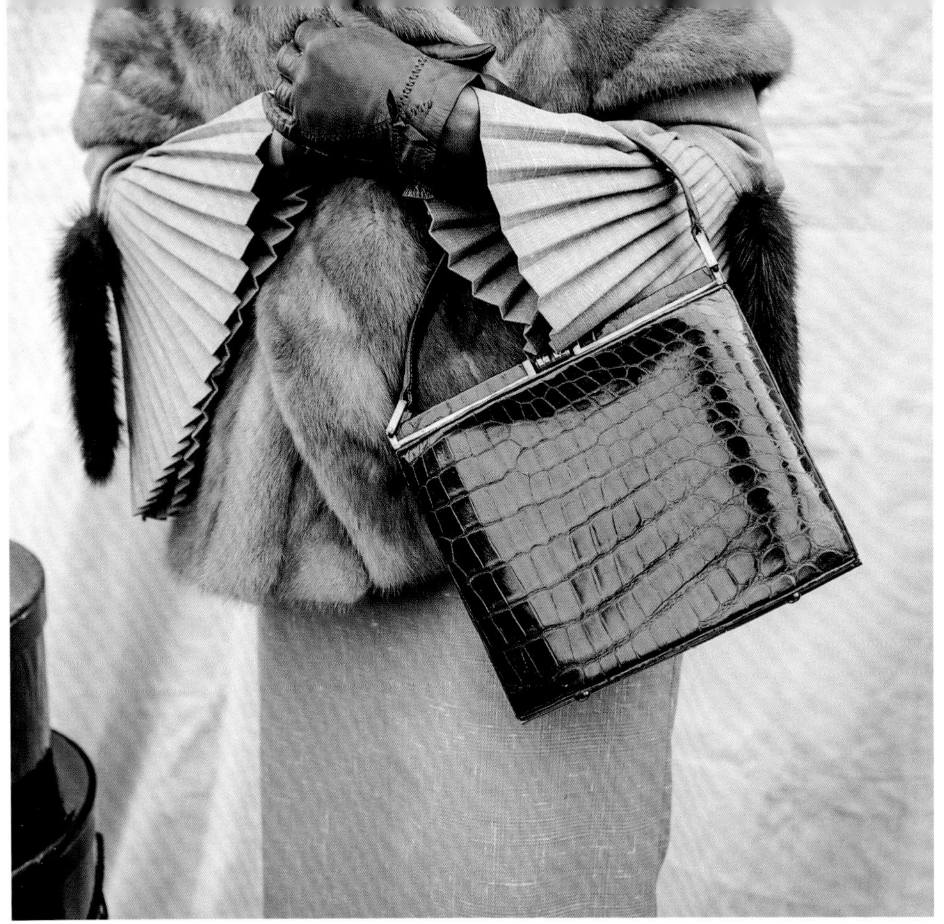

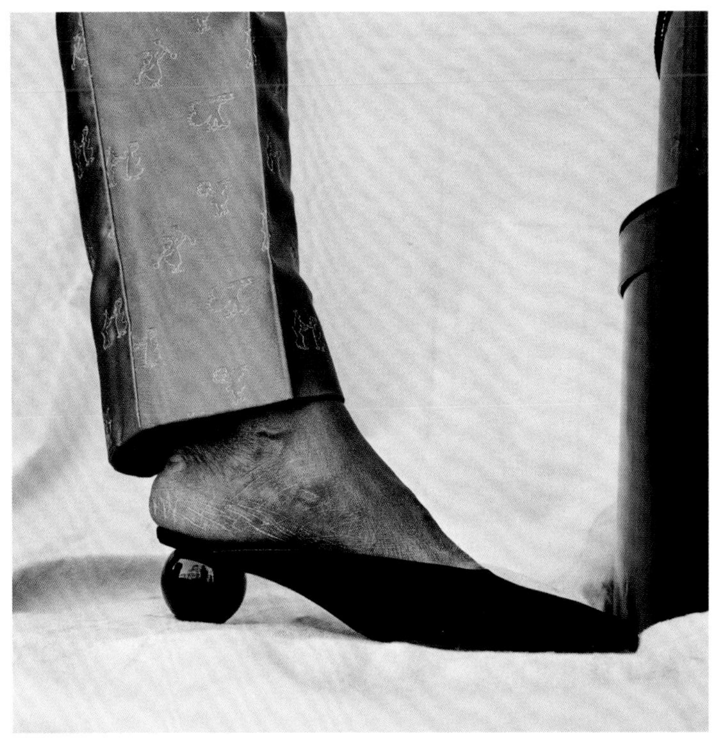

Melissa Alcena

A Word in your Shell-like

Nassau-based portrait and documentary photographer Melissa Alcena aims to dismantle some of the most enduring stereotypes and narratives about the Caribbean islands, namely, the dichotomy that posits them either as a paradise and getaway or as a place of poverty and violence. Alcena focuses on what often gets left out of these narratives: the people of the islands themselves. Understanding the power photography has to shape how we see people and places for far longer than the moment in which we first view an image, Alcena's vivid, colourful photographs celebrate everyday life in the Bahamas and the comings-and-goings of its people.

Her subjects, who span a range of ages, are often photographed at eye level, with the intention, it seems, of removing as many barriers as possible between them and her, and them and the viewer. In a few of the photographs, the subjects are sat at an angle, looking at the camera through the sides of their eyes, not out of contempt or disdain but rather a knowingness regarding being observed. It is a gaze that asks for acknowledgement of that exchange as opposed to participating in another exploitative and voyeuristic exercise. "I want you to look at this person, and I want you to respect them in all their glory," said Alcena in an interview with *Vice*. "I'm trying to celebrate the beauty that I see in people and the many forms that they come in."[18] The Bahamas' natural beauty also shines, with Alcena reframing common images like conch shells, palm fronds and market stalls as intimate settings for her vivid portraits. No unpeopled stretches of beach or thronging crowds, her photographs remind us that these are the everyday surroundings of many people, and the islands don't cease to be when the tourist is not looking.

Black masculinity is another complex topic that Alcena interrogates, looking at the self-conceptualization of men in the face of myriad sources that have for centuries defined masculinity for them. What does it mean to challenge these views of Blackness with photography? What does it mean that the approach to that challenge so often involves displaying a tenderness still so seldom associated with Black men as to often be deemed radical? These are questions Alcena explored in a 2017 exhibition, *Some Re(assembly) Required*; even the title of the show referred to the building and breaking down of ideas surrounding the images of Black men.

> "Alcena's vivid, colourful photographs celebrate everyday life in the Bahamas and the comings-and-goings of its people"

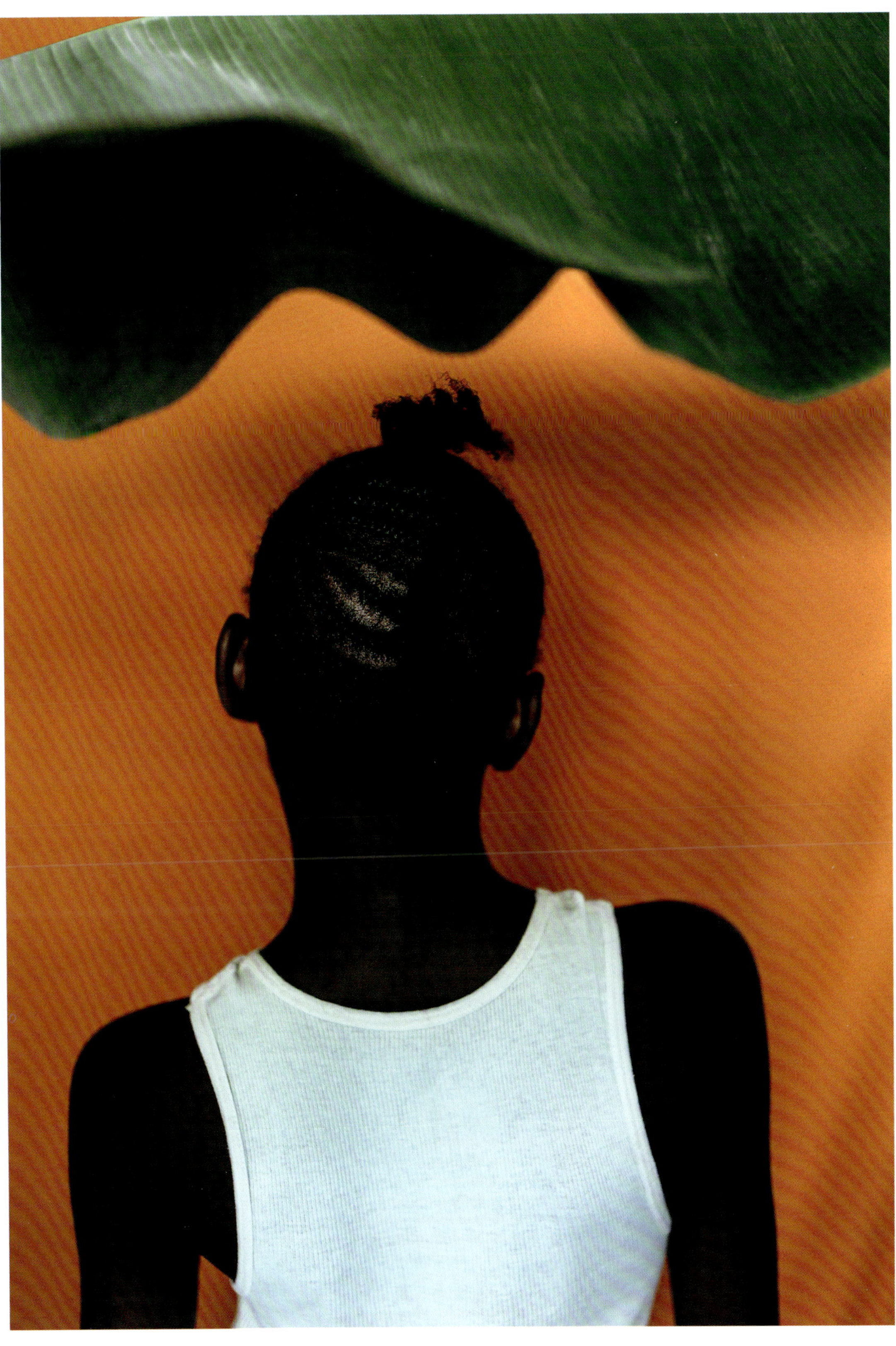

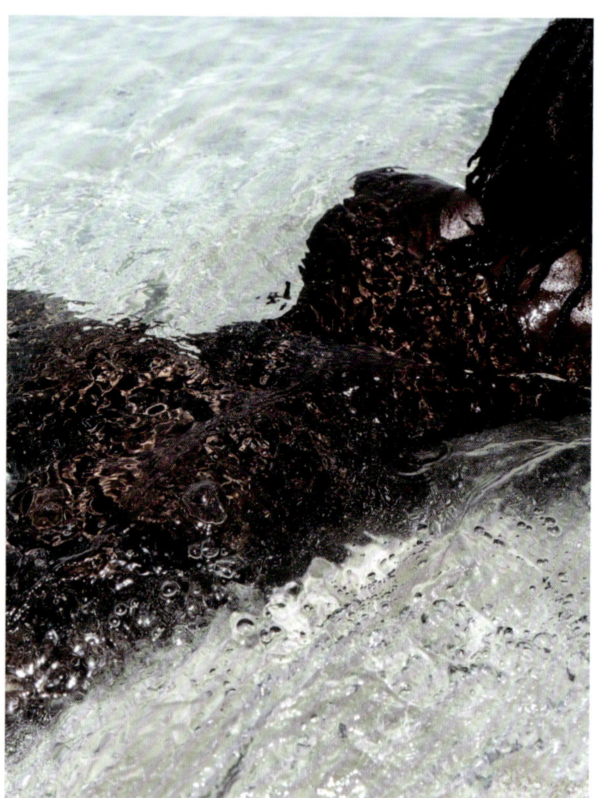

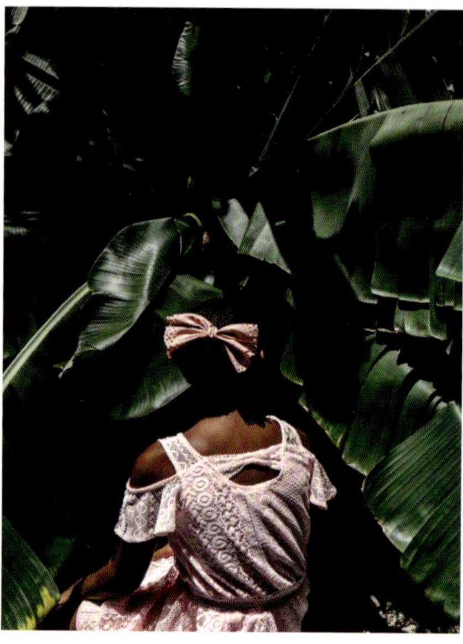

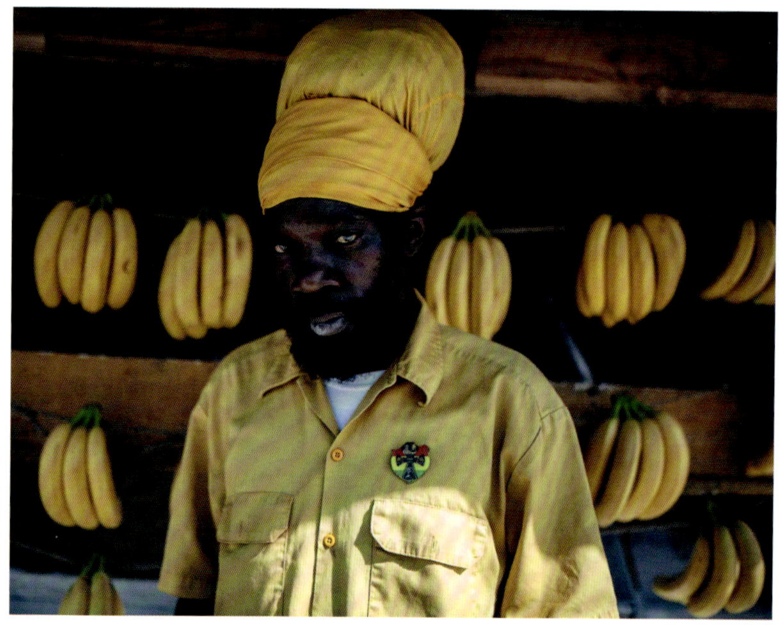

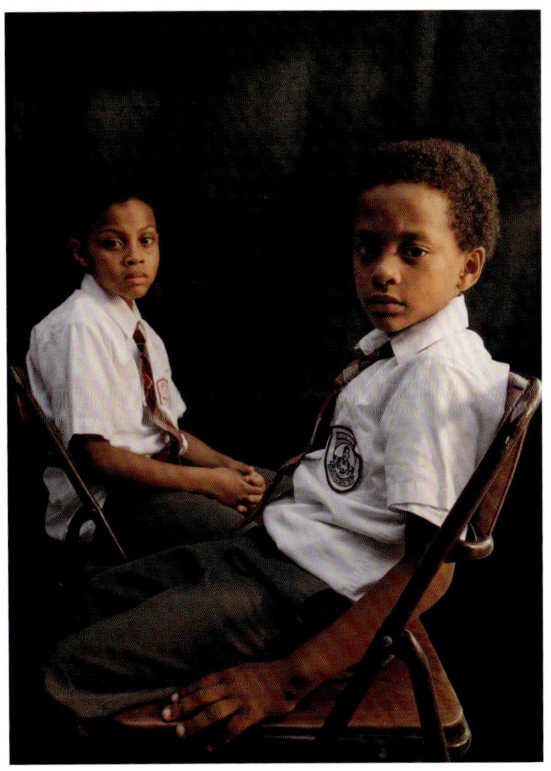

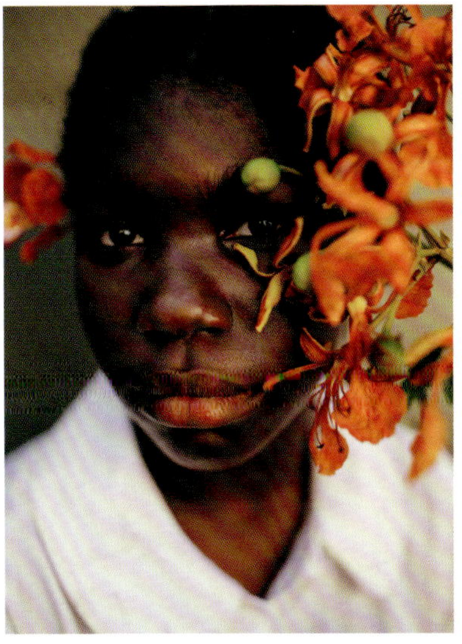

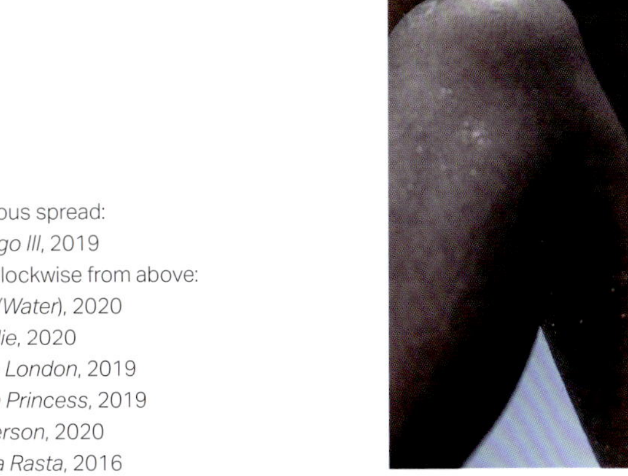

Previous spread:
Mango III, 2019
These pages, clockwise from above:
Khalid (Water), 2020
Ellie, 2020
Ocean & London, 2019
Poinciana Princess, 2019
Anderson, 2020
Banana Rasta, 2016

Davey Adesida

Searching for Softness

New York-based photographer Davey Adesida finds inspiration in the colours of French director Éric Rohmer's films. His photographs have a dreamy and cinematic quality and flirt with nostalgia without getting mired in it. Shot on Kodak film for the tones it produces for skin colour (ironically, until Kodak Gold, Kodak's film historically did not photograph darker skin tones well at all), Adesida's work, from fashion editorials to celebrity portraiture, combines intimacy with slight whimsy. His work exudes a gentleness, innocence and quiet sense of contentment, which a colour palette that occasionally juxtaposes block primary colours with more powdery tones helps evoke. This can be seen in a photo shoot with *Stranger Things* actor Caleb McLaughlin. In one image, the young actor, dressed in a bold red tank top, reclines, propped up on his elbows, a blue-violet backdrop reflecting purple light onto his face. He looks intently at the camera and the viewer, a bunch of long-stemmed yellow flowers in his left hand.

"I want Black people to be seen in a softer manner because we're seen as aggressive and dramatic most of the time, and I want the world to see us as something calmer, more therapeutic,"

> "His work exudes a gentleness, innocence and quiet sense of contentment, which a colour palette that occasionally juxtaposes block primary colours with more powdery tones helps evoke"

says Adesida in a discussion about his series of photographs submitted to *Love* magazine for its Love Diaries series.[19] The series does not depict Black subjects exclusively, but all the models are seen through that eye that wants to afford Black people the fullness of their humanity under the scrutiny of the camera lens. He uses intense close-ups, the faces of his subjects taking up most of the frame, drawing the viewer's focus to every facet of their facial features, not allowing them to be distracted by surroundings, inviting our gazes to linger without the feeling of invasion. Just as his extreme close-ups invite the viewer to contemplate the relationship between the lens and the subject, *Polaroids, Peel Back* looks at the photograph as an object too, depicting the contact sheet of Adesida's portraits.

Adesida is outspoken about contributing alternative images of Black men to the realm of visual art and culture that is considered mainstream, and he has also been vocal about the importance of increasing the presence of Black people behind the camera, calling out the elitist gatekeeping he sees in the fashion industry and advocating for more Black fashion photographers and stylists to be hired on a long-term basis.

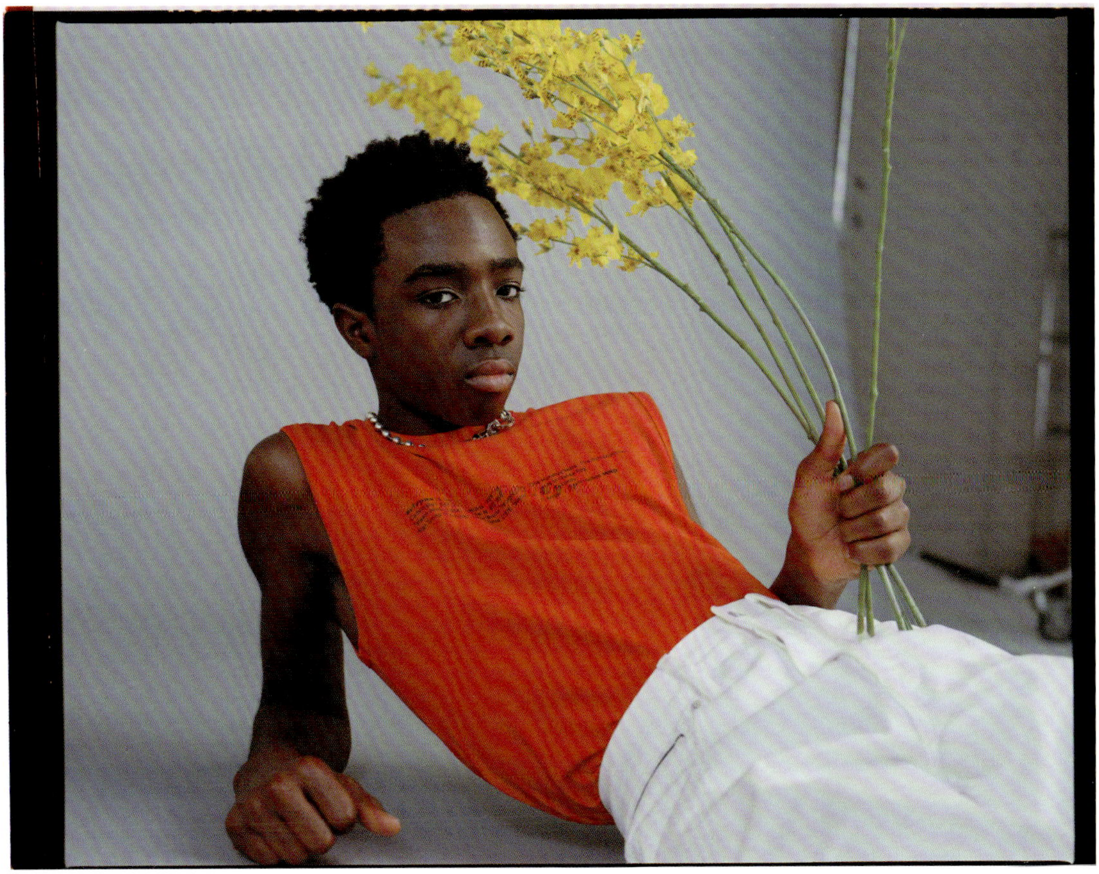

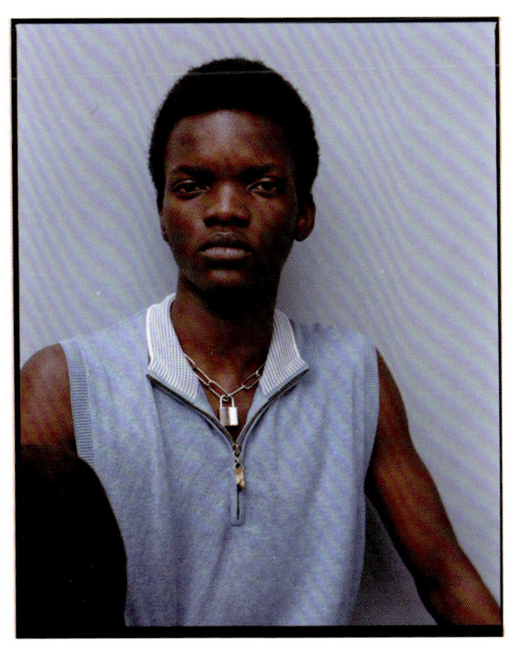

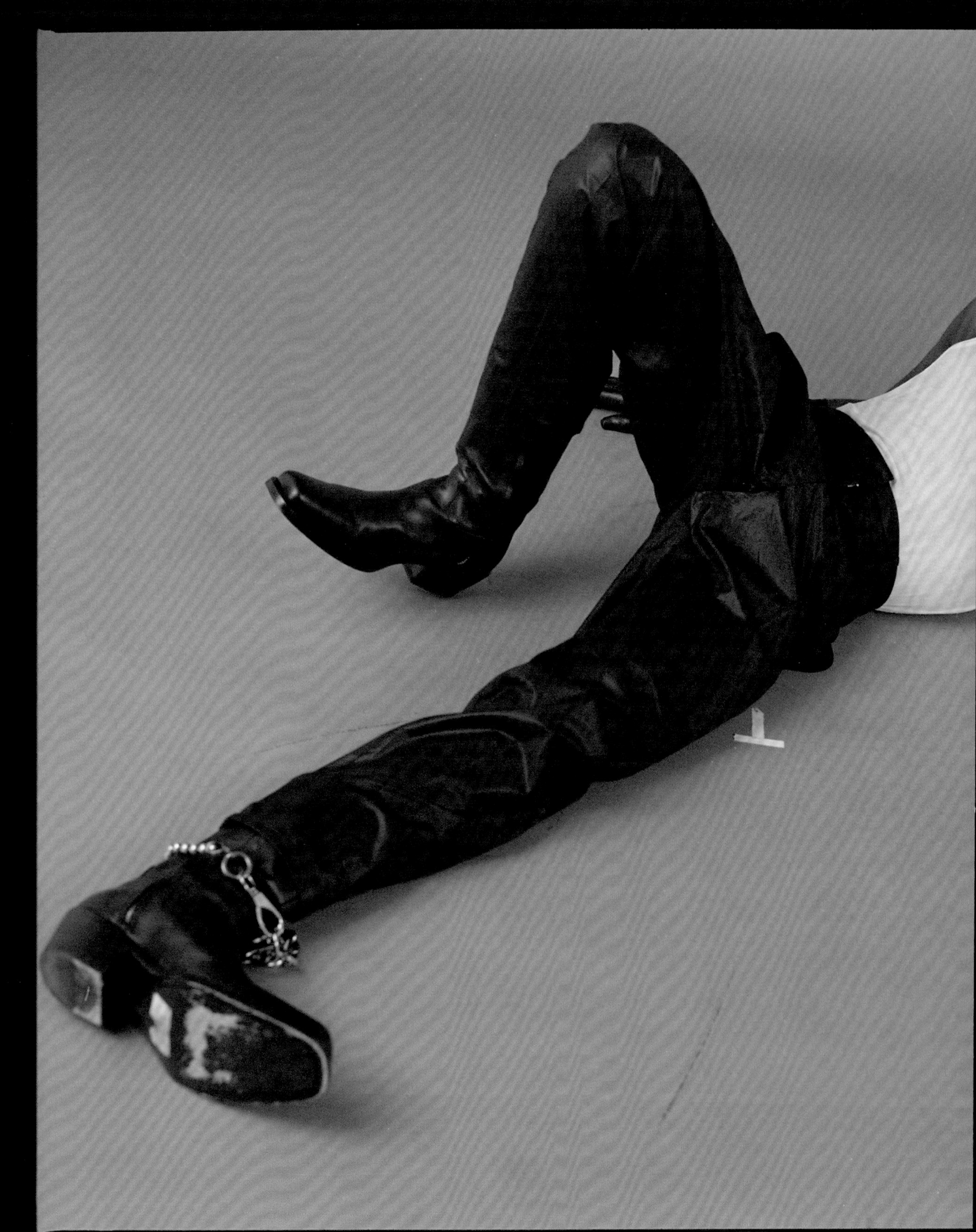

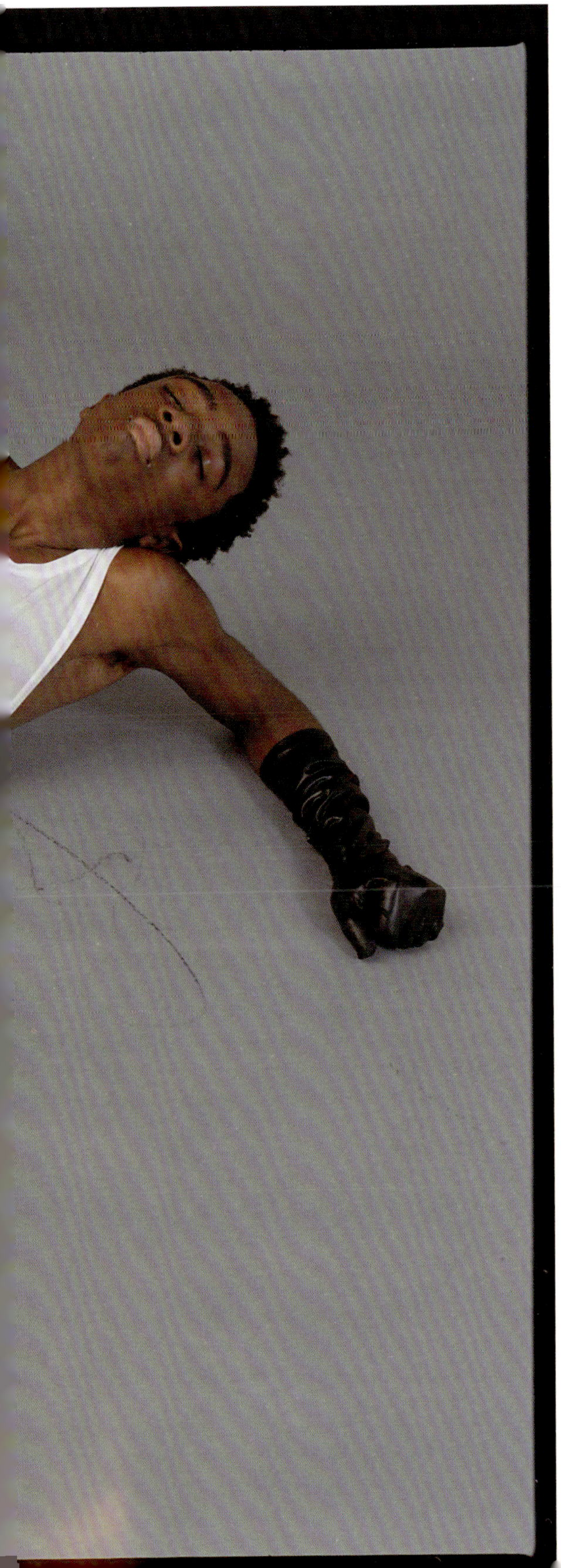

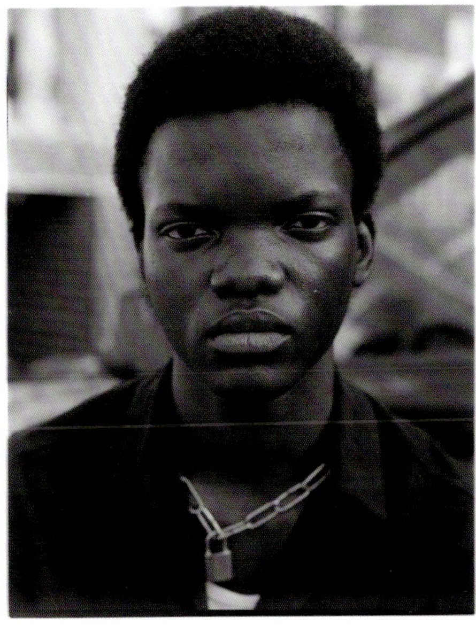

Previous spread, from top: *Neue Journal*, March 2018
Personal Work, May 2020
These pages, from left: *Neue Journal*, March 2018
Love, August 2020

Takeisha Jefferson

Preservation in Print

The familial has always been a source of inspiration for American photographer Takeisha Jefferson. The US Air Force veteran began taking photographs of her siblings as a child and then, as an adult, started photographing her own children influenced by Sally Mann, whose most known works were her controversial large-format black-and-white images of her three children.

Spurred by the revelations of ancestral DNA tests, Jefferson uses her portrait photography to honour and "bring to life forgotten and unknown members of her family".[20] She emulated the wet collodion and tintype photography of the mid-to-late nineteenth century. In doing so, she steeps her work in a sense of historicity, finding an imaginative way into her ancestral past through the faces of her modern-day family members.

That melding of fantasy and history gives her images a sense of drama and romance, perhaps most strikingly evoked in *Grandma's* (2020) and *I'm Not a Killer But Don't Push Me* (2020). The former depicts a beautiful young Black woman, the tintype effect creating a mist around her. This is an effect duplicated in the latter photograph, which depicts a young Black man with shiny, dark eyes and his head covered. *The Revolution* (2018) also creates the sense of the discovery of a historical artefact, the portrait of a man with tribal marks on his face almost having the quality of a drawing. While the manipulation of the images gives us a sense of the era Jefferson wishes to evoke, there is no real sense of place, which gives the images a slightly ghostly quality. That sense of a void makes the faces of her subjects appear like flashes of memory and emphasizes the attempt to capture something ephemeral, the attempt to retrieve something from history and preserve it.

Jefferson prints her photographs on archival paper, an act given greater significance by the themes Jefferson is exploring of family lineage and hidden history. Every deliberation has gone into making work that not only has the appearance of having survived centuries but that is also itself designed to last and not degrade over time.

Jefferson's fantasy Victoriana explores the idea of work surviving beyond you as a physical object at a time when digital photography not only dominates but when it is where most people now look to for the immortality of images.

> "She steeps her work in a sense of historicity, finding an imaginative way into her ancestral past through the faces of her modern-day family members"

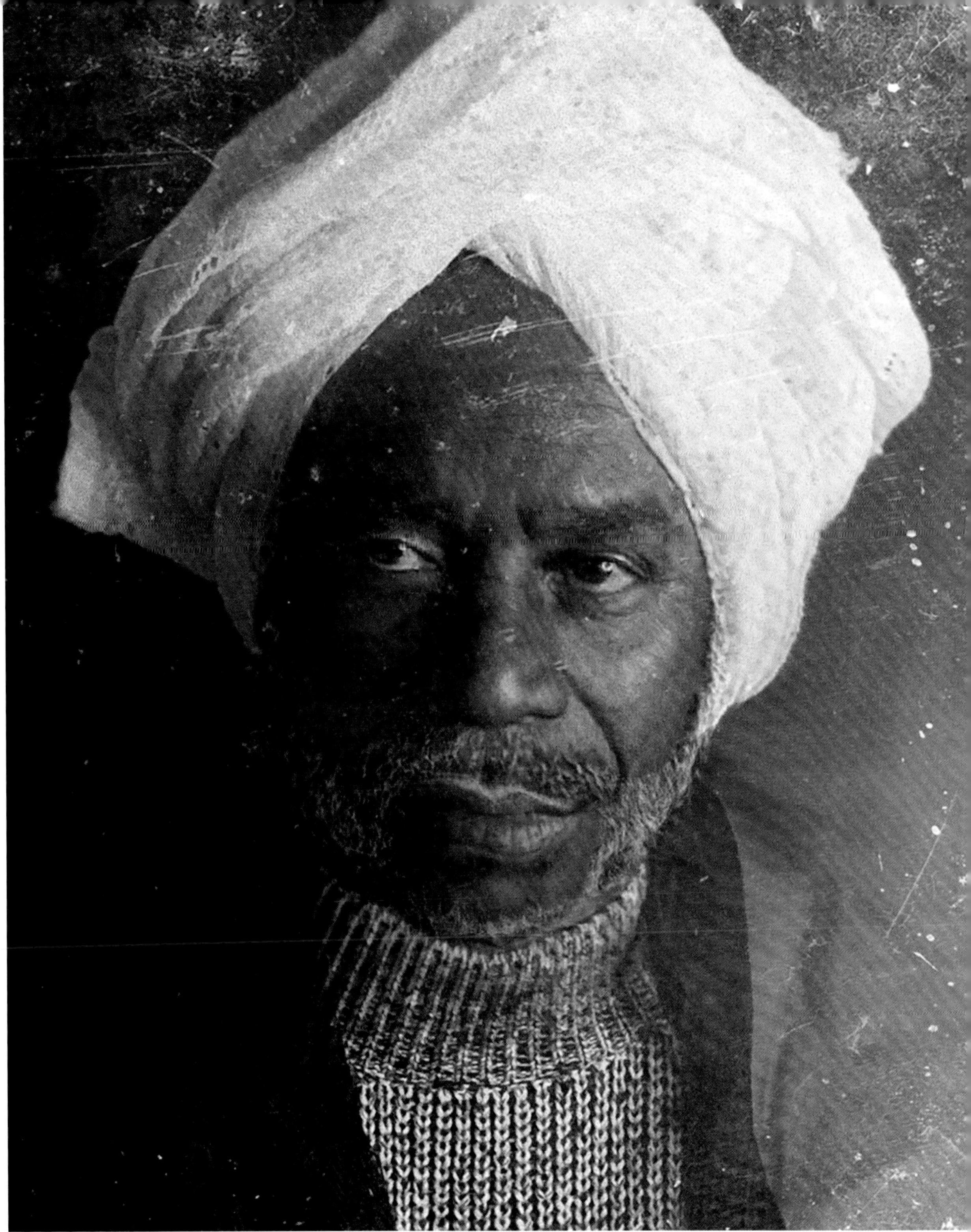

Descendants, 2020

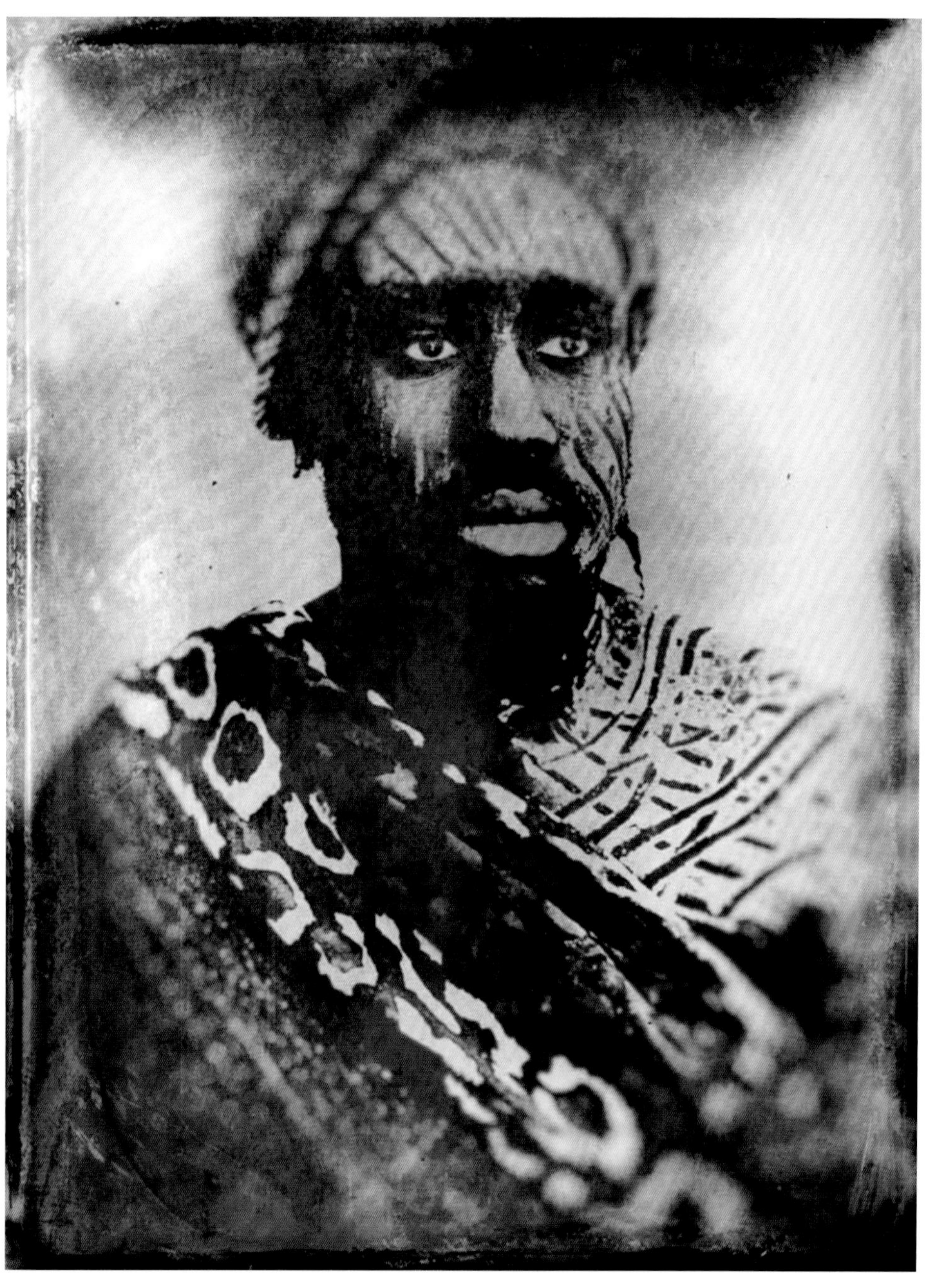

The Revolution, 2018

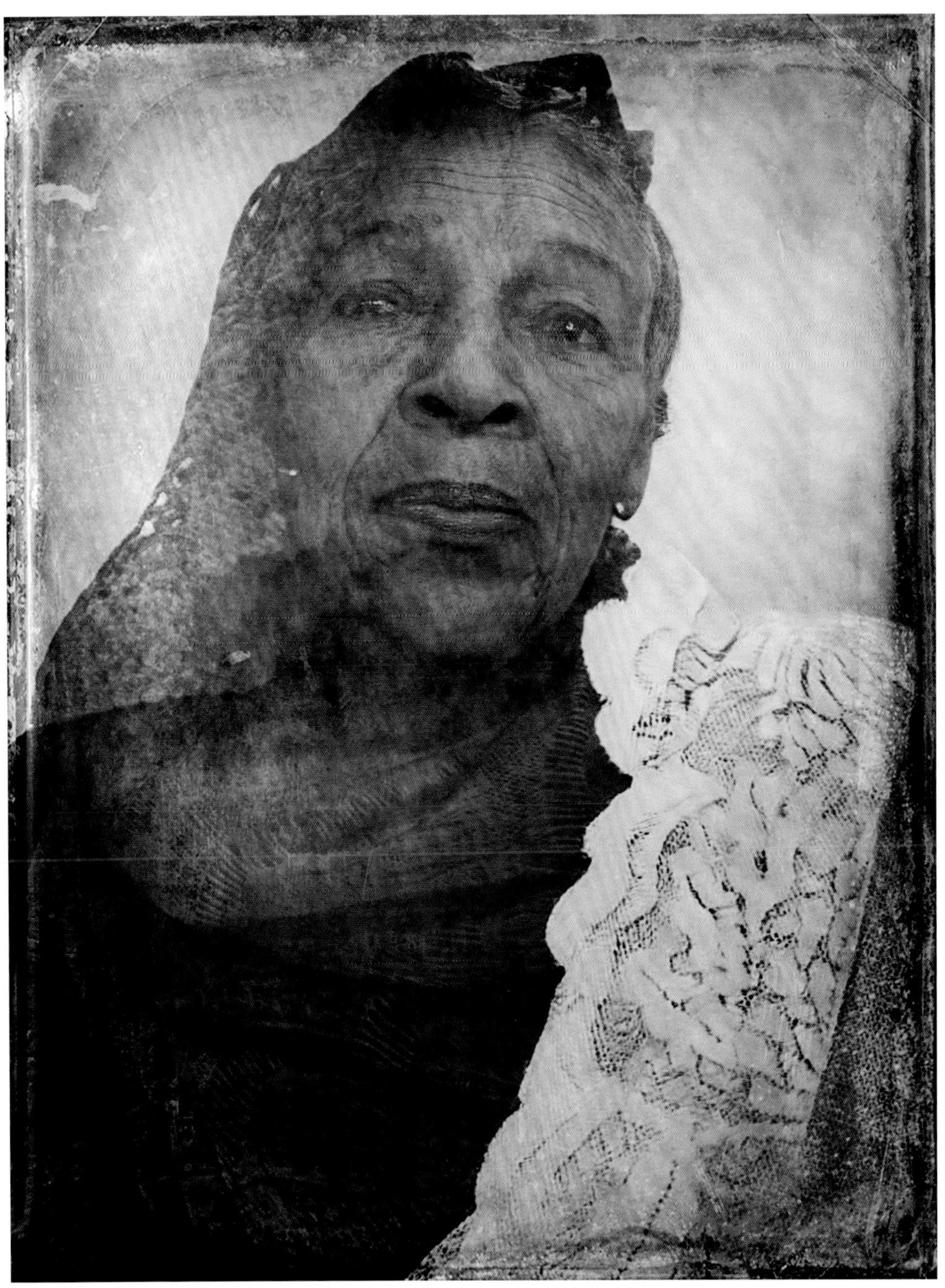

Big Ma, 2019

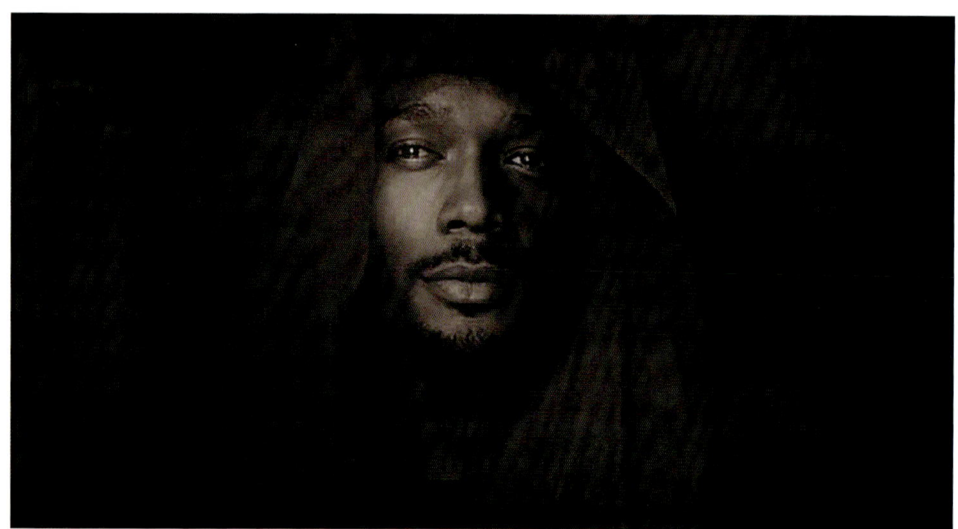

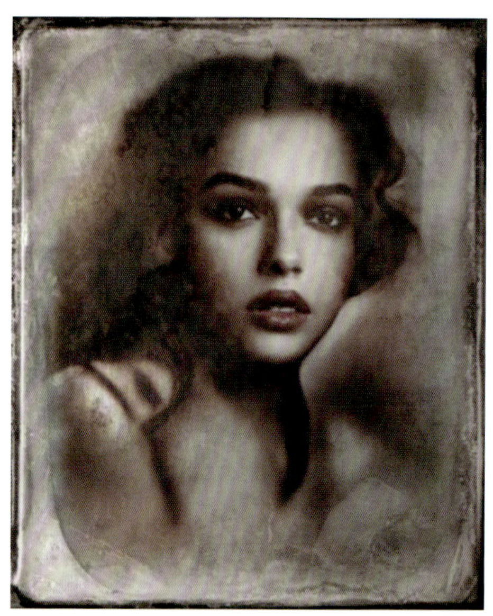

From top: *I'm Not a Killer But Don't Push Me*, 2020
Grandma's, 2020

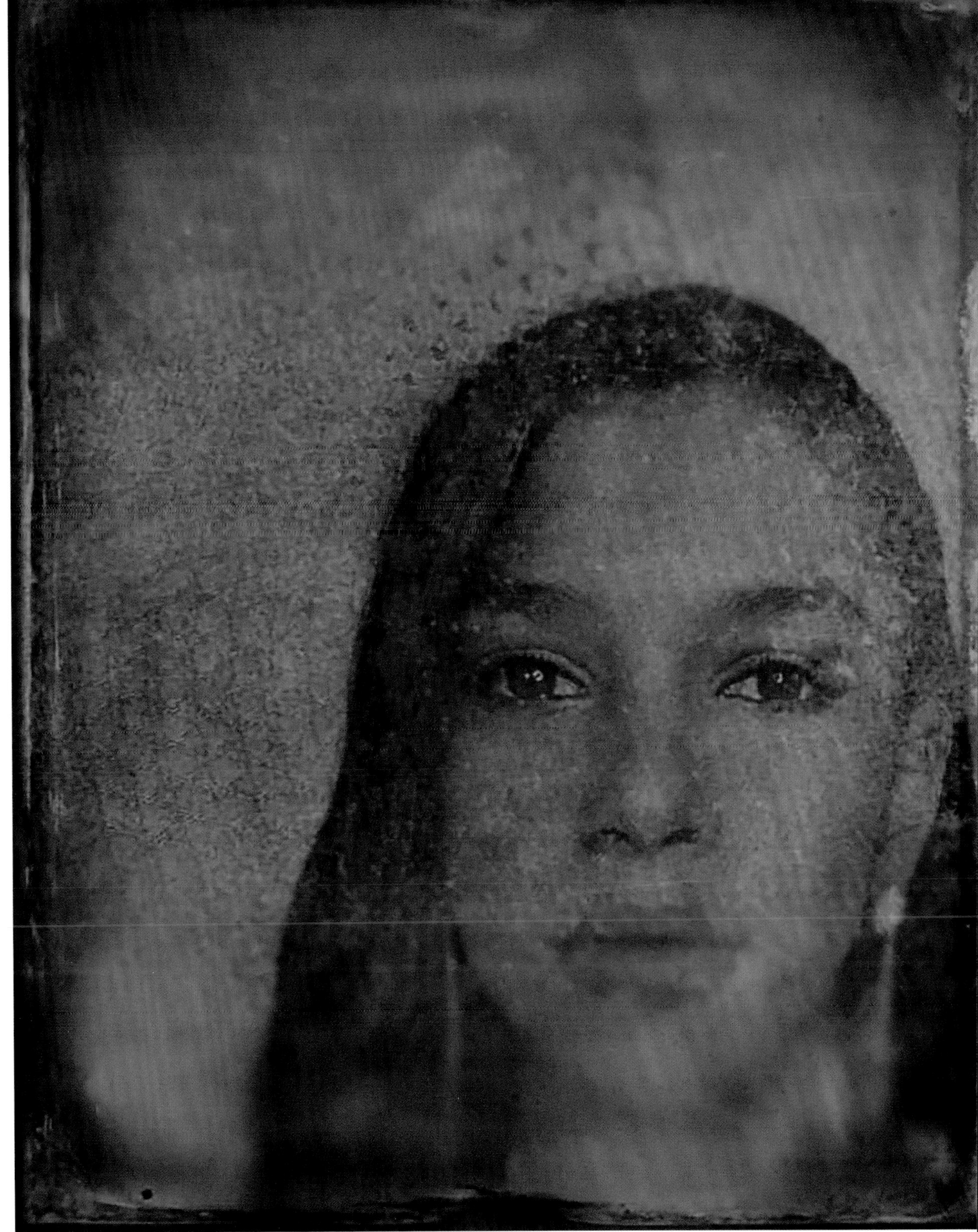

Voiced, 2018

Atong Atem

A Radical Gaze

Based in Melbourne, Australia, writer and artist Atong Atem uses her multidisciplinary approach to explore themes of postcolonialism and looking. Moving to Australia as a refugee in 1997 cemented the importance of storytelling for her, and finding Black African artists and activist communities who created their own spaces in response to the exclusivity and inaccessibility of the art world in Australia was also a boon. Wary of the "anthropological" way indigenous art was explored at school, Atem stresses in her work the persistence of issues perpetuated by colonial expansion in the countries those powers once controlled, with the warning that we are not living in the postcolonial times that the titles of so many university modules would suggest.[21]

Working with photography and video, Atem does not see her work as overtly political but rather as implicitly so, partly because of the multiple identities she inhabits. She sees her work instead as being about herself, how she sees and is perceived by the world. "I've described my work in general as an ongoing self-portrait because there is so much self-discovery in learning about world history," she told the *Sydney Morning Herald*. "It feels like I am constantly making work about myself, and it just happens that it resonates with other people."[22]

What Atem gleans from studying history and looking into archival material from the last two centuries, she transmutes into her work both visually and conceptually. Speaking to *Nataal*, Atem credited studio photographers Malick Sidibé, Seydou Keïta and Philip Kwame Apagya for "changing the European narrative of photography from one of ethnography and consumption, to one of ownership on our part".[23] It is this – what she has termed "the radical gaze of Black studio photography" – to which Atem's work pays tribute.[24] Her earliest photographic series, *Studio Series* (2015), drew inspiration from those aforementioned artists. Her subjects posed in vibrant wax-print fabrics in celebration of those studio photographers who, in the midst of African nations beginning to find political independence, responded to the ethnographic style of photography that had dominated in depictions of continental Africans by demonstrating how they depicted themselves. With her work she aims to generate and bring to the fore conversations that are less narrow and more reflective of the vastness of Black history and lived experience, exploring the relationship between image manipulation and the concept of truth in photography. You can see this in her *Photo Weavings* series (2021), where the images have been cut and woven through each other to create surreal, abstract and textured work that seems to speak to the complexity of subjectivity and identity by complicating the image we see.

> "Her work generates conversations reflective of the vastness of Black history and lived experience, exploring the relationship between image manipulation and the concept of truth in photography"

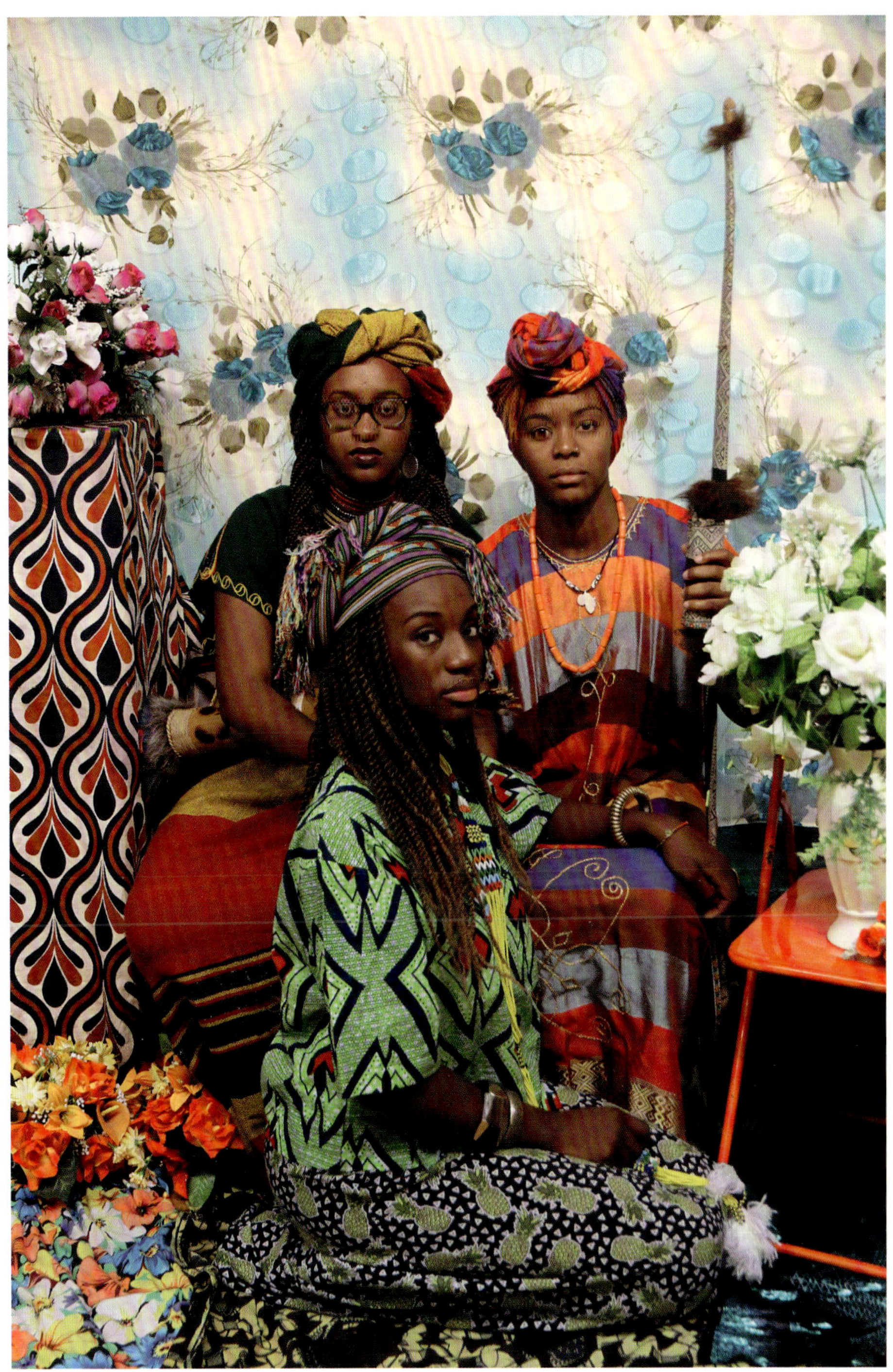

Paanda, 2015

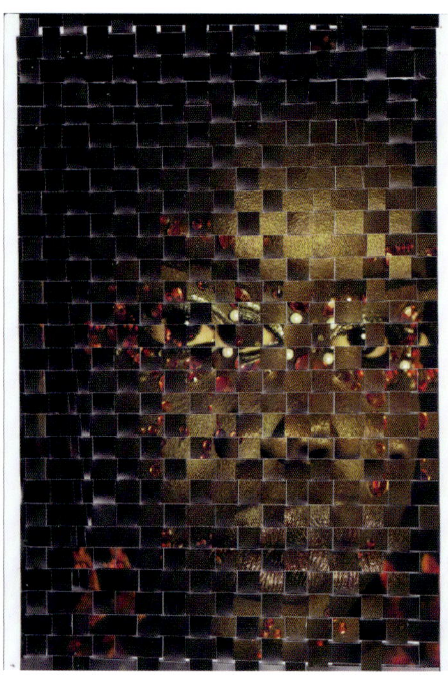

From top: *Red Weave*, 2021
Hamam 6, 2021
Hamam 5, 2021

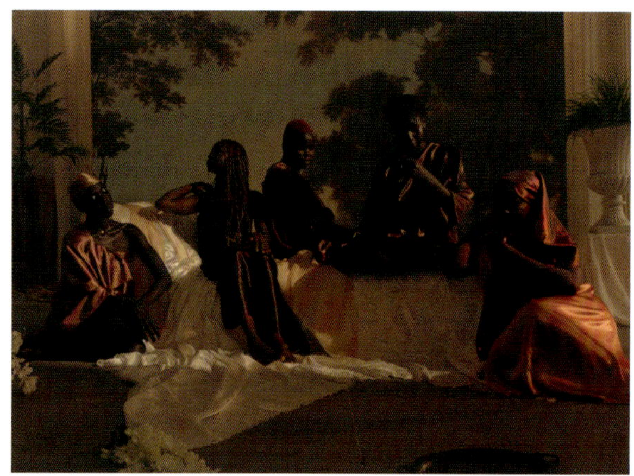

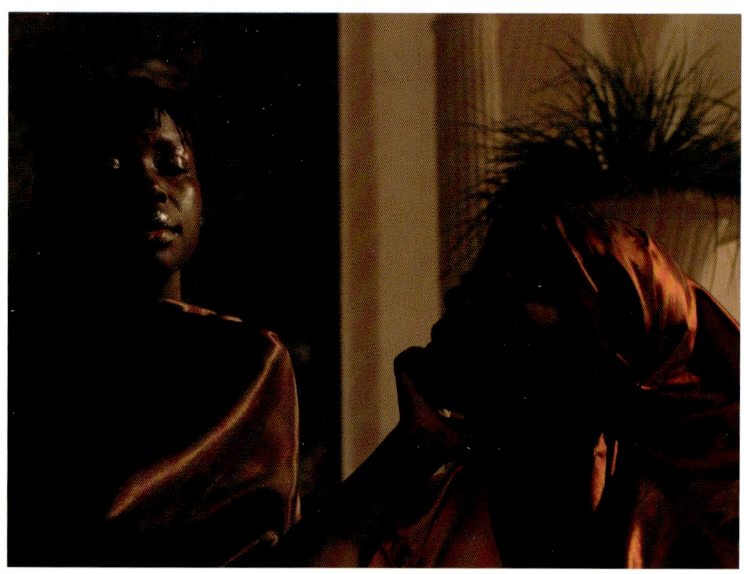

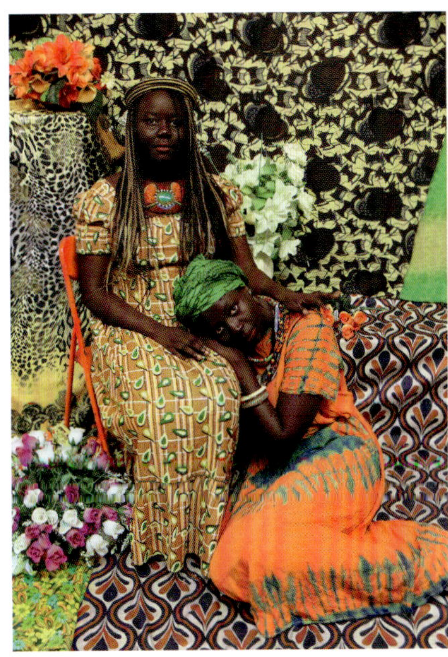

From top: *Adut and Big*, 2015
Eva in Green, 2020

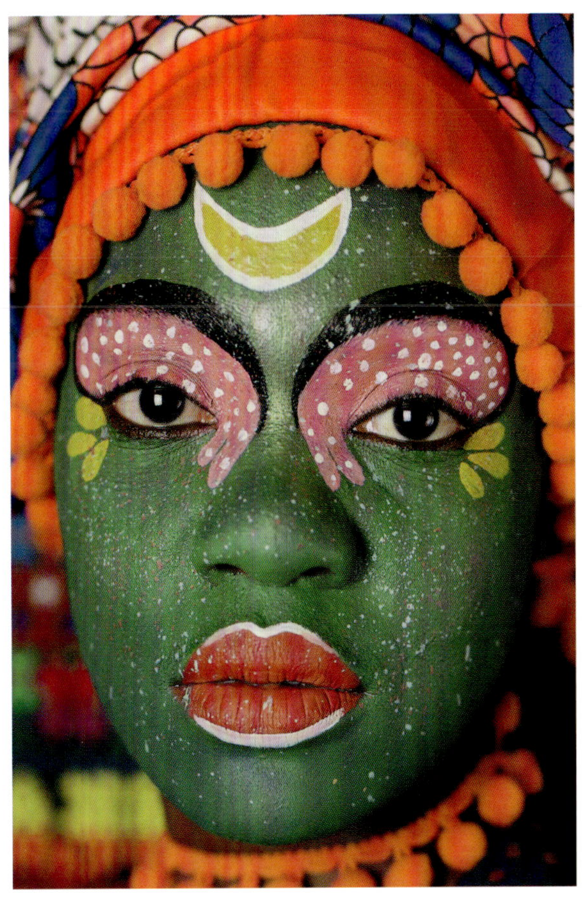

Donavon Smallwood

Solace in the City

Self-taught New York-based photographer Donavon Smallwood published his first monograph, *Languor*, in 2021. A "lyrical series of images made as a means of exploring escape, home, nature, and tranquillity", the photographs were taken in New York's Central Park in 2020 as the city became an epicentre for the COVID-19 pandemic in America. In a year which contained both the eerie emptiness and silence of less-travelled streets and the shouts for racial justice in the protests that arose after the killing of George Floyd, Smallwood's photographs were made to "escap[e] the pressure cooker that was 2020".[25] In his images, the wilder northwestern part of Central Park is transformed into another world, far away from the bustle and tension of the city. But it is not only the city itself that can hold tension. Shortly before creating this series, Smallwood learned of Seneca Village, a nineteenth-century community of mostly Black landowners that was forcibly evicted and razed to create Central Park. A high-school teacher once told Smallwood, who had considered as a child becoming an archaeologist, that "archaeology and photography were in many ways the same".[26] This sense of uncovering, amalgamated with an appreciation of nature inspired by the poetry of William Blake, results in a collection of portraits and landscape photographs of the park that seem to explore space

that has not been encroached upon and that could provide solace, however temporarily, for Smallwood's Black subjects.

Shot on medium-format film, Smallwood's images promote isolation but not loneliness. They do not emit an atmosphere of bereavement or deprivation, but rather calm assuredness. In one particular image, a young man wearing a black du-rag sits on the ground, one leg tucked underneath him, the other extended. His arms rest languidly on them, fingers grazing the grass. He is completely out of focus, the leaves of a tree dangling in the foreground instead as though objecting to the camera's – and our – intrusion. Another image in this series emphasizes this idea. It is shot through the leaves, the park in the background blurred and abstract, the leaves creating a patterned veil that begs to be swept to the side to reveal the hidden space behind. A relationship between Smallwood's subjects and nature is set up, one where the latter protects the former. In October 2020, he accompanied *Financial Times* writer Oluwakemi Aladesuyi to Idlewild, an unincorporated community in rural west Michigan, which was once known colloquially as the "Black Eden of Michigan" until the 1964 Civil Rights Act passed. This more reciprocal relationship between green, open spaces and Black people is a salient theme explored repeatedly in Smallwood's work.

> "The reciprocal relationship between green, open spaces and Black people is a salient theme explored repeatedly in Smallwood's work"

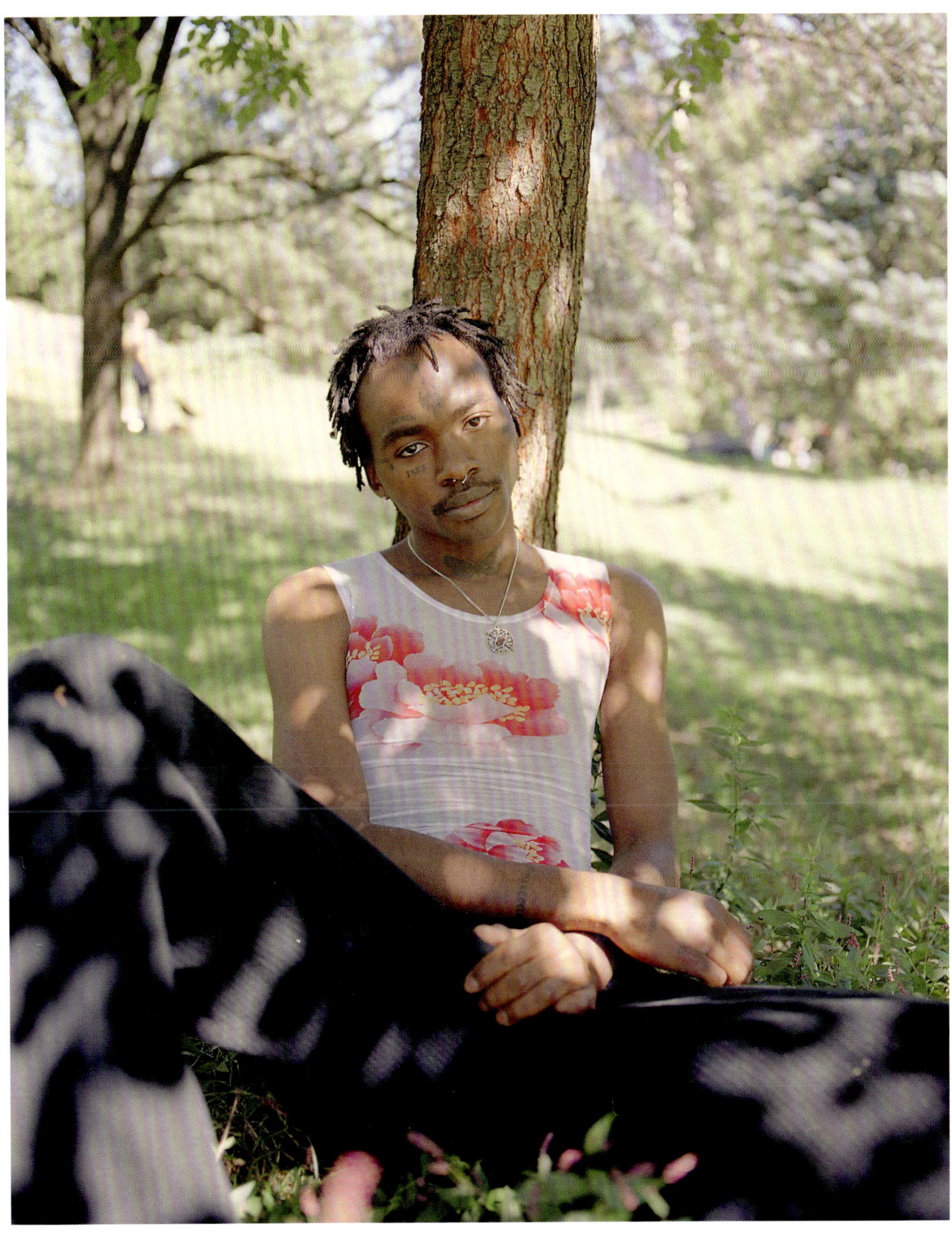

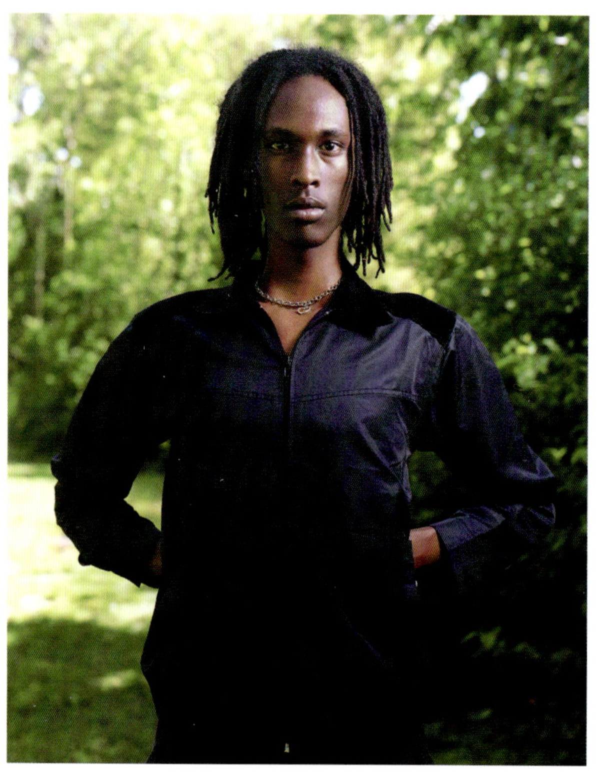

Previous spread: *Terry*, 2020
This page, from top: *Haroon*, 2019
Untitled #35, from *Languor*, 2020
Opposite, clockwise from top left:
Untitled #30, from *Languor*, 2020
Untitled #7, from *Languor*, 2020
Asante, 2020

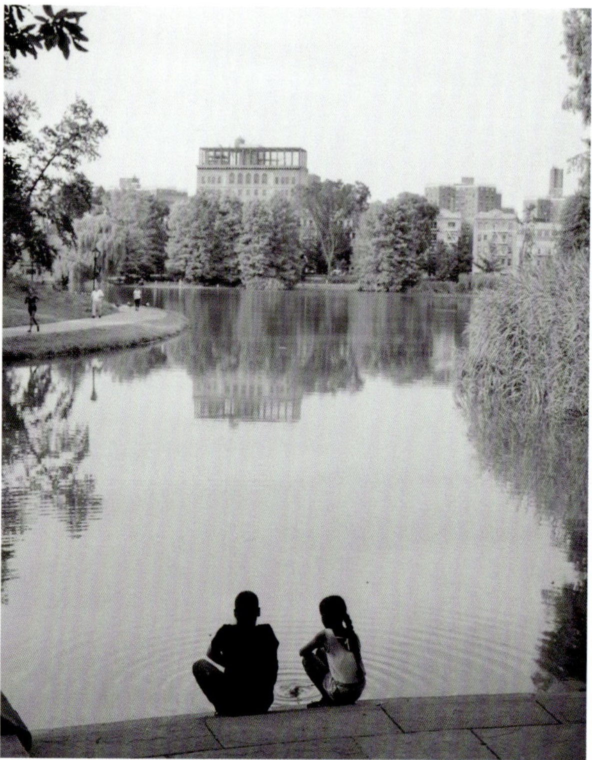

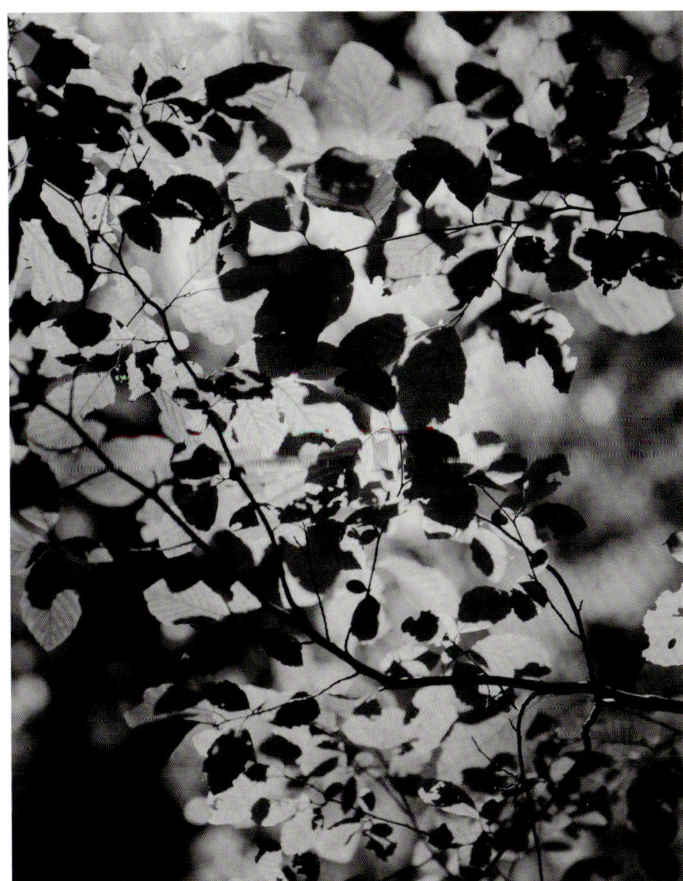

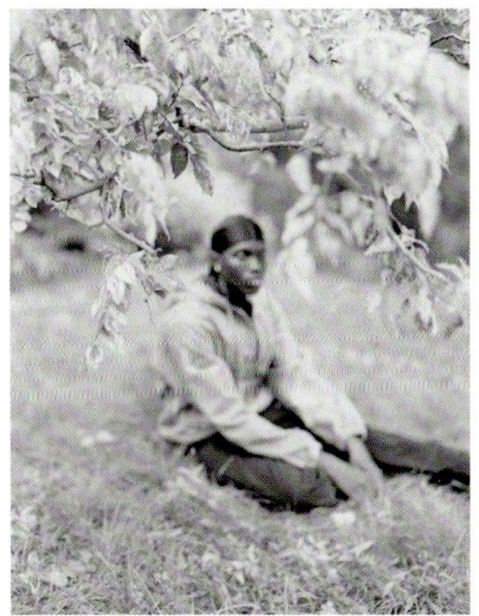

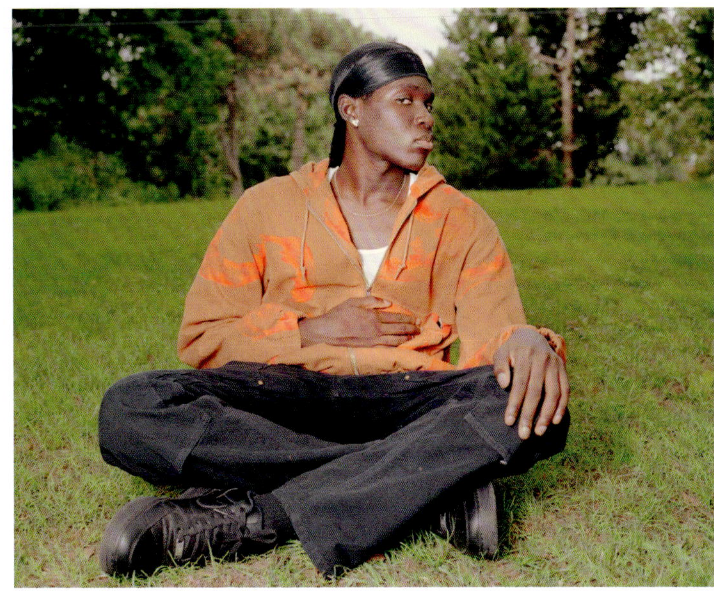

Henry J. Kamara

Looking for the "I"

British-Sierra Leonean artist Henry J. Kamara has described his work to *It's Nice That* as a way to "better understand the mechanisms that make up my sense of 'I' in this world". The exploration of his subjectivity, informed by the experience of being a first-generation immigrant born in the United Kingdom to a Sierra Leonean-Lebanese father and Sierra Leonean mother, took him to the West African nation his parents emigrated from, where he began a lifelong project to document the lives and stories of its people. *Two Sim*, named for the slang phrase meaning dual identity and referring to the swapping of two mobile phone SIM cards, embodies the idea of moving between two places one might consider home. Kamara travelled to his father's village wanting to find the things that influenced his life from more than 4,000 miles away and shaped the experiences of his parents – including their decision to migrate to the UK – more directly. The photographs Kamara created tell a story to which many children of the African diaspora can relate: the desire to find yourself in what looks both familiar and unfamiliar to you. He photographs children playing games, the girl in the foreground captured mid-leap, a little toddler standing behind her, preoccupied with a fascinating pot. Kamara's camera is right in the midst of the action, not observing from afar with detachment but not evoking a sense of intrusion either.

While his work explores the push and pull of places we call home, Kamara also seeks to challenge, if not dismantle, the restrictive and often offensive narratives and stereotypes through which the world gets a limited view of the African continent. Avoiding a sense of exploitation with street photography is therefore something the artist strives for, aware of the justifiable distrust on the part of many ordinary people about how Sierra Leone has often been portrayed in the media. His point of view, like that of a few other artists in this book, is situated in the "in-between", as he told *i-D* magazine: the feeling of being "never quite one or the other". Again, like other photographers featured here, Kamara took photographs of the Black Lives Matter protests which spanned the globe in the summer of 2020. Shooting the crowds, signs and speeches in London's Trafalgar Square, Kamara's images contribute both to a repository of future visual sources on the resurgence of the movement after the killing of George Floyd and to a growing modern tradition of new civil rights protest photography.

> "Kamara's camera is right in the midst of the action, not observing from afar with detachment but not evoking a sense of intrusion either"

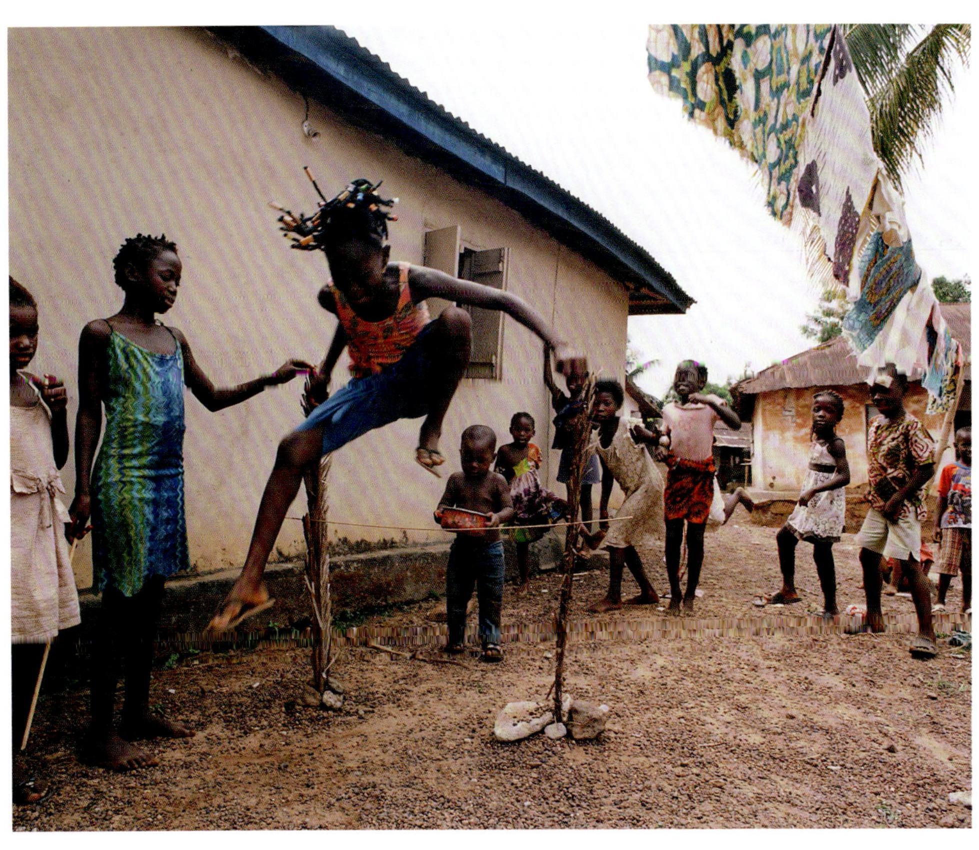

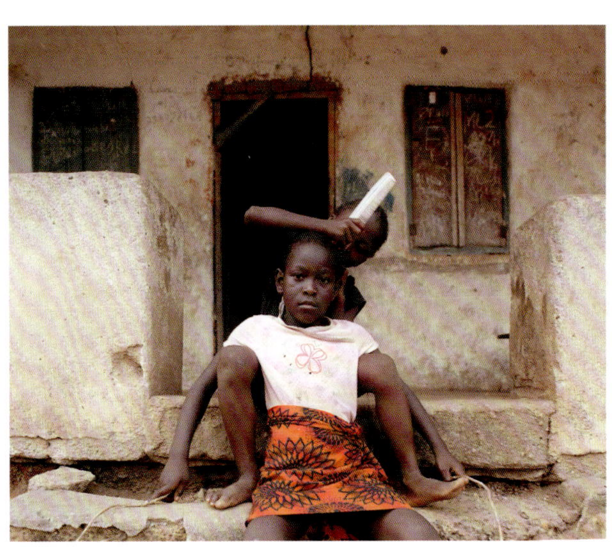

This page, from top: *Children of Blama, Sierra Leone*, April 2019
"Kam siddom make ar plant you eya." A Young Girl Braiding her Sister's Hair, Blama Eastern Province, Sierra Leone, April 2019
Following spread: *Oloya Alex Hassan, Also Known as Loyalty, Freetown, Sierra Leone*, April 2019

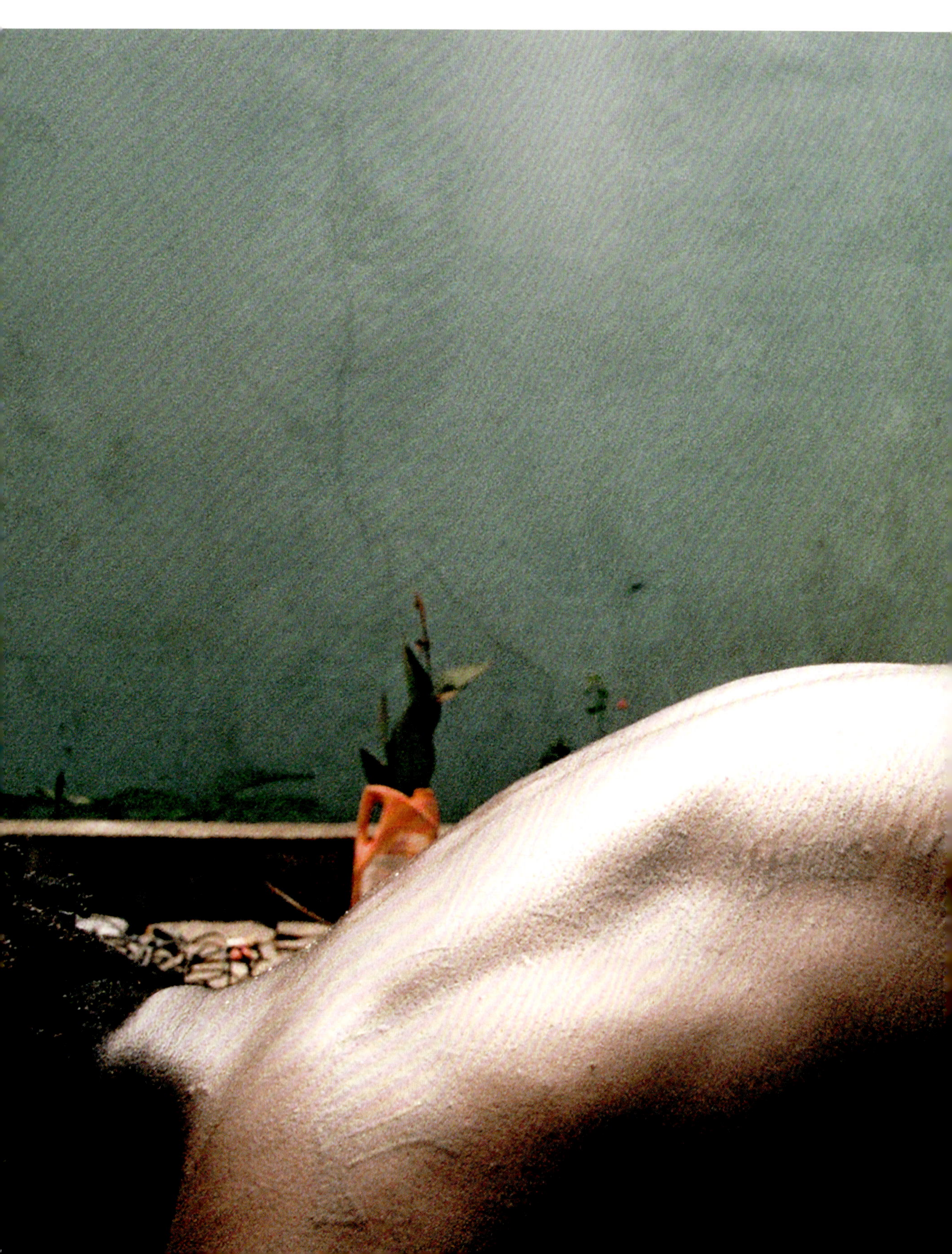

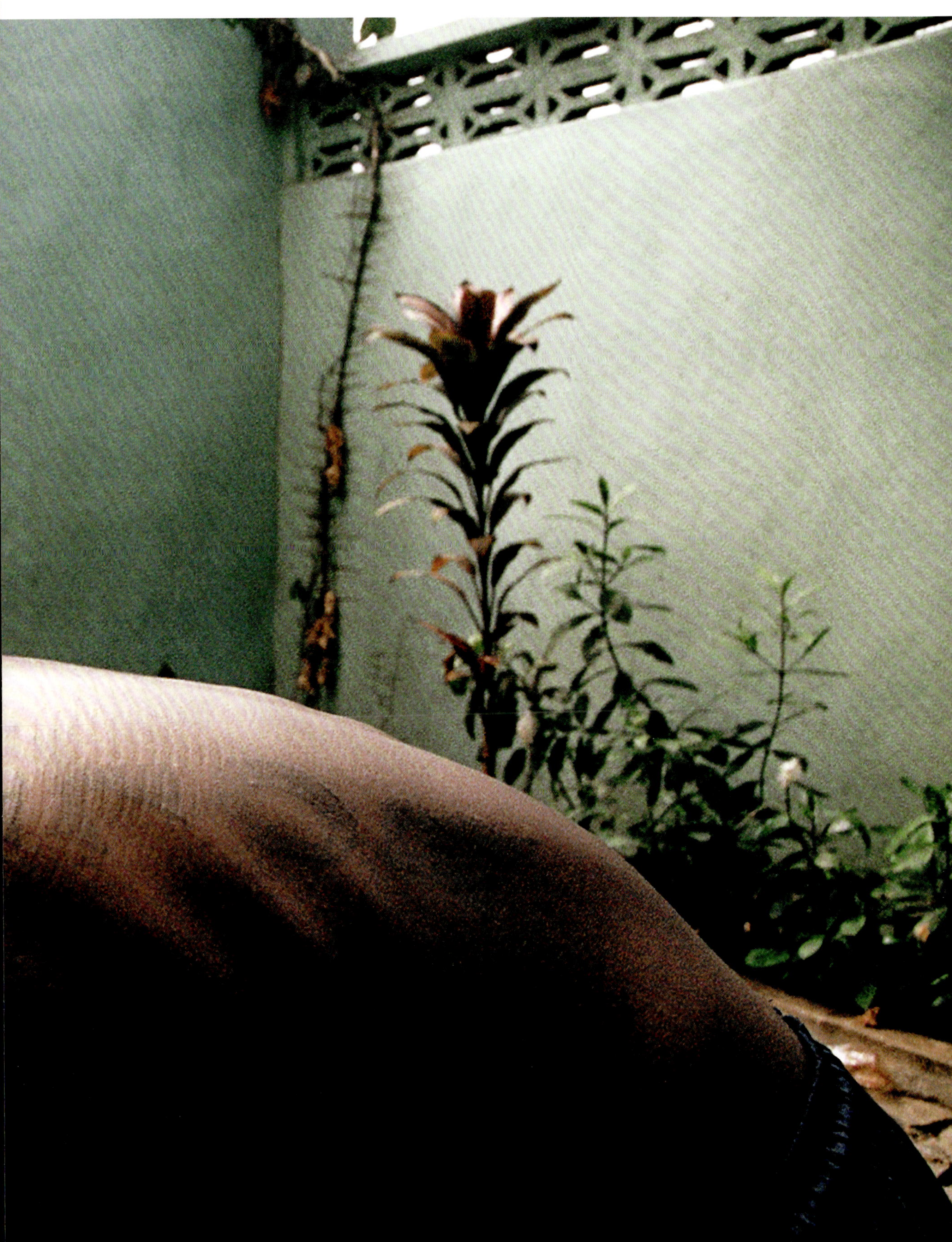

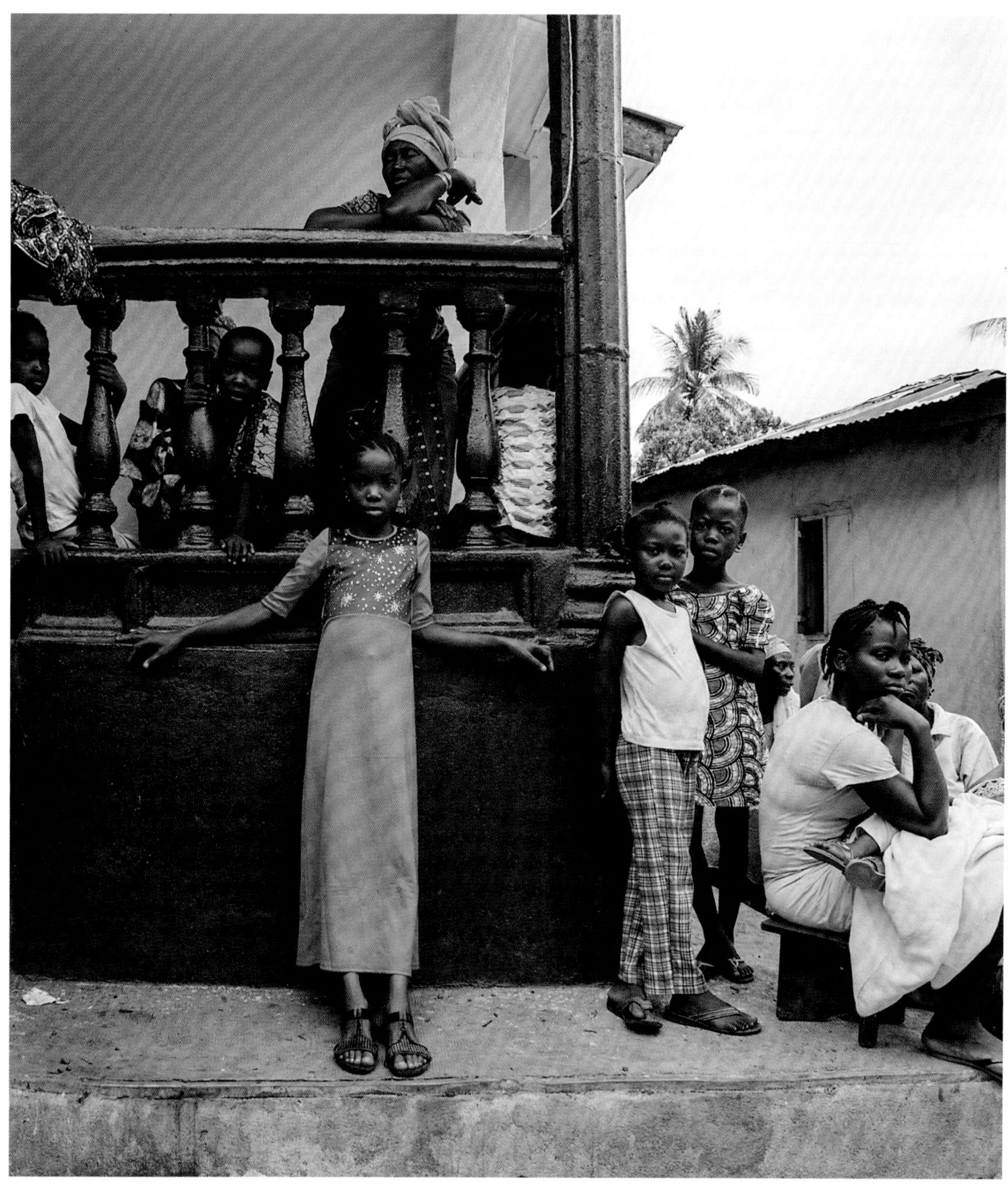

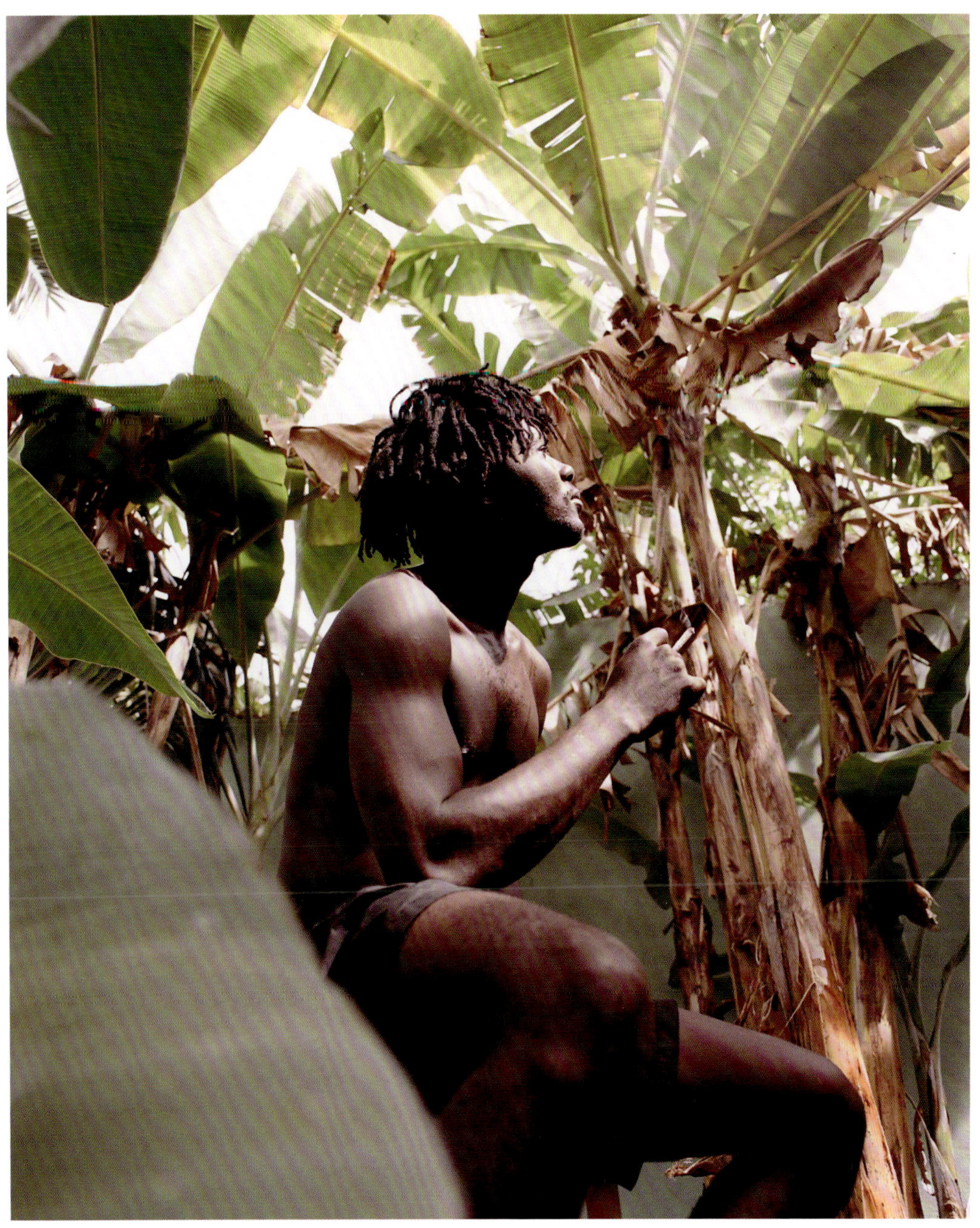

Above: *Oloya Alex Hassan, Also Known as Loyalty,
Freetown, Sierra Leone*, April 2019
Opposite: *Women of Blama, Sierra Leone*, April 2019

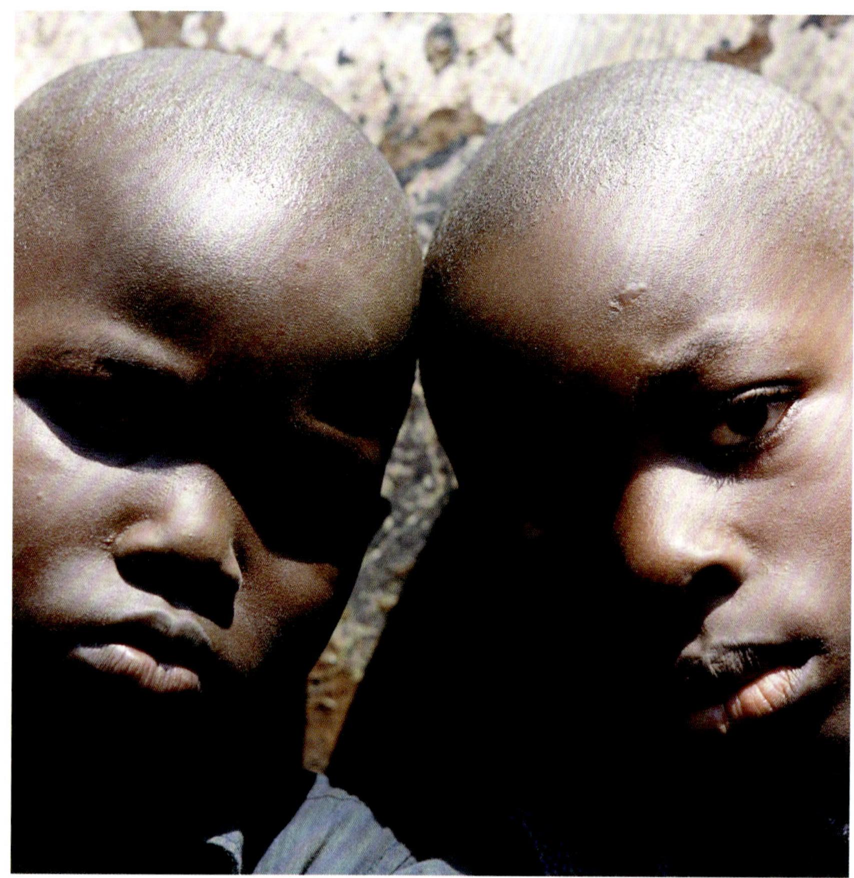

Daniel and Valentine at Carrying Colour Studio in Freetown,
Sierra Leone, April 2019

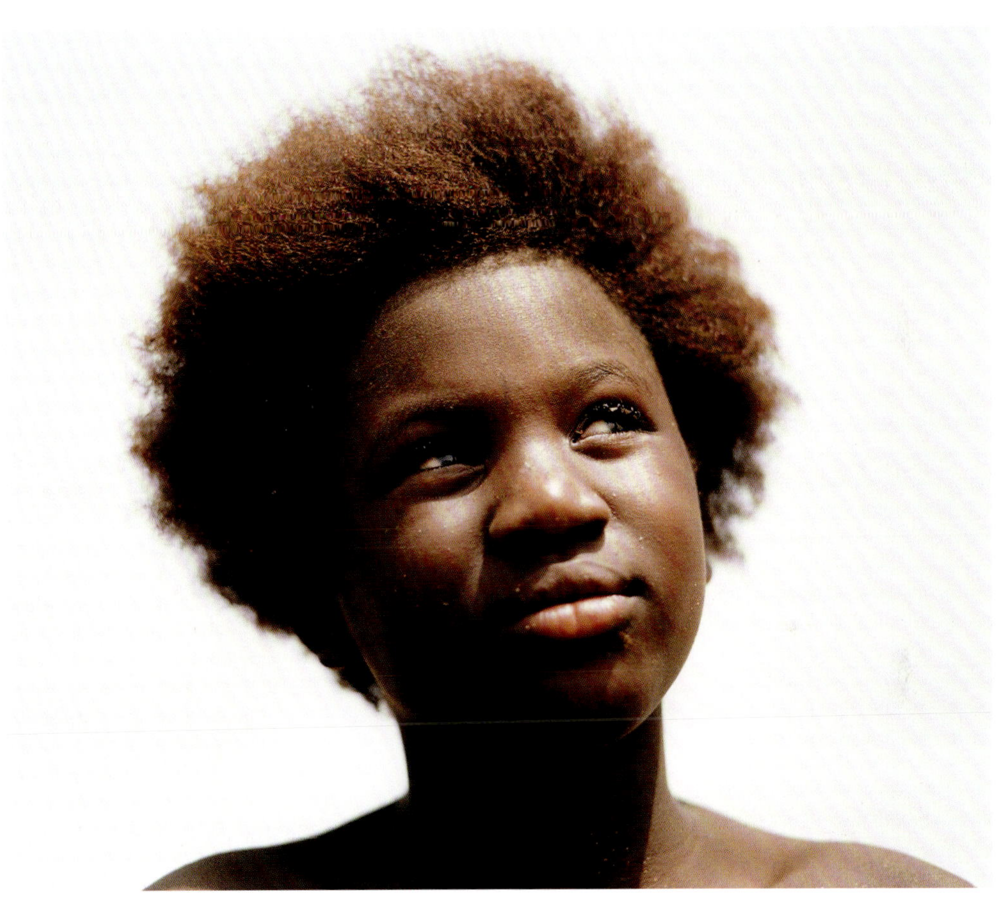

Children of Mania Beach, Sierra Leone, April 2019

Zithelo Bobby Mthombeni

Who Gets To Be Irish?

Dublin-based photographer, filmmaker and producer Zithelo Bobby Mthombeni's award-winning short documentary *This Land* (2020) takes a look at the question of what it means to be Irish. Mthombeni spoke to people from many walks of life – from artists to musicians, activists to entrepreneurs – curious about their experiences of racial discrimination and racial identity, and particularly wanting to know how they self-identify. The film connects a powerful series of vignettes depicting the daily lives of Mthombeni's subjects, woven in with interviews to form not a linear narrative but a collage in which immigrants and the children of immigrants tell their own stories about racial discrimination, integration and assimilation, balancing new and old identities in a place that can sometimes be hostile.

Mthombeni himself emigrated from South Africa to Dublin with his family when he was ten years old. That lack of a straightforward linear narrative flow expresses Mthombeni's aim to draw questions out of the viewers rather than be conclusive and attempt to provide answers. A significant amount of the 20-minute film focuses on the policy of Direct Provision, a system that aims to allow those waiting for official refugee status in Ireland to apply for housing, but it has been regarded by many as a failure, flagged by civil rights groups for leaving people in poor, cramped conditions without access to food, an issue that has only been exacerbated by the COVID-19 pandemic. The documentary can be heavy in places, but what is clear is the effort on Mthombeni's part to positively highlight the contributions immigrants and their children have made to Ireland, contributions that span every sector of society from hospitality to music. In 2022, *Our Land*, a three-part documentary series expanding on this film, premiered on RTÉ Player.

Music plays a large part in Mthombeni's work as he photographs musicians and their live performances under the name Bobby Zithelo. This deep interest in music also led him to begin filming *Up Next*, a documentary about the rise of Irish hip-hop, in early 2019. Taking the same approach as with *This Land* in centring the voices of the contributors, he invites several artists to tell the stories of their connection to music in an attempt to bring the Irish hip-hop scene to the fore. Booming sound and slow-motion images for the gigs and natural light and casual conversation for the interviews create the sense of the scene as a world underexplored, boosted by the collaboration of mostly young men who feel like people you could know. It is that sense both of relatability and of the unknown and intrigue that makes Mthombeni's films so compelling.

> "Immigrants and the children of immigrants tell their own stories about racial discrimination, integration and assimilation, balancing new and old identities"

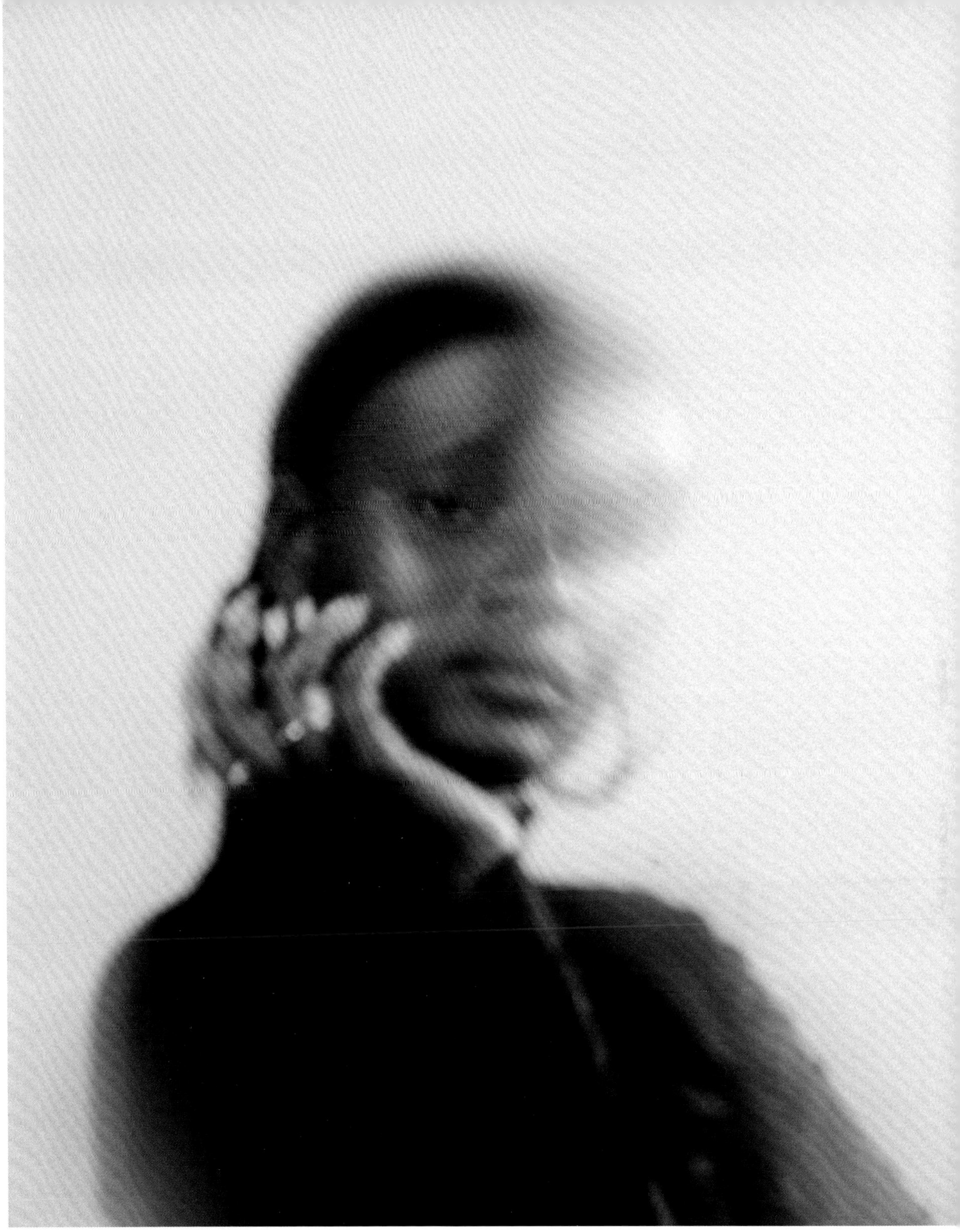

Tolü Makay, 2020

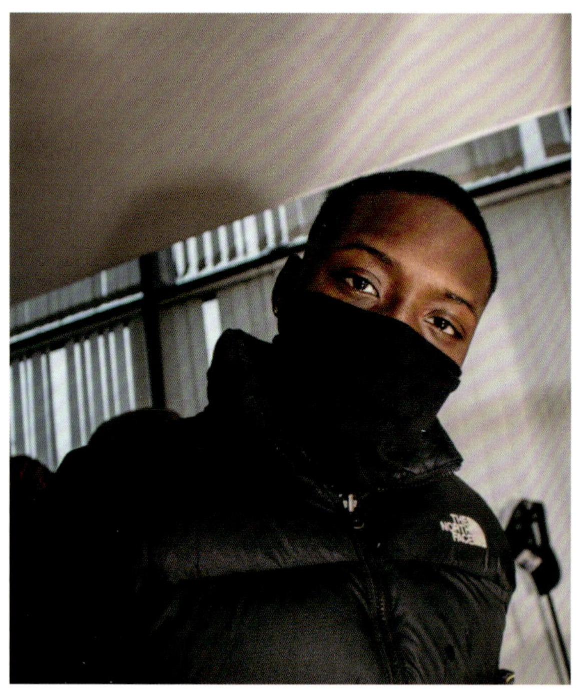

From top: *Mo*, 2019
Tobi Iroli, Howth, 2021

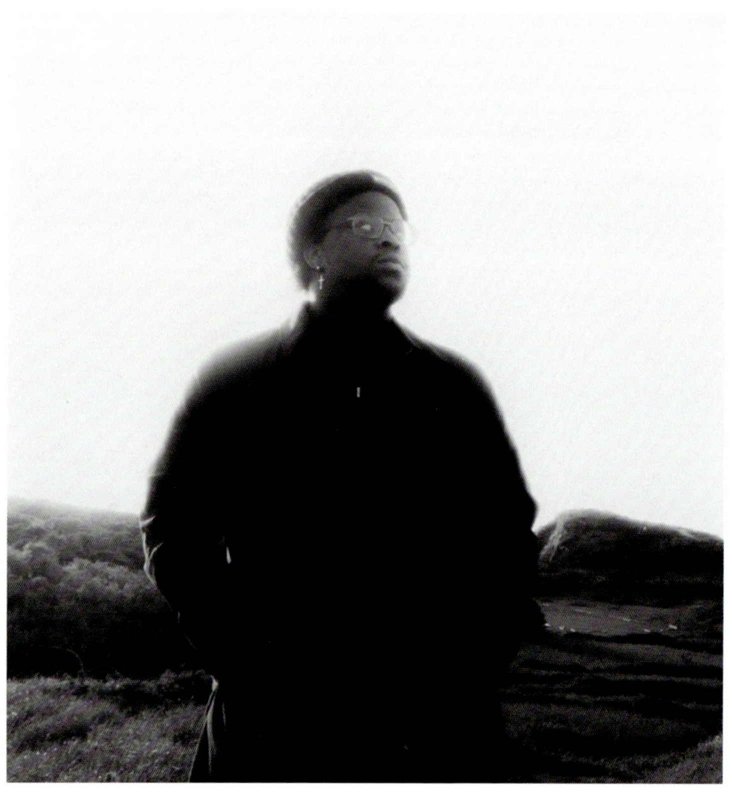

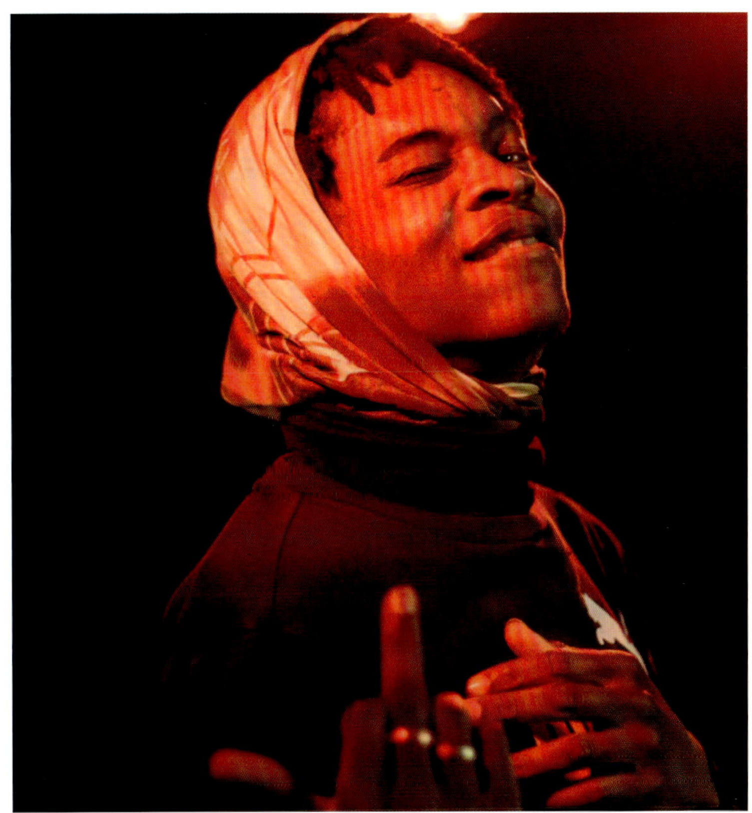

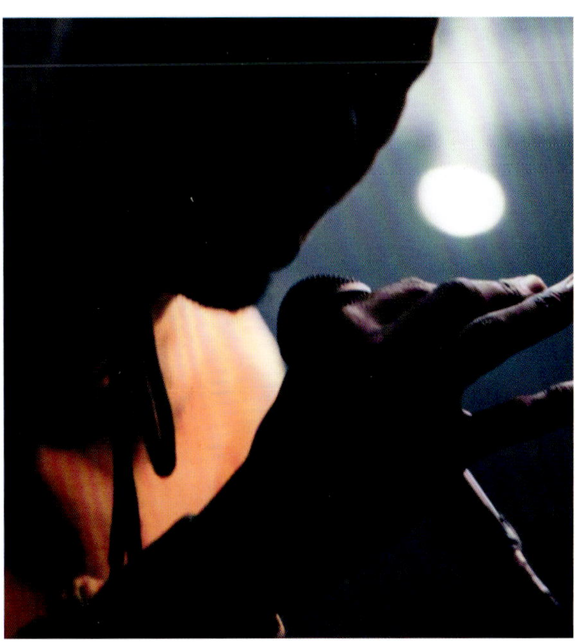

From top: *Eeddaayy*, The Workman's Club,
Dublin, 2019
Paye Fox, The Sound House, Dublin, 2019

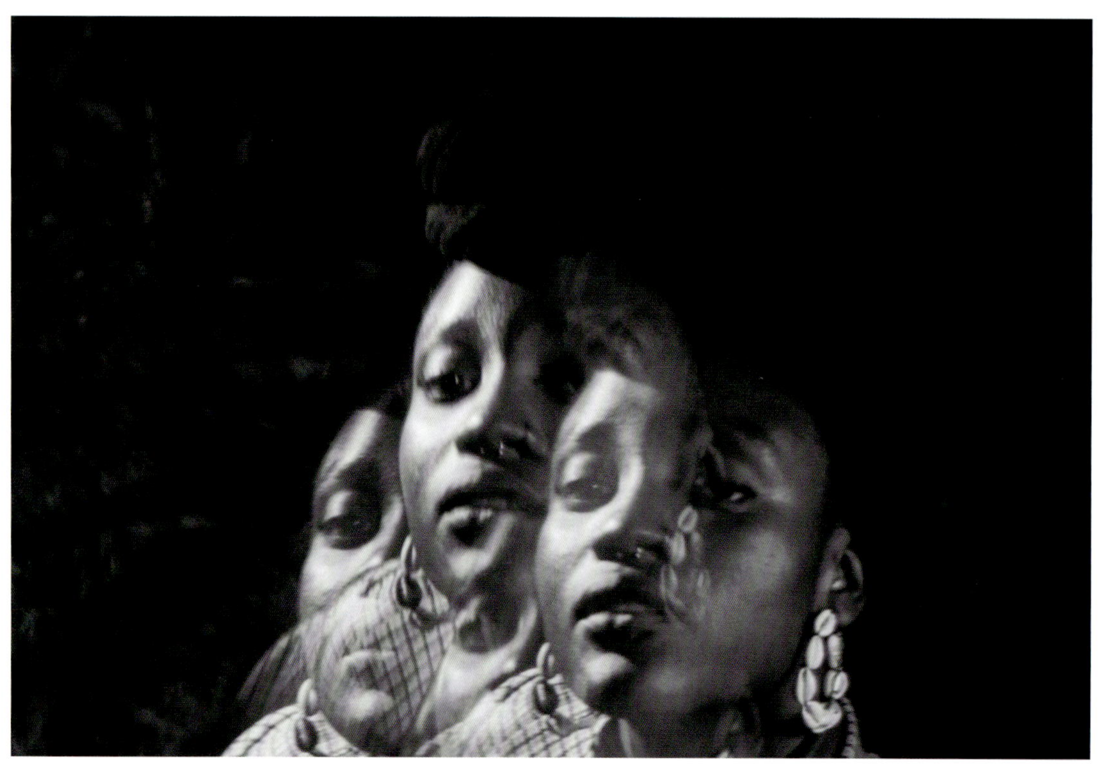

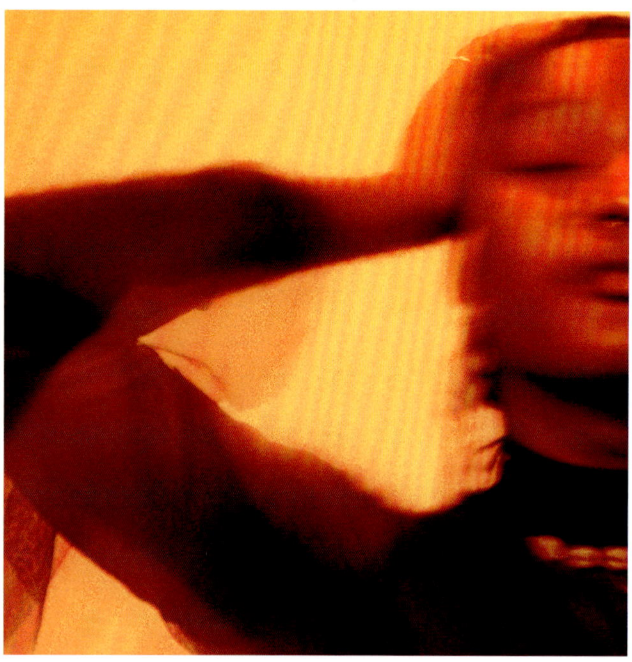

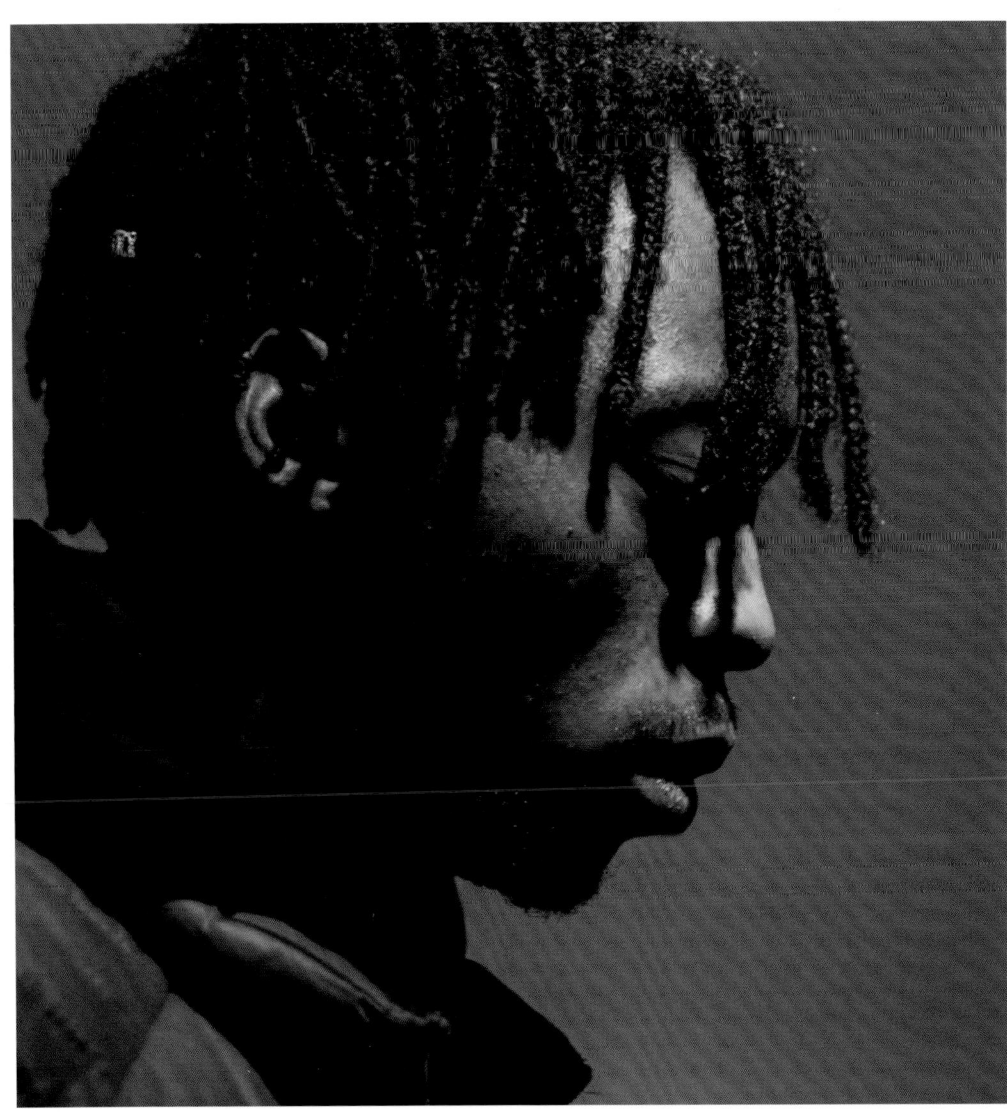

Above: *Daniel Jayden Duho*, 2019
Opposite: *Tolü Makay*, 2020

Ronan Mckenzie

Building Home

London-based photographer and director Ronan Mckenzie has described her work as an attempt to photograph "real people in a stylized way that creates more aspirational imagery".[27] Her editorial work does not evoke the sense of distance or high sheen that the idea of phrase "aspirational imagery" might sometimes suggest. Instead, Mckenzie's images radiate a strong sense of warmth and community. Editorials such as *Present, Finally*, shot for *Luncheon* magazine in 2019, exude both glamour and domesticity in their portrayal of what appears to be a family celebration. In several of the images in *Present, Finally*, Mckenzie's subjects are all dressed in white, some wrapped in pearls as well, and they are photographed against the brick walls and outdoor furnishings of an ordinary family home.

The domestic is a common theme for the self-taught artist. In a 2018 campaign for Our Place, Mckenzie photographed designer Akua Shabaka's family in Los Angeles as they prepared and ate a meal together. Here too are warm colours, yellows, mahoganies, as well as gentle light and limited space that doesn't feel claustrophobic but intimate. In 2018, Mckenzie curated *I'm Home*, an exhibition featuring Black British female photographers whose work she felt was often sidelined in favour of more well-known African American names in exhibitions designed to showcase Black art. Mckenzie outlines, "I wanted to use this thread to explore these differences in relation to how we respond to home and family", a question also explored in *Our Place*. Expanding on this exhibition, Mckenzie created the HOME space, a co-working gallery and community space for young artists to socialize and collaborate with each other. The spirit of collaboration runs across her work from the process to the images themselves, many featuring multiple subjects standing close together. The name HOME conjures feelings of comfort and familiarity that fall in line with the artist's desire to create a space for the work of her peers that wouldn't feel hostile to them or those who came to view it, a contrast to how many have described the experience of the white cube.

In creating this space, as with the exhibition, Mckenzie wanted to fill a void. She has described it as a "physical manifestation" of questions she had been asking herself about the struggle to find a place to fit in as a child of the African diaspora.

> "The name HOME conjures feelings of comfort and relatability, and expresses the desire to create a space for the work of her peers that wouldn't feel hostile"

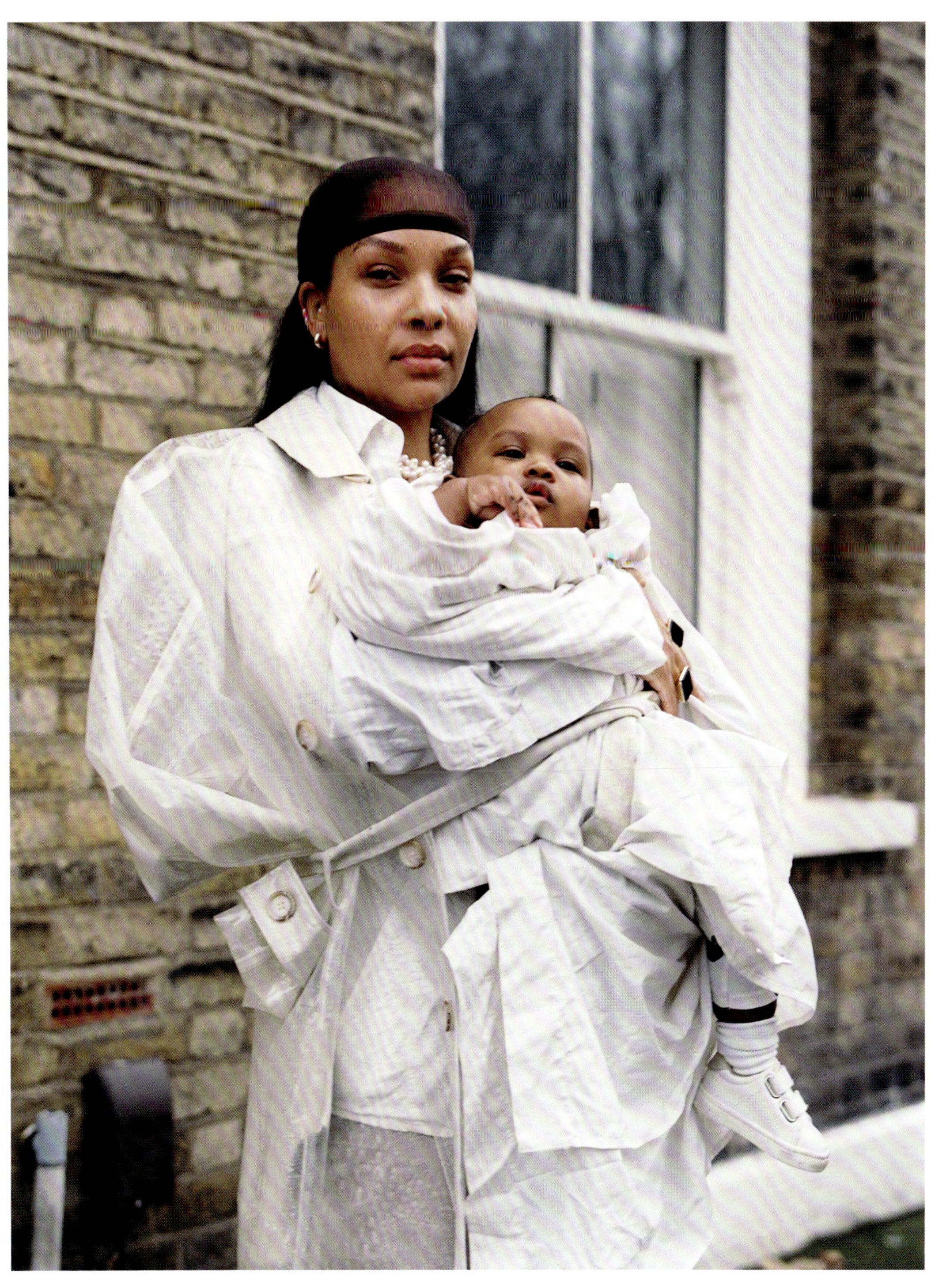

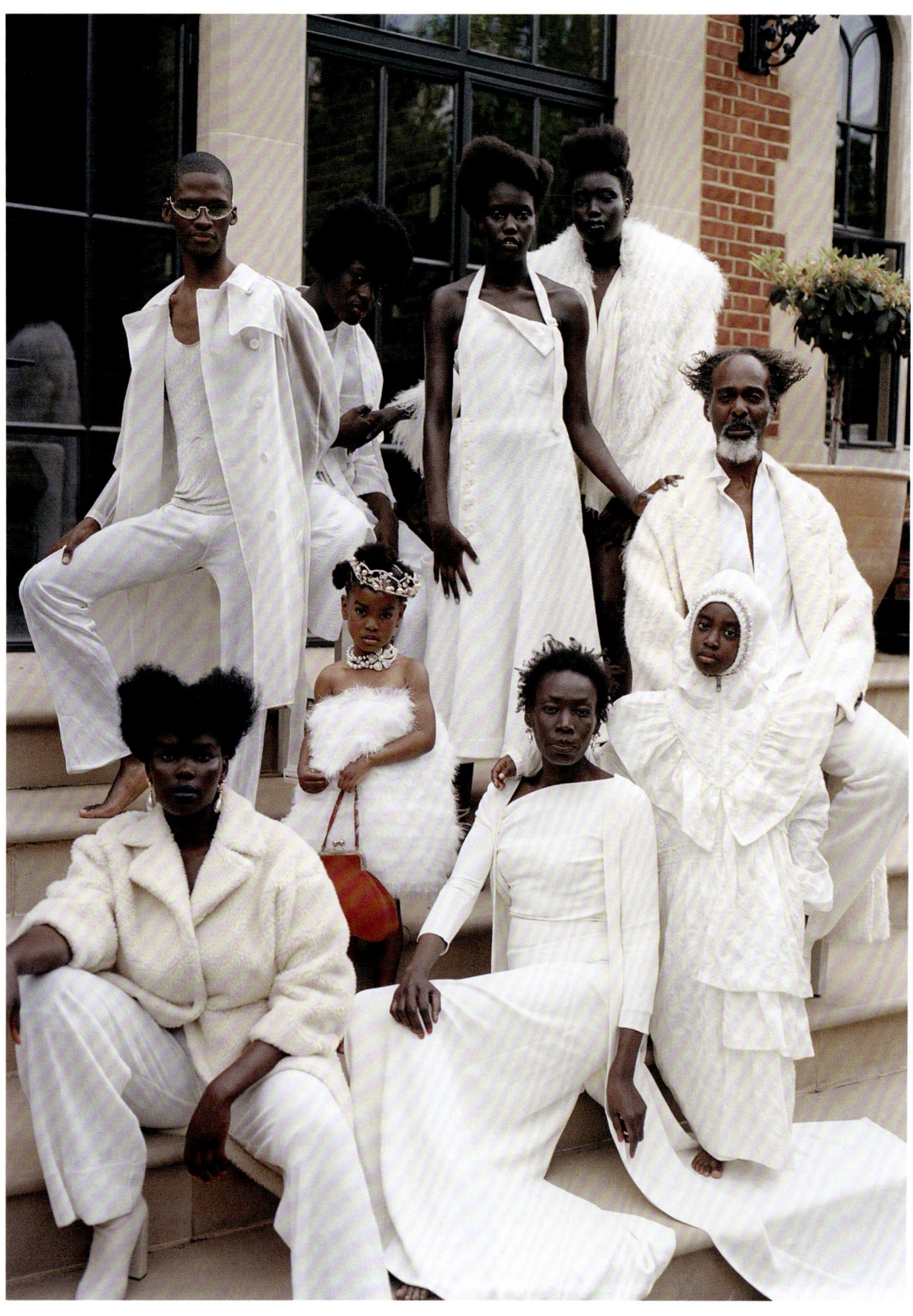

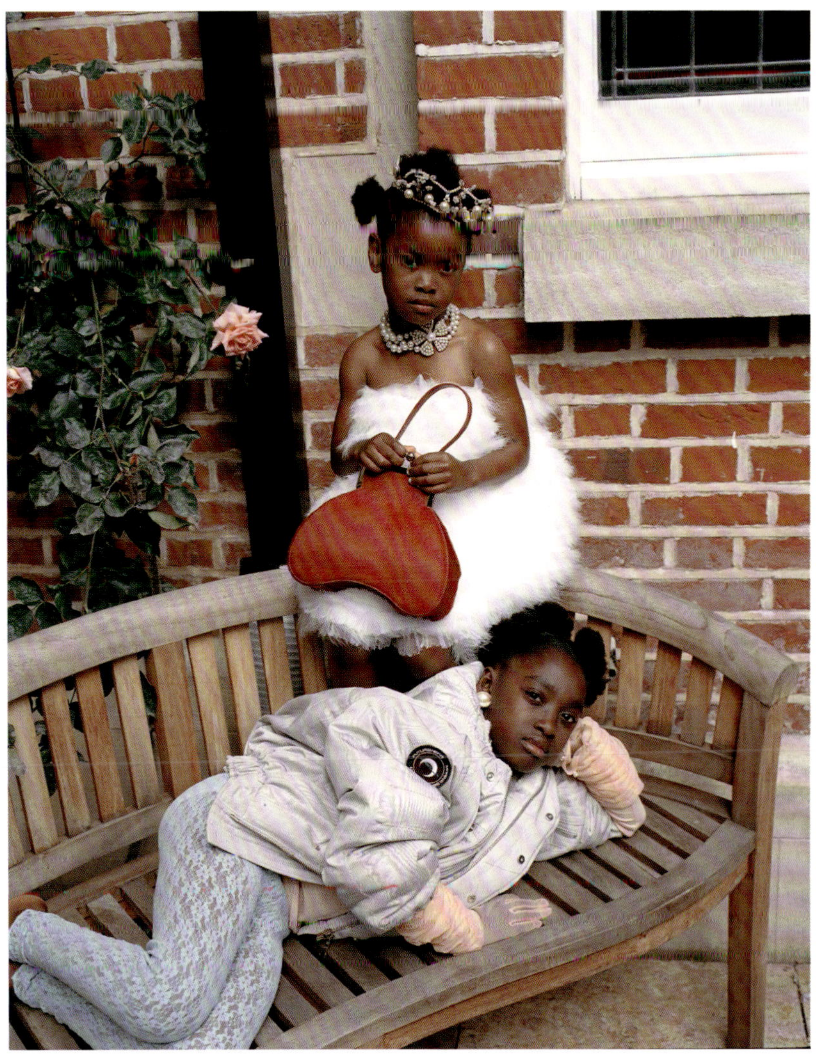

Previous spread: *Jennifer and Genesis*
These pages: from *Present, Finally*, 2019

As We See It

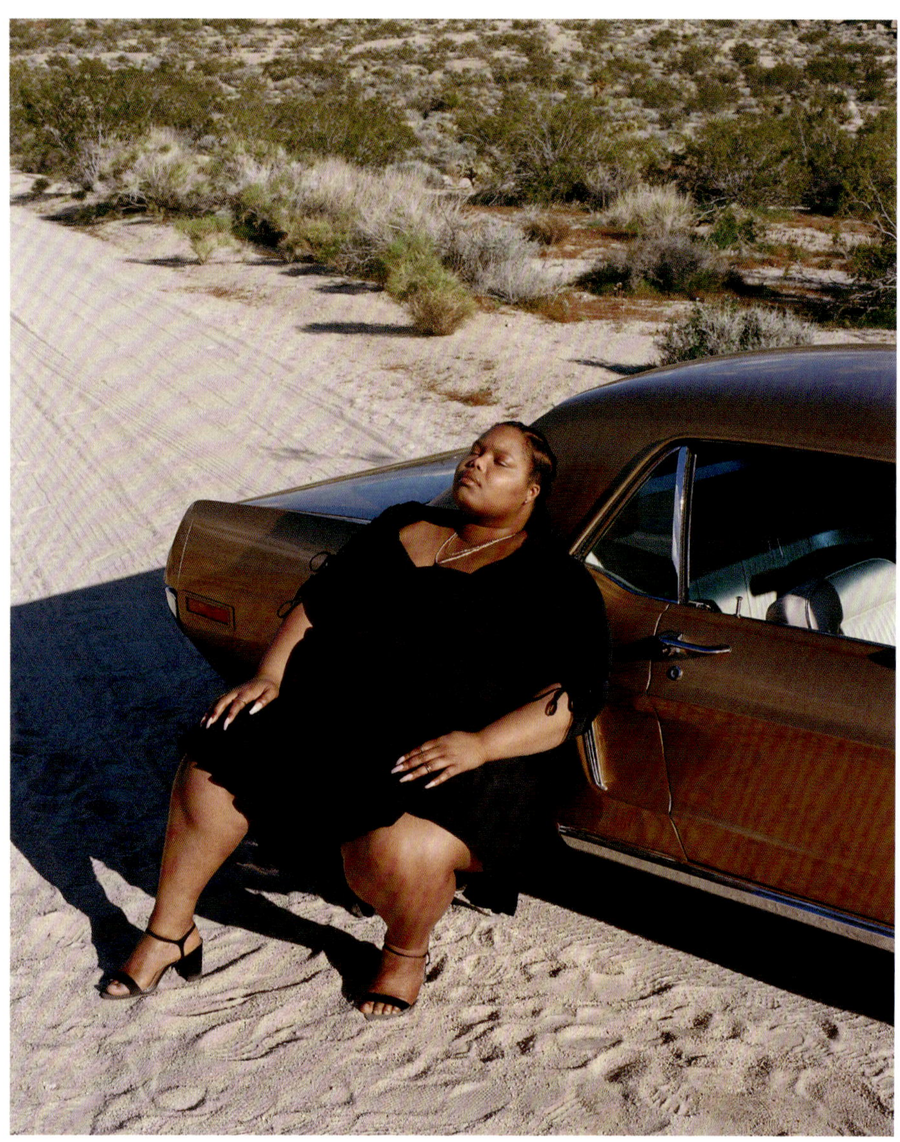

Above: *Enam*, for Rodarte x Universal Standard, 2019
Opposite: *Nya in Melissa Eakin*

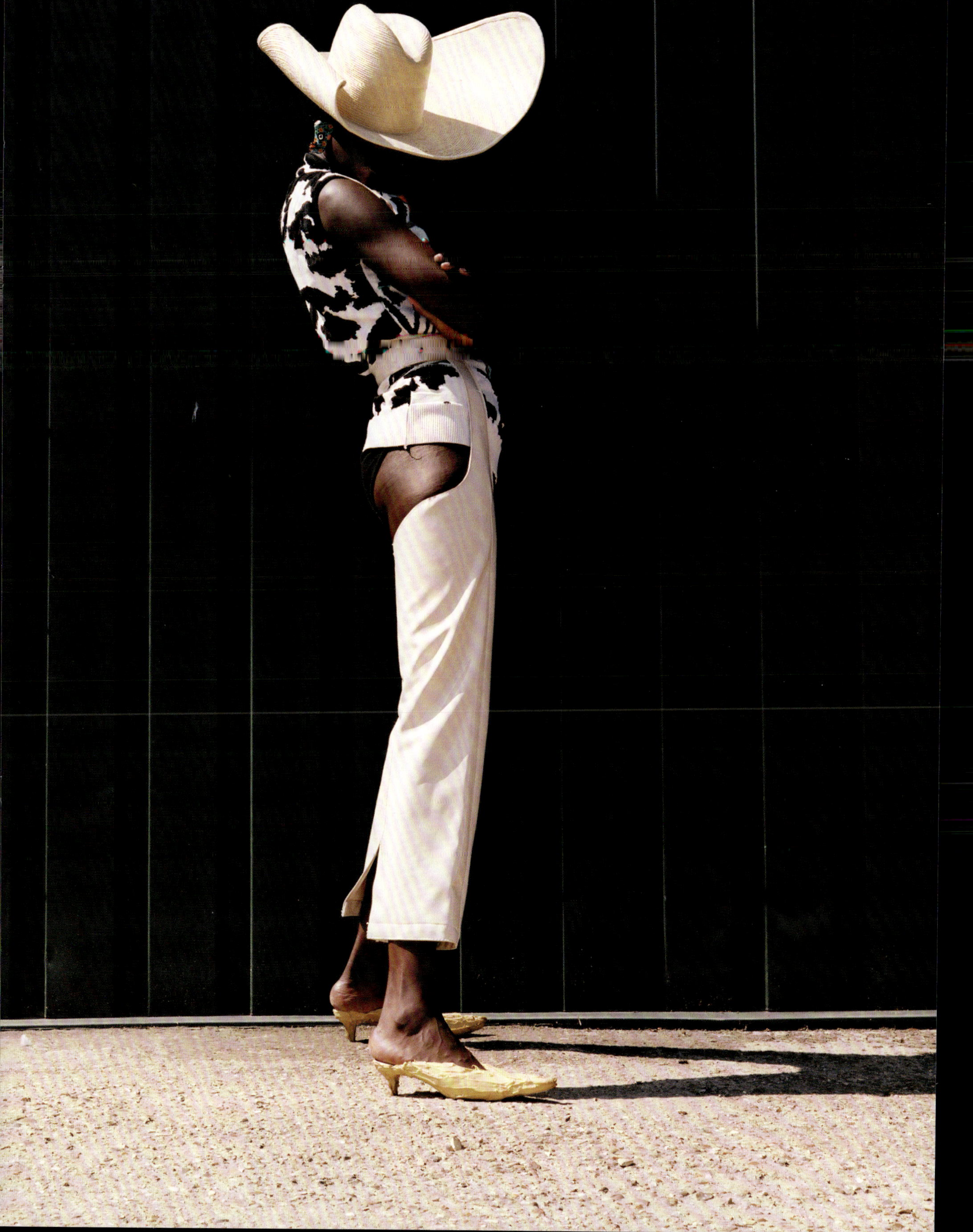

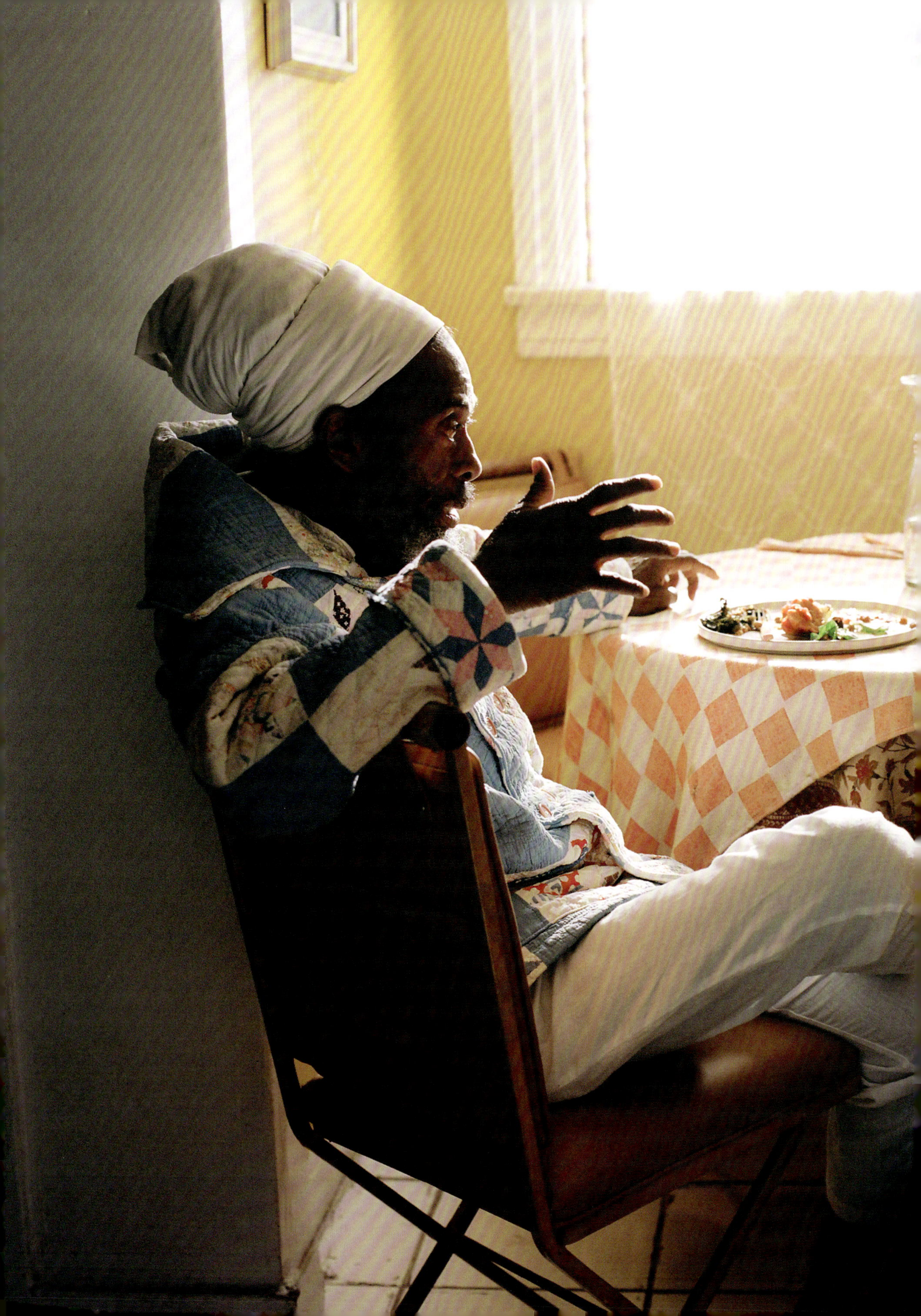

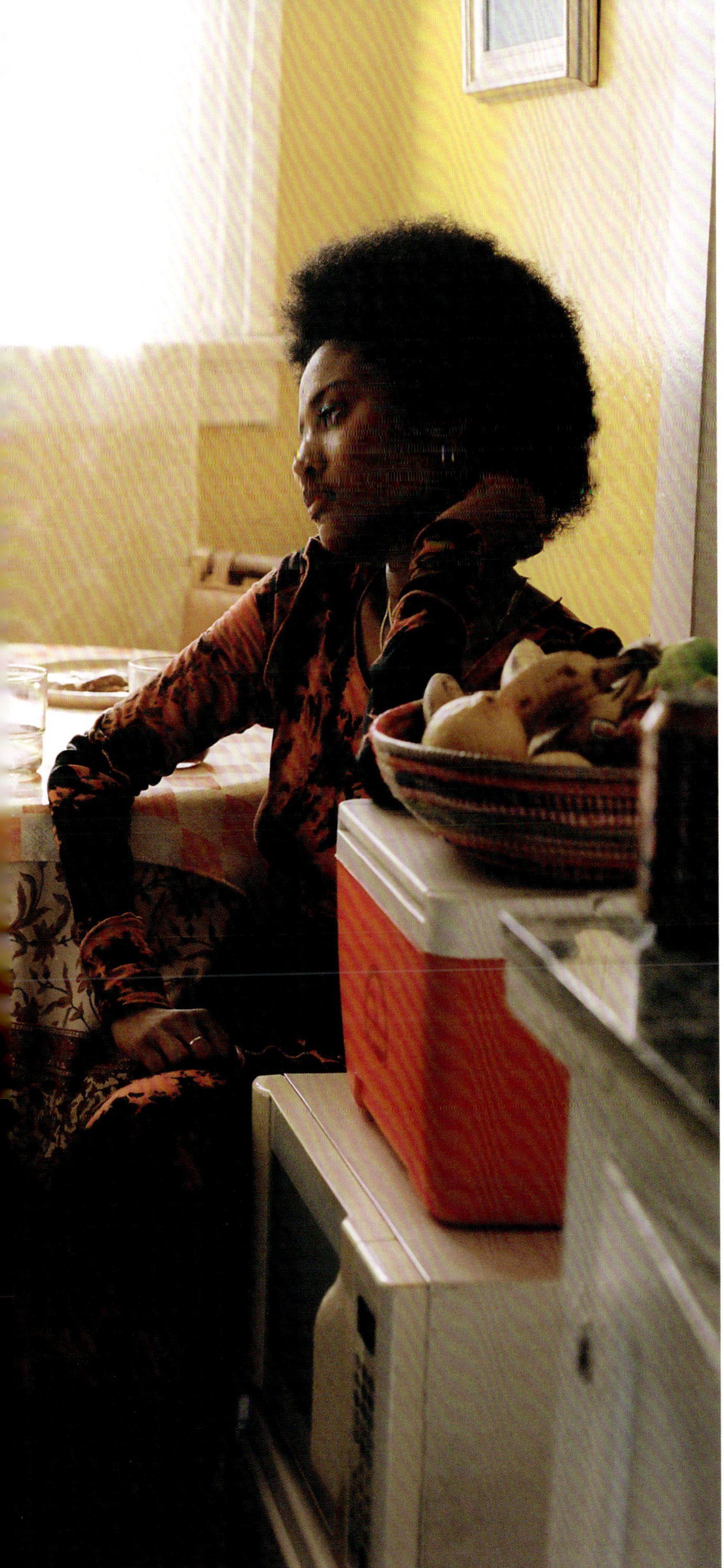

Our Place, 2019

Rahima Gambo

Lingering Trauma

Rahima Gambo is an artist and photographer based in Nigeria's capital city, Abuja. Her multimedia work engages with the themes of collective memory, gender, urbanism and the act of autobiography. Her first major series, *Exiled from Home* (2014), documented the story of a man from Nigeria seeking asylum in New York due to homophobic persecution and the passing of laws that prohibit not only same-sex marriage, but also the establishment of gay clubs and the physical expression of affection between people of the same sex.

Since then, Gambo, who studied for a Master's in journalism at Columbia Graduate School, has shifted away from the more traditional photojournalism of her first project, taking an almost collage-like approach to what in some cases still feels like reporting, to create a quite distinctive method of visual storytelling. Gambo's technique of drawing in other visual elements, such as illustration, video and sculpture installations, is almost like an exercise in world-building, which allows the viewer an intense and immersive experience of the artist's explorations of topics like community, trauma and grief.

You can see Gambo's experimentation with presenting the long-lasting effects of traumatic experiences in *Education Is Forbidden*, a series she created between 2015 and 2016. The project combines prose, illustration, photography and film to present the lives of students in north-eastern Nigeria as they try to get an education amidst the rise of Boko Haram (the series takes its title from a rough translation of Boko Haram ("Western education is forbidden"). Exploring collective experience and the complexity of memory, the prose is written in the style of a newspaper or magazine feature, with quotations from the staff and pupils; infographics are woven in, depicting in one example the statistics on the violence that occurs at schools. An image taken by Gambo of a huddled group of schoolgirls is attached to a still from the video of the Chibok schoolgirls abducted by Boko Haram in 2014. They look roughly the same age; their uniforms are identical save for the colour. In another image, a photo of schoolgirls is superimposed over a bullet hole-riddled blackboard, a reminder that schools, which were supposed to be a place of safety, play and education, were turned into scenes of horrific violence. The placement of all these elements in an interactive narrative is Gambo's way of communicating more than the hard facts but also what she described in *LensCulture* as "the lingering trauma and infrastructural decay evoked by the conflict", particularly to those who may be thousands of miles from the conflicts.[28]

> "A photo of schoolgirls is superimposed over a bullet hole-riddled blackboard, reminders that schools were turned into scenes of horrific violence"

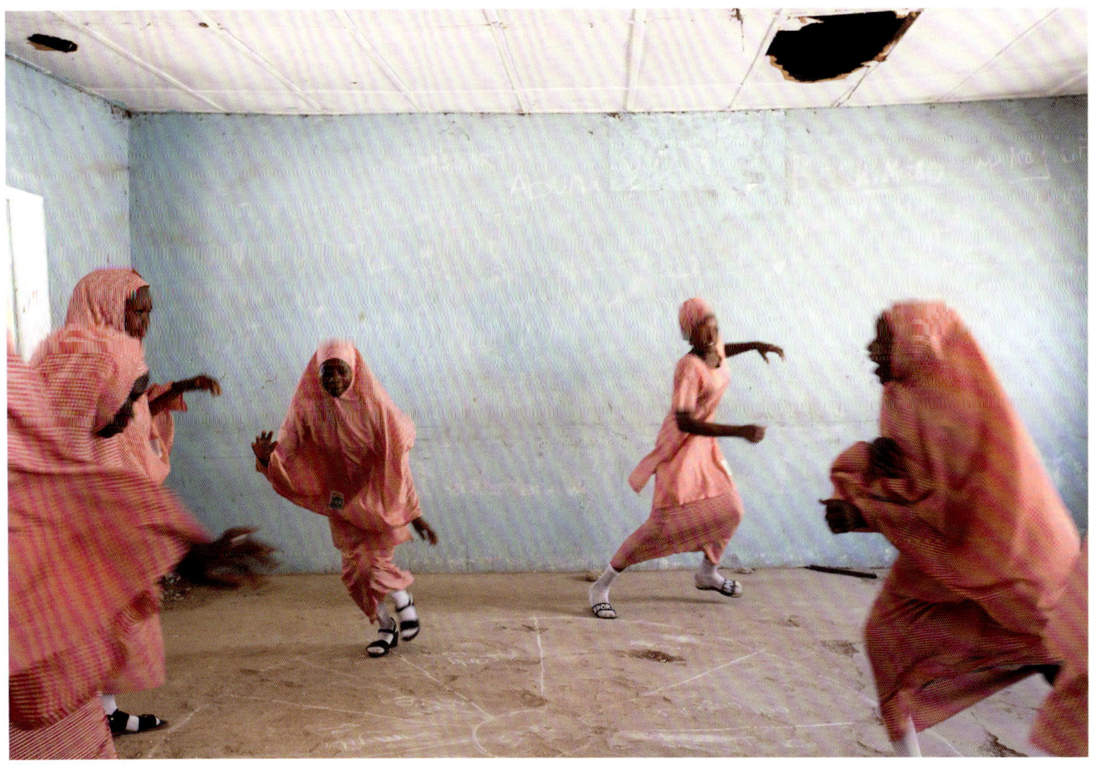

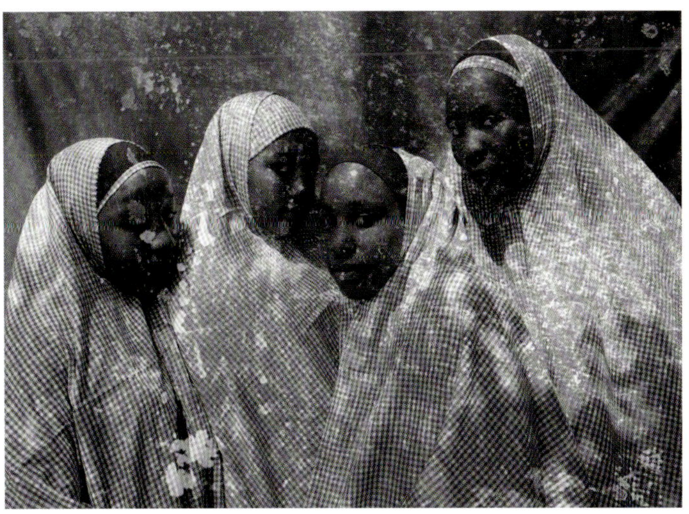

From top: *Ruth, Amina, and the Three Aisha's Play "In and Out"*, from *Tatsuniya*, 2017
Rukkaya and Friends, from *Education Is Forbidden*, 2015–16

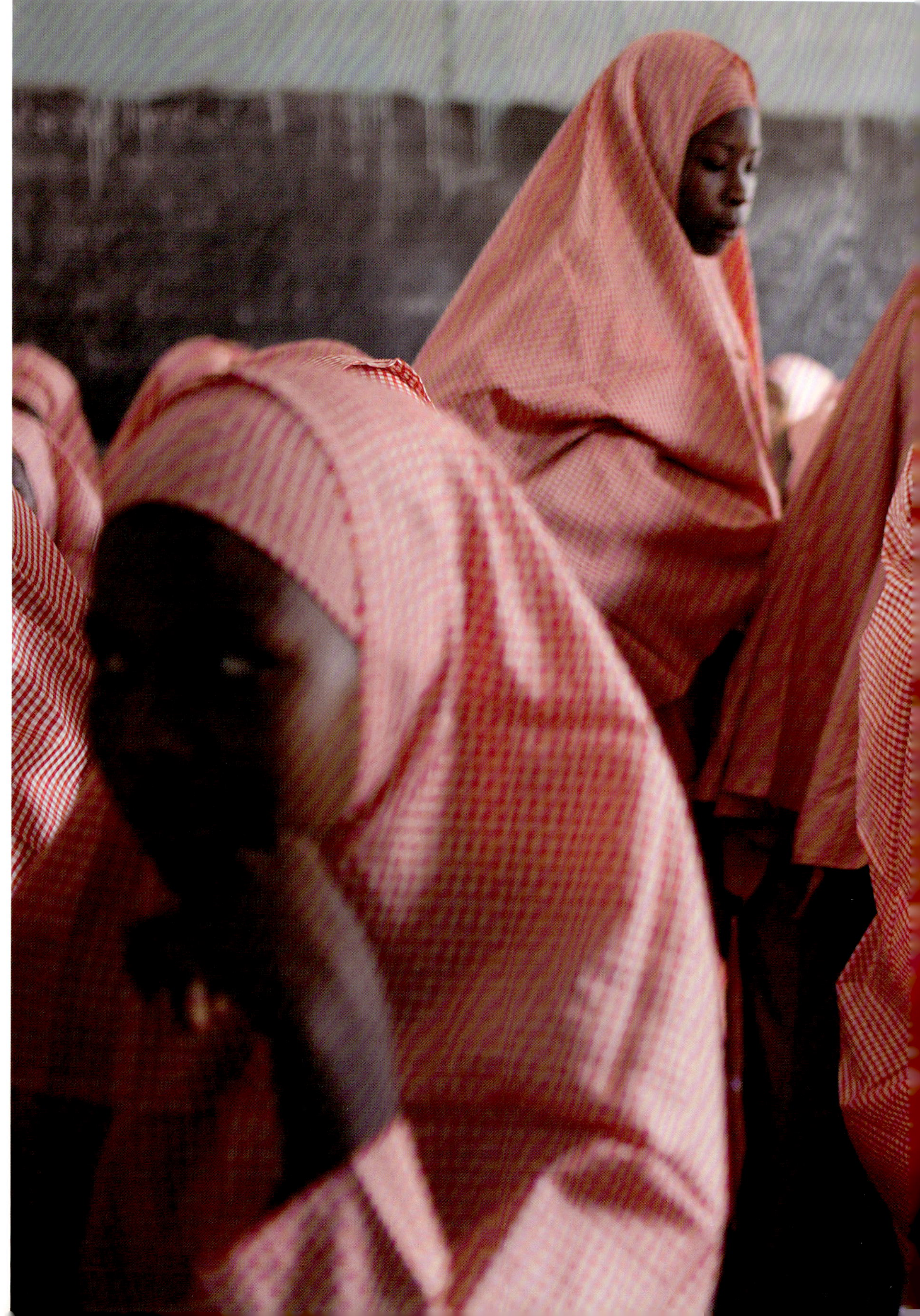

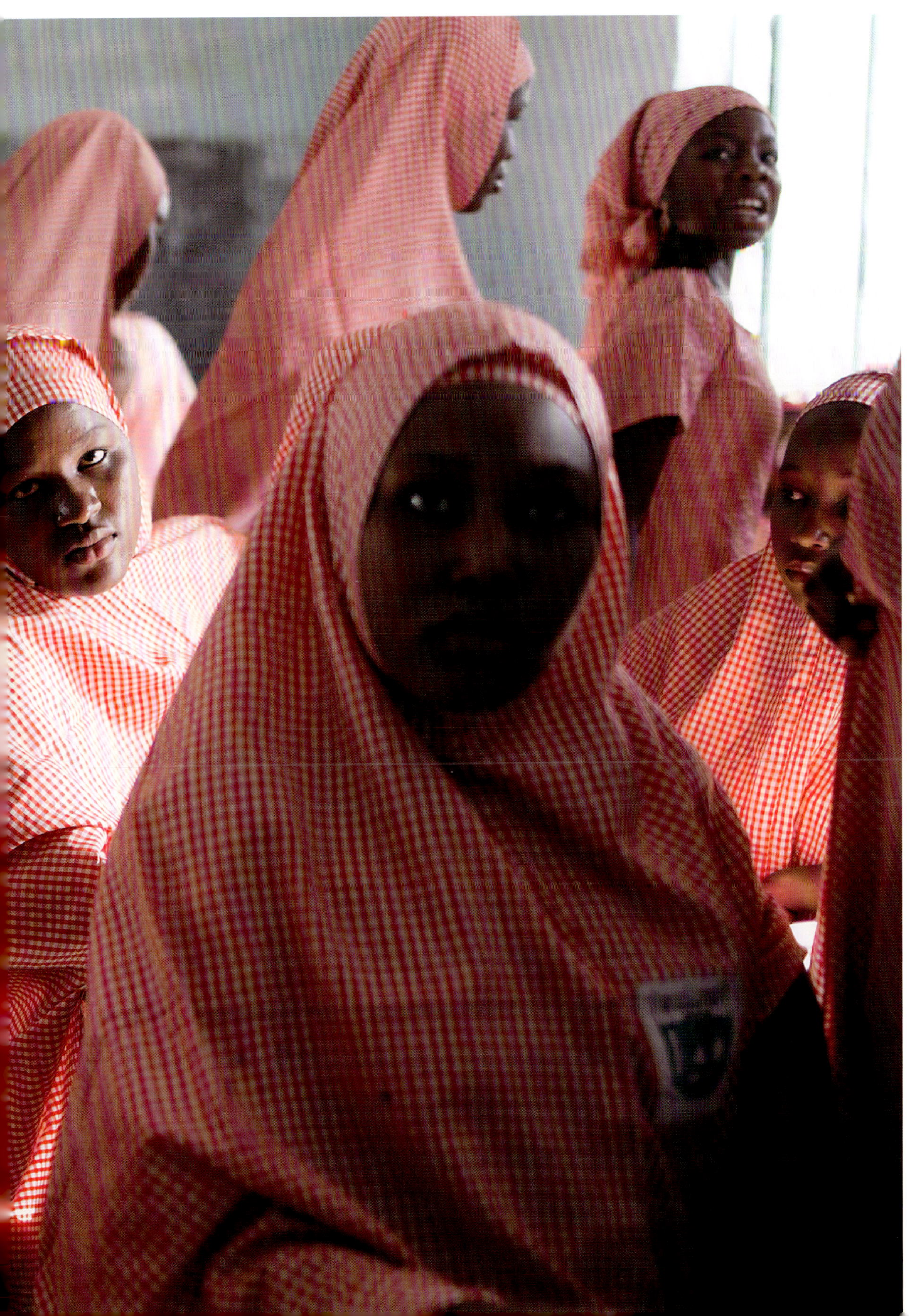

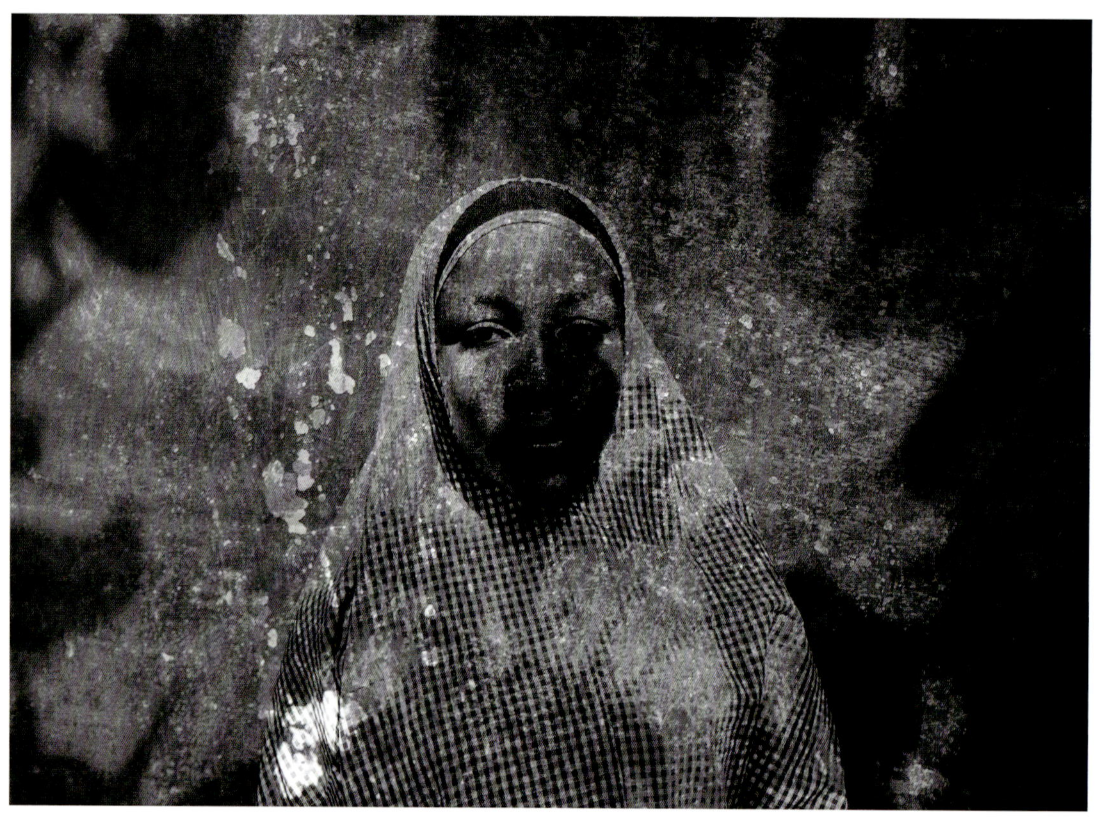

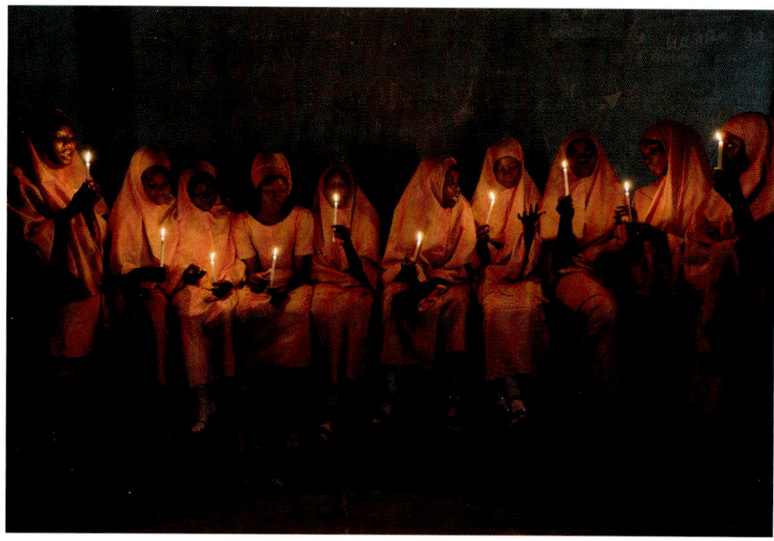

This page, from top: *Rukkaya*, from *Education Is Forbidden*, 2015–16
School Girls with Candles (1), from *Tatsuniya*, 2017
Previous spread: *Students Wait for Class to Begin at Shehu Sanda Kyarimi*
Government School, from *Education Is Forbidden*, 2015–16

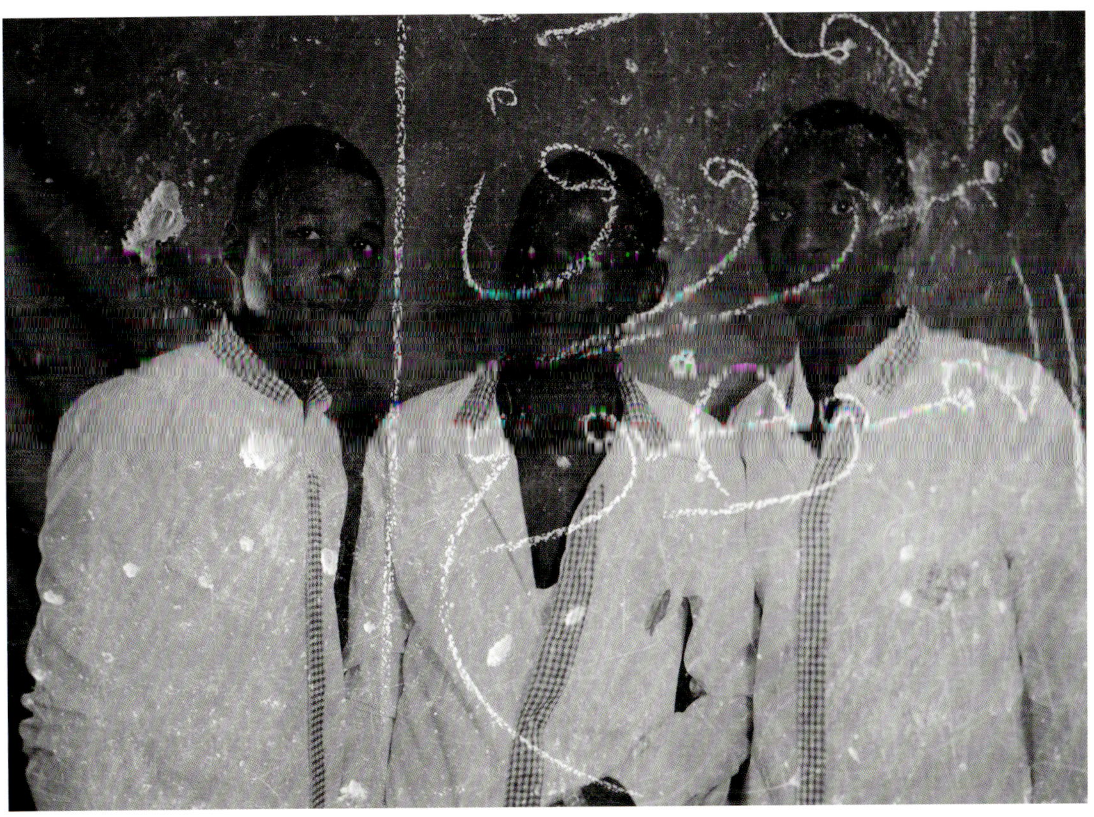

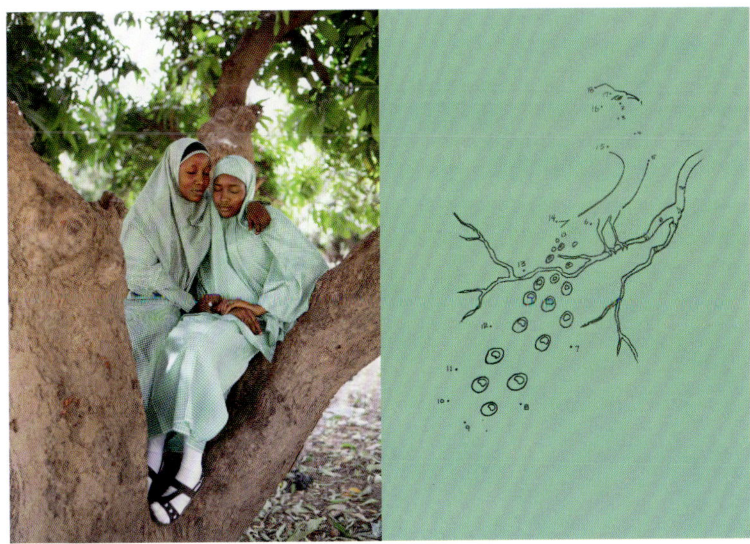

From top: *Three Students from Shehu Sanda Kyarimi Government School*
Rukkaua and Hadiza
Both from *Education Is Forbidden*, 2015–16

Allison Janae Hamilton

Picturing the South

Allison Janae Hamilton is a multidisciplinary artist working in photography, video, sculpture and installation to explore the mythologies of the American South and climate change. The landscape of northern Florida, which Hamilton feels is left out of the image of the South in the collective imagination, takes precedence over the people in her images: "place is the centre of my practice," she told *BOMB* magazine.[29] The camera lingers on gently wavering reeds in shallow water in her video *Wacissa* (2019). The forests of the tough, extreme weather-resistant sabal palm – Florida's state tree – are also a significant landscape, which Hamilton turns into a Brothers-Grimm-meets-Southern-Gothic-style land in her series *Sweet Milk in the Badlands*. The series *Florida Water* (2019), which depicts a young girl dressed in white floating in murky water, exudes the same sense of simultaneous playfulness and unease, a sense of impending disaster or of the aftermath of one.

This is in line with Hamilton's interest in the disastrous effects of climate change which manifests itself in site-specific installations and exhibitions for which the artist re-creates environments such as deforested spaces. Hamilton's work also pays particular attention to the disproportionate effect of climate change and natural disasters on communities of colour. Inspired by true accounts of deadly weather events across America, such as the Okeechobee hurricane, one of the deadliest in the history of the United States, Hamilton has paid tribute with her work to those who lost their lives, many of whom were Black workers, as well as to the persistence of African American communities in the face of disaster and hardship, both meteorological and not.

Folklore forms a key theme in Hamilton's work and lends a slightly surreal quality to her photographs and films, so that the figures within them become mythic creatures. In *Sisters, Wakulla County FL* (2019), sisters are dressed alike to resemble twins, who for millennia have had the symbolic significance of dualism projected upon them, in white Sunday dresses and red berets. Hamilton herself features in *Scratching the Wrong Side of Firmament* (2015), running across the frame in front of what appears to be a Baptist church, her face covered with an animal skull mask. Masks are another feature of Hamilton's work. Some are made with the skulls of animals such as deer or made to look like bird skulls, which also evoke medieval plague masks. Others are made from fencing masks and woven with flowers and palm leaves. Unworn, they look like totems; installed at higher than standard gallery height, they intimidate, again looking to the idea of folklore, this time the traditions of West African mask-making.[30]

> "Folklore forms a key theme in Hamilton's work and lends a slightly surreal quality to her photographs and films, so that the figures within them become mythic creatures"

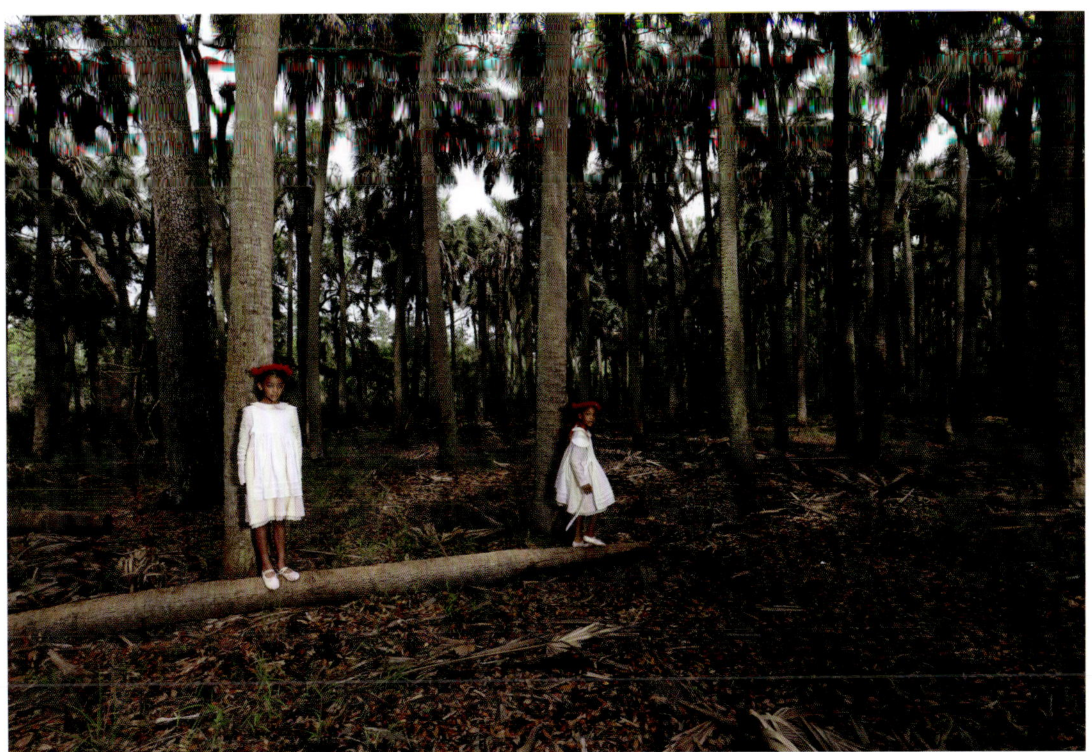

Sisters, Wakulla County FL, 2019

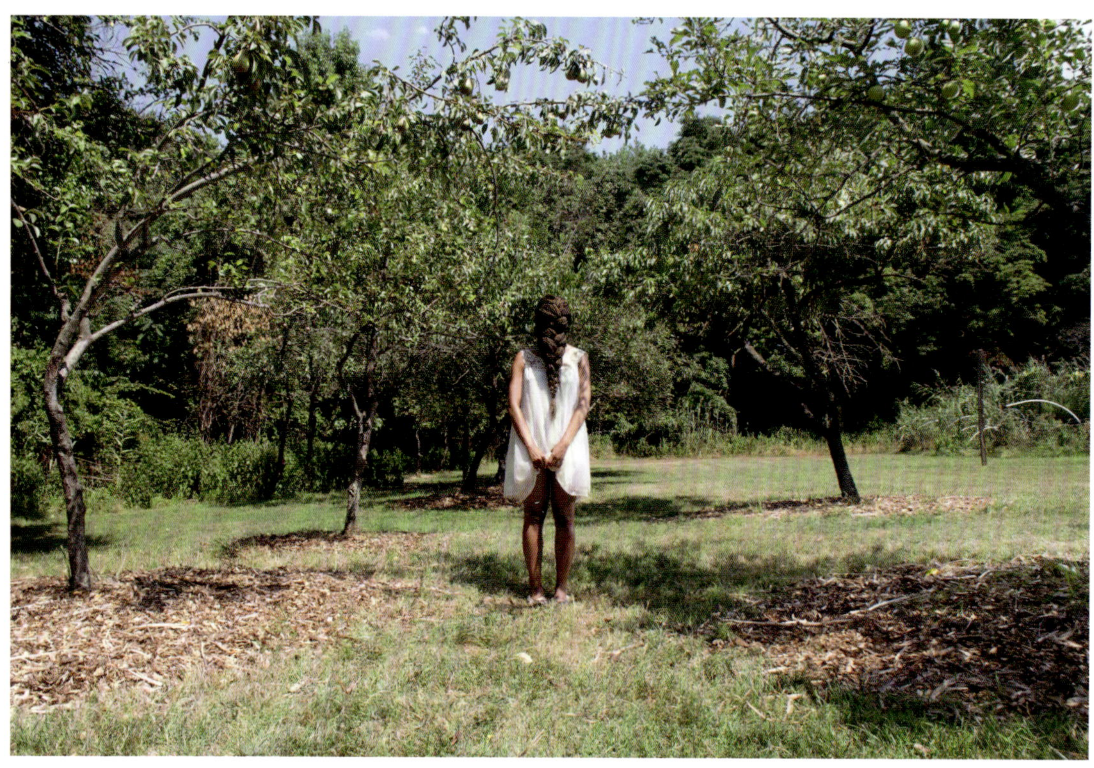

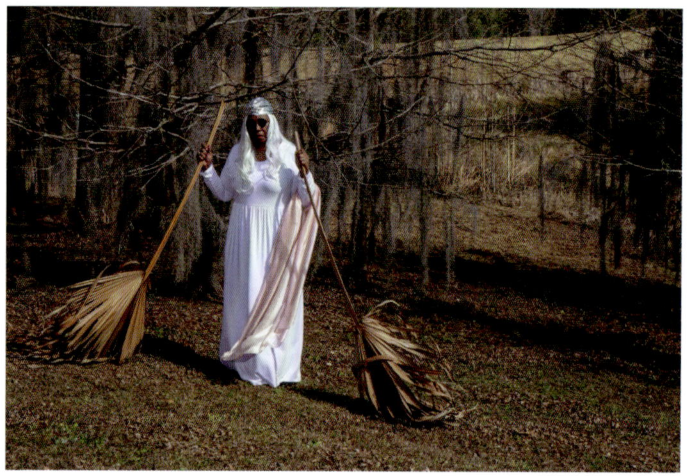

From top: *Dollbaby Standing in the Orchard at Midday*, 2015
All the Stars Appointed to their Places, 2021

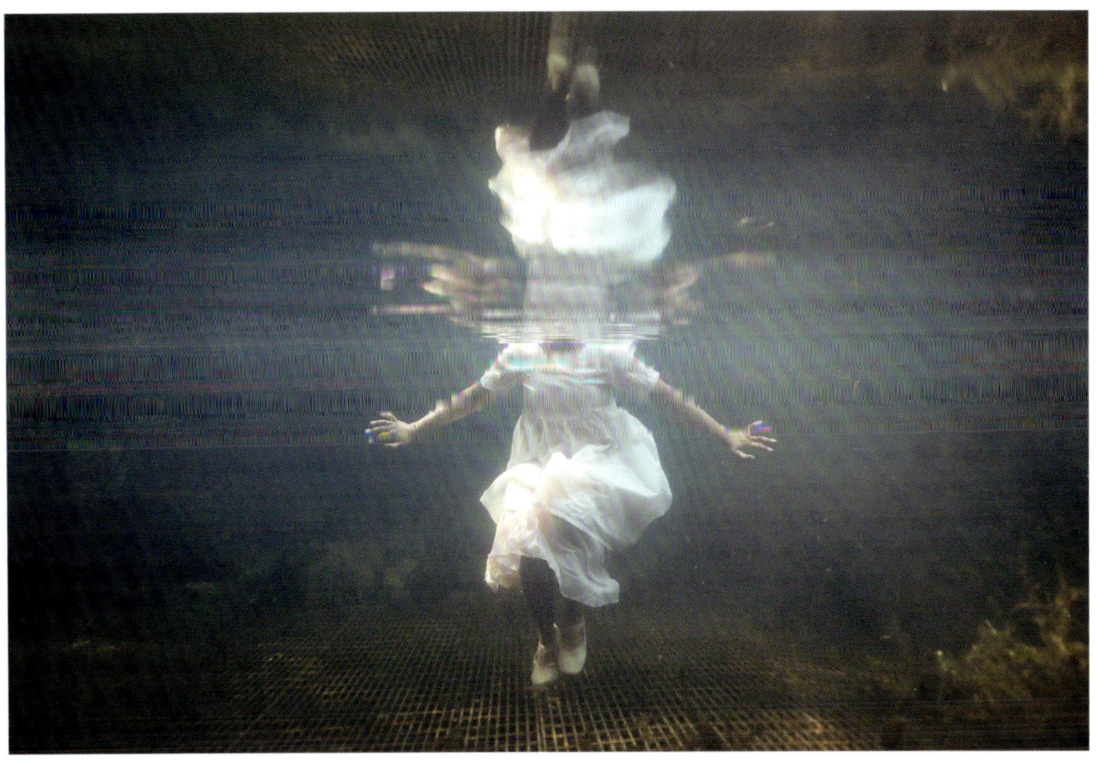

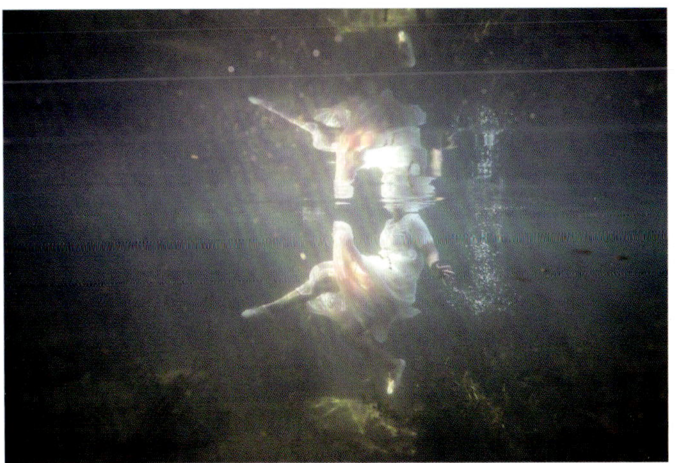

This page, from top: *Floridawater IV*, 2019
Floridawater II, 2019
Following spread: *Scratching the Wrong Side of Firmament*, 2015

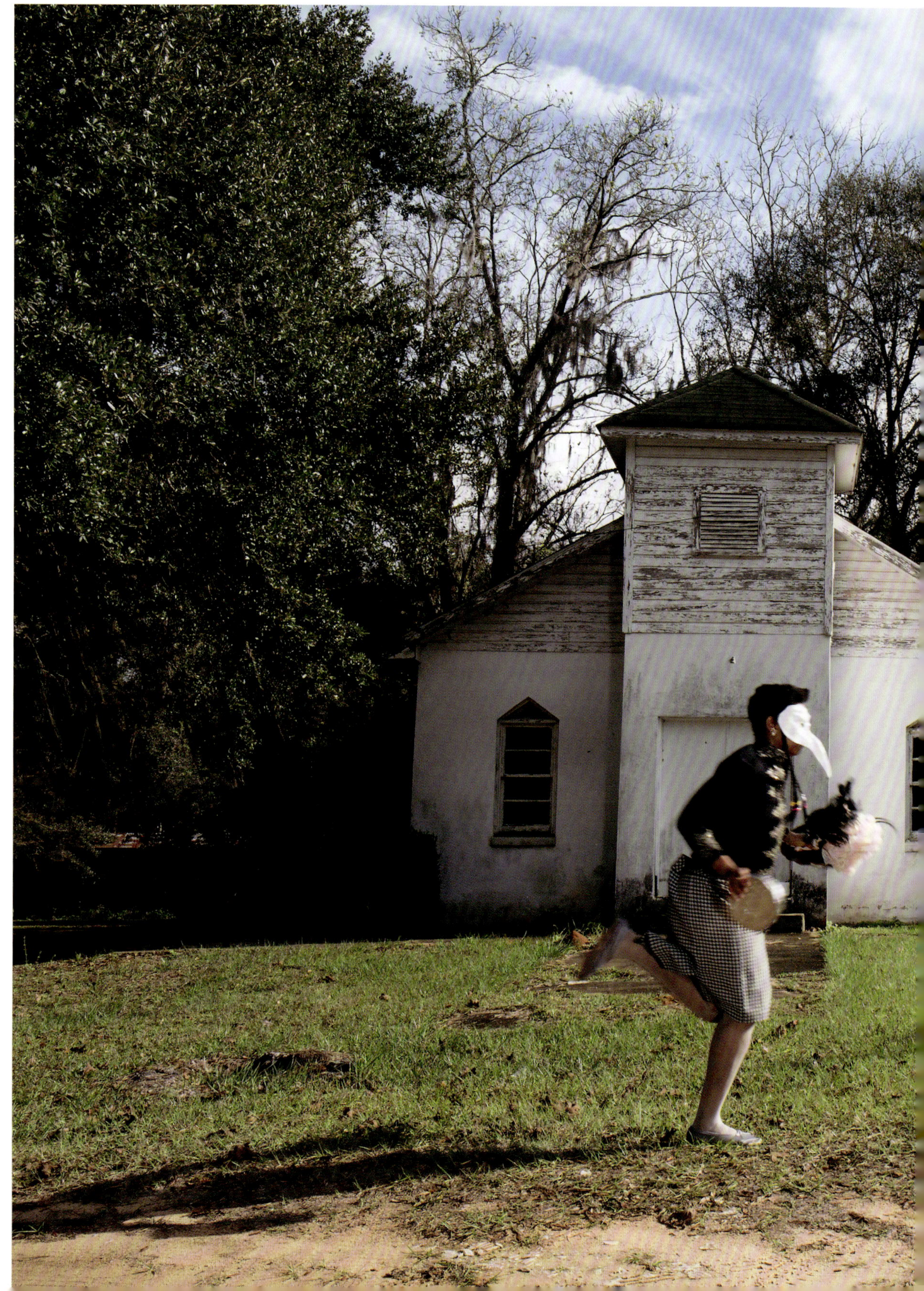

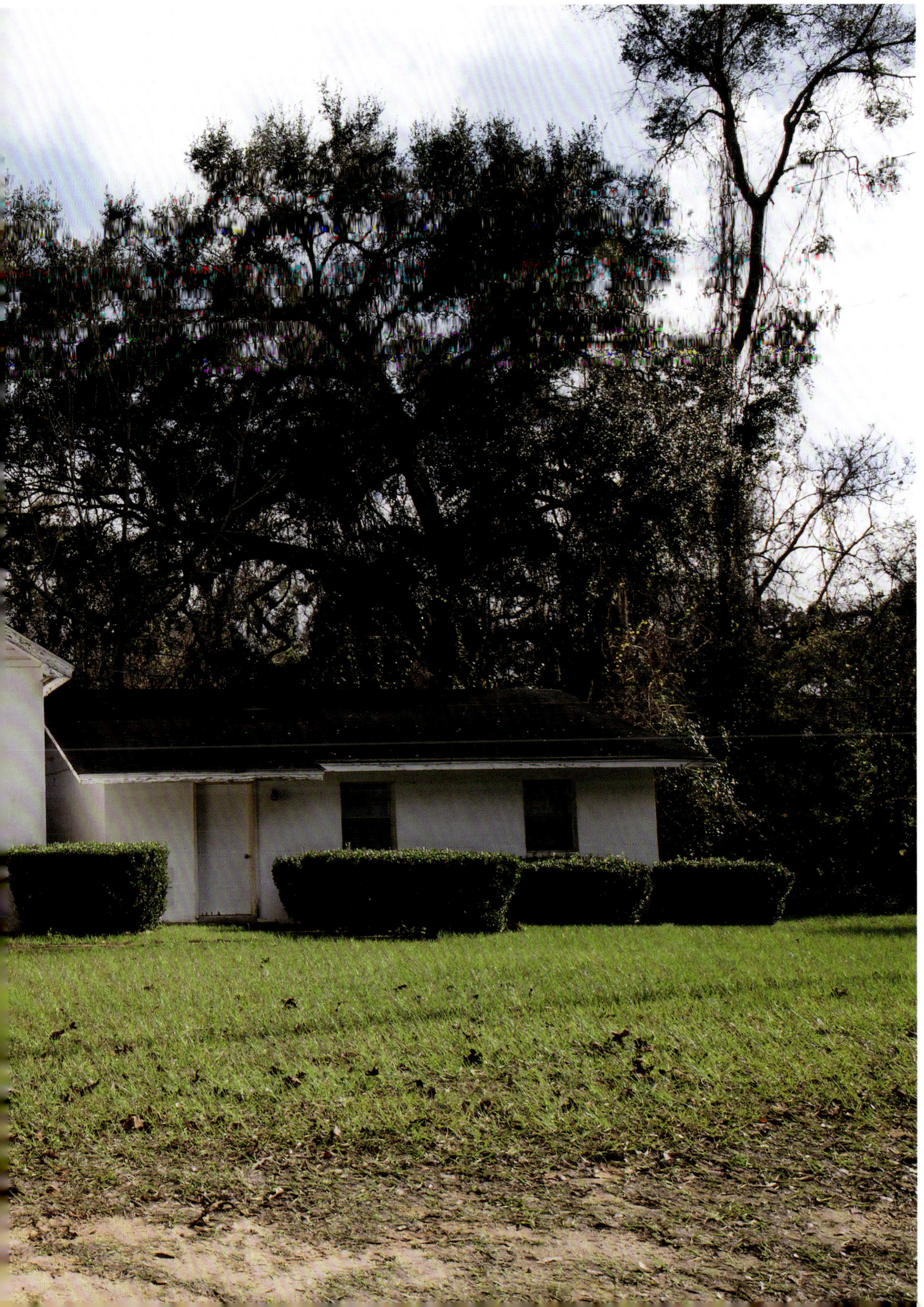

Sedrick Chisom

Monstrous Defiance

The Philadelphia-born, NYC-based fine artist Sedrick Chisom describes himself as a painter, writer and mythmaker. His paintings do have the feel of a literary epic, so distinctive are his narratives which are often also revealed in the characteristically long titles of his works. For example, *The Fugitives of the Southern Cross Gathered with the Monstrous Races beneath a Juniper Tree along the Outer Realm of the Savage South* (2021) alludes to American Civil War history but also to much older ideas about race and monstrosity inspired by books such as John Friedman's *The Monstrous Races in Medieval Art and Thought*.

Some of his earlier works explored race and the monstrous by depicting Black people as zombies in a way that evokes the work of renowned cultural theorist Jeffrey Jerome Cohen, who suggested that monsters reveal a culture's anxieties.[31] In this case, that fear is one of the derangement of boundaries (between life and death) and the idea of a maligned group having power over the grave: the one thing that is supposed to stop everybody and everything.

However, since 2018, Chisom's works have followed a new particular narrative thread.[32] He has been world-building, envisioning a post-apocalyptic landscape that delivers an inspired twist on Afrofuturism. Black people are noticeably absent as he focuses on a civilization built on the myth of white supremacy, called Altrightland, whose inhabitants are a pitiful mutant race slowly succumbing to disease.[33] Chisom reminds the viewer of the story of white supremacy through his references to the Confederacy, and mocks it. *The Wholly Avoidable Death of the Mighty Whitey, the Last Drunk Dionysian Hero, AKA The Wholly Tragic Birth of Fragile Narcissus* (2020), for example, is a charcoal piece depicting a character seemingly "hoisted by their own petard", a spear sticking out of their abdomen as they stare down at it and the pool of blood at their feet with incredulity.

Chisom's engagement with mythology, both addressing the more colloquial meaning (a shorthand for "something that is not true") as well as the meaning that suggests an epic attempt of a culture to explain the world around it, asks us to look at it with an irreverent eye. However, he does not encourage an approach that is dismissive of the very real effect these stories have. Instead, the artist opts for a method – a philosophy, perhaps – that can simultaneously see the inherent ridiculousness of some of these foundational tales, while also marvelling at the human ability to tell stories that are so compelling they appear to bend reality.

> "He has been world-building, envisioning a post-apocalyptic landscape that delivers an inspired twist on Afrofuturism as he focuses on a civilization built on the myth of white supremacy"

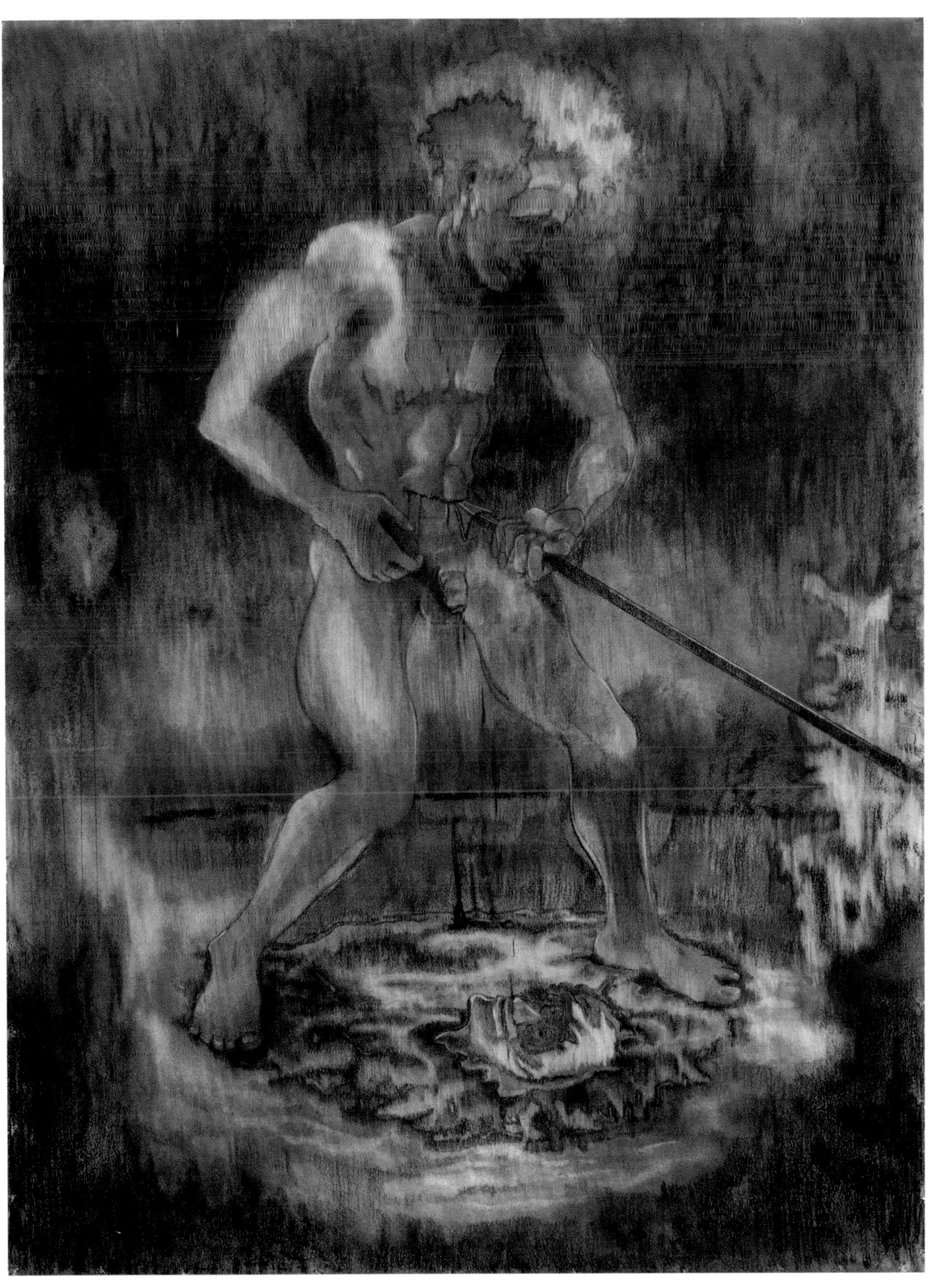

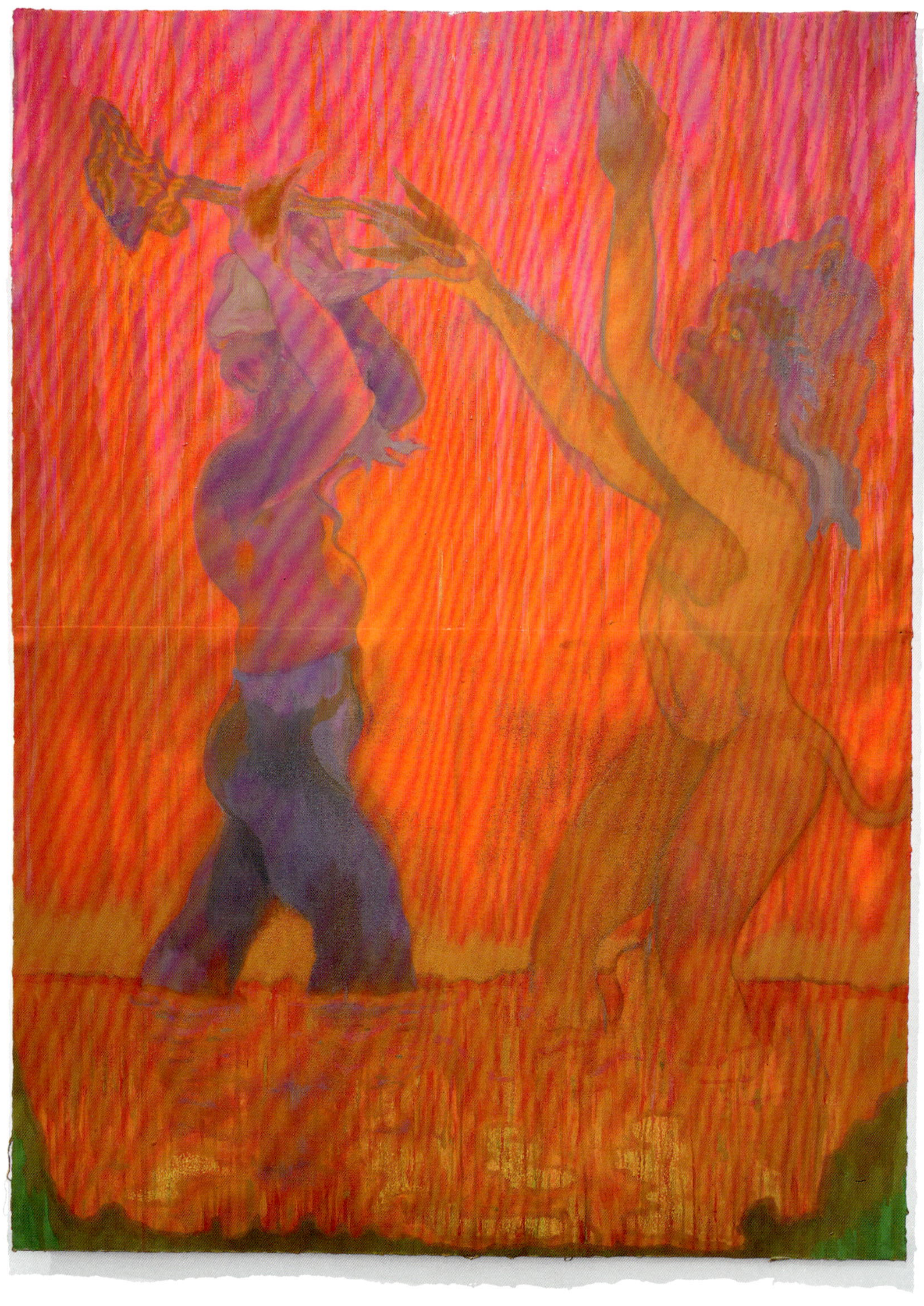

Previous spread: *The Wholly Avoidable Death of Mighty Whitey, the Last Drunk Dionysian Hero, AKA The Wholly Tragic Birth of Fragile Narcissus*, 2020
Above: *An Early Episode of the Empire's Preemptive Counterattack on the Monstrous Races in the Savage South*, 2019

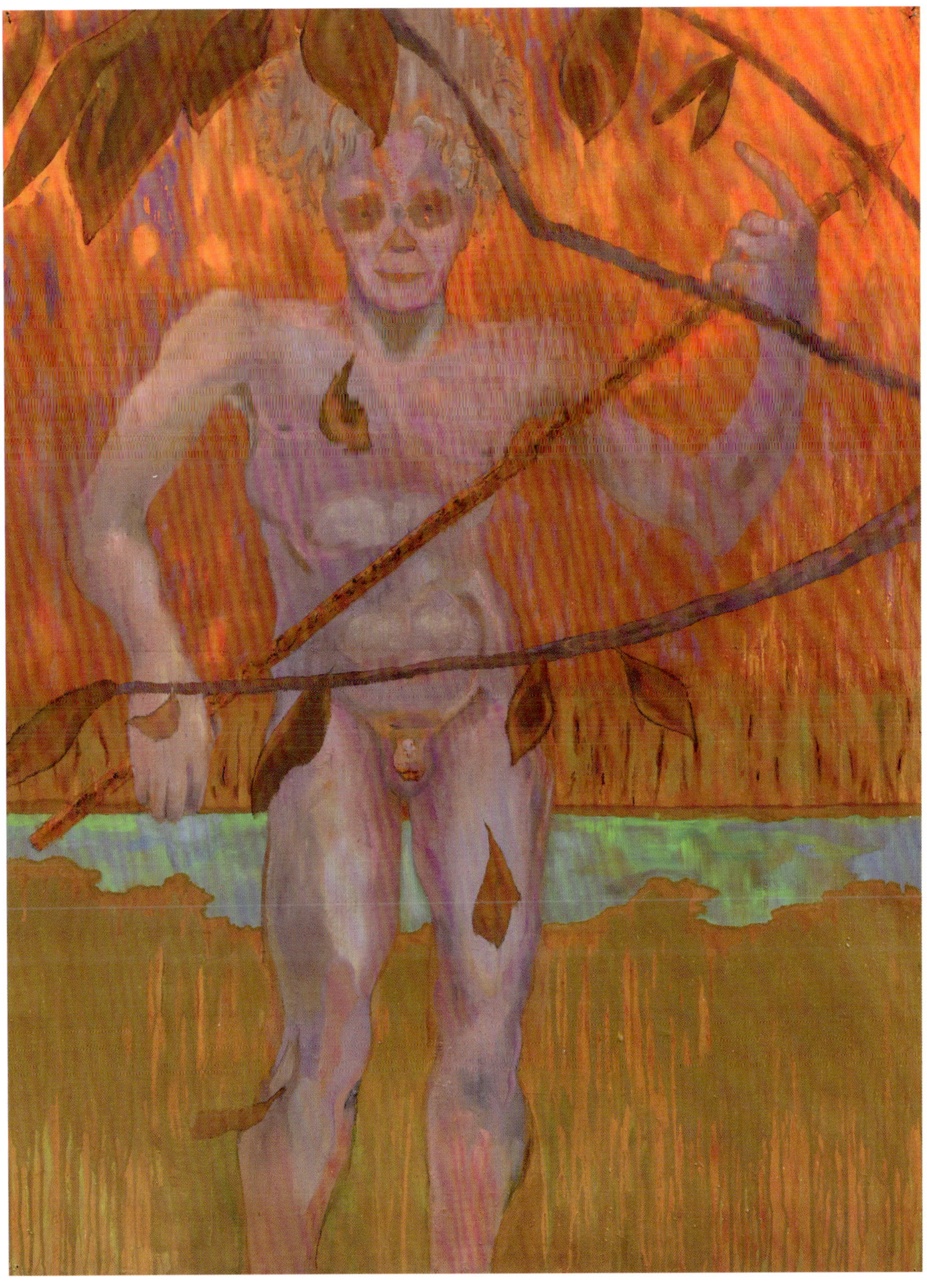

The Hero of Dionysus Emerged Inching through Umbrage, 2020

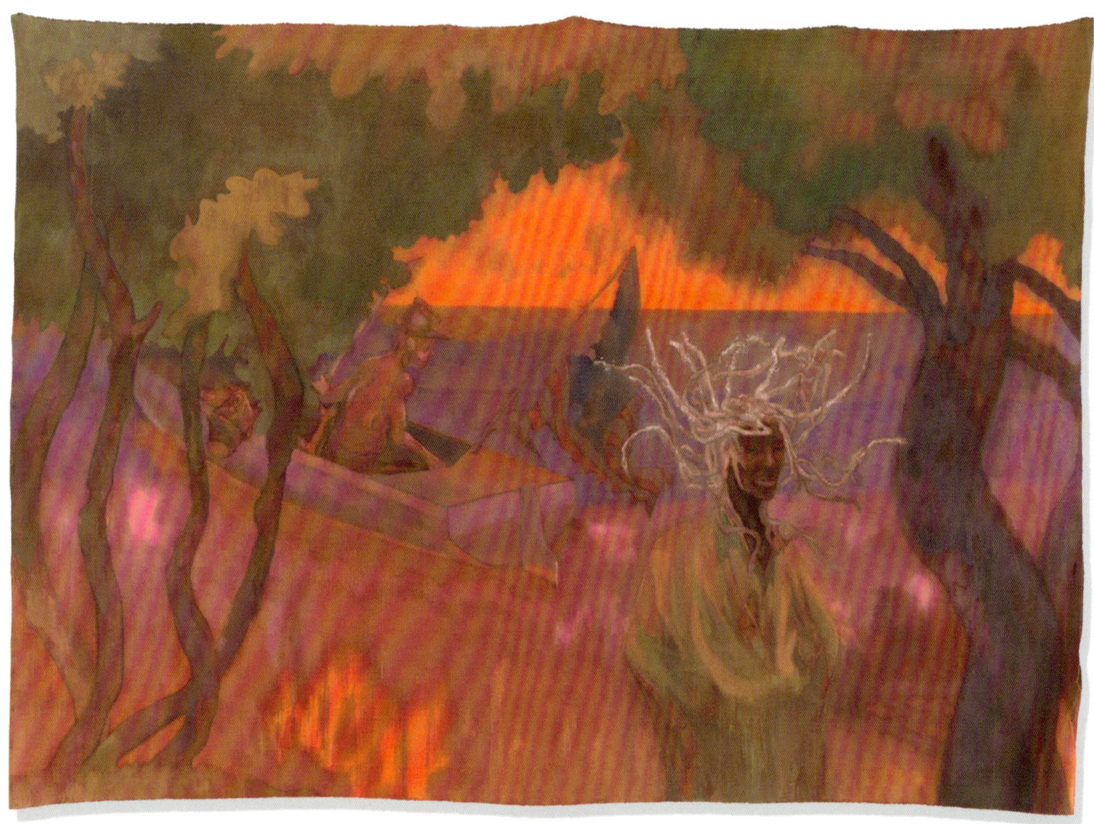

Medusa Wandered the Wetlands of the Capital Citadel Undisturbed by Two Confederate Drifters Preoccupied by Poisonous Vapors That Stirred in the Night Air, 2021

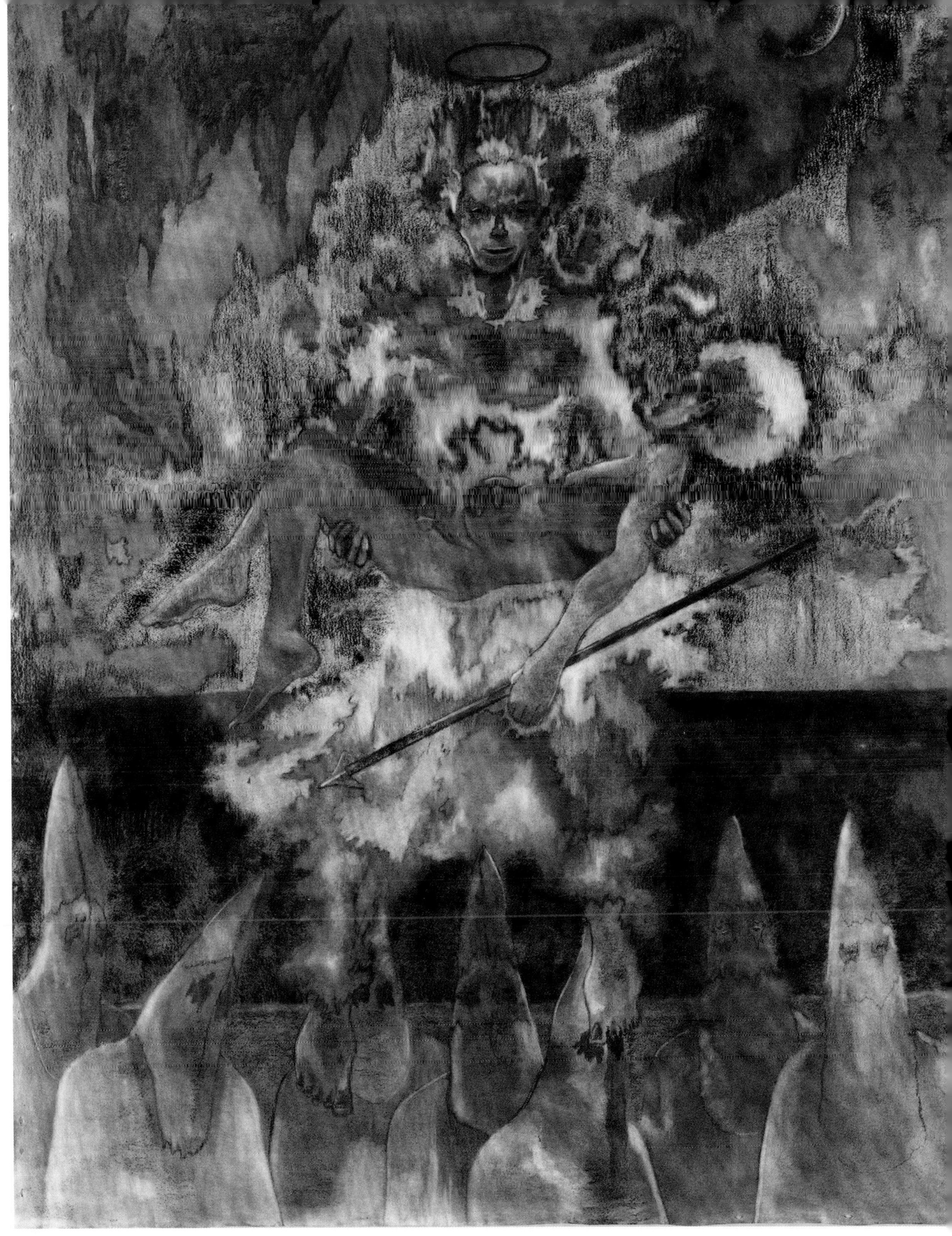

The Woes of the Westward Kingdom Were Such That the Angel Moroni Delivered a Dionysian Hero to the Daughters and Sons of the Southern Cross, 2020

Lunga Ntila

A Seamless Composite

South African fine artist and photographer Lunga Ntila is known mostly for her distorted photographic self-portrait collages. Her experience being raised by diplomat parents in South Africa, Germany, Benin and the Netherlands influenced this exploration into the fragmentation and reconfiguration of identity. "Every time I moved to a different country, I felt like I had to mould myself into a different culture and re-adjust my identity to unfamiliar surroundings," she said in an interview with *Contemporary And*.[34] Her photo-collages break up, enlarge and exaggerate the features of the face, but where one might expect sharp right angles, there is a roundness to the way she cuts her pieces which evokes a sense of fluidity that in some pieces blurs the join lines and from afar seems to present a new seamless composite whole. Ntila's 2021 work *Jabulani* does this, enlarging and multiplying eyes, playing with distortion around the ears, from which two oversized diamond cluster earrings hang, as well as the shape of the head itself. Ntila cleverly utilizes the artistic effects that might in another circumstance connote monstrosity and alienness, to instead remind us of the inherently compositional nature of individual human identity.

Fashion and street photographer Anthony Bila, as well as expressionism and Francis Bacon,

> "Effects that might connote monstrosity and alienness instead remind us of the compositional nature of individual human identity"

are inspirations. You can see the influence of fashion editorials in the 2020 works *Father Stretch My Hands* and *They Still Watching Me*. Her series *God Among Us!* is a mix of portraits and documentary-style photographs in her signature cut-and-paste style, with striking, almost violent, pops of red amongst all the monochrome – accentuating lips and hats, symbols of sensuality and authority respectively. "The black and white shows the viewer the confidence that I have in my work… I play with red as it marks a connection to this other dimension," she explained in the same interview with *Contemporary And*. In these digital collages, this other dimension is inspired by concepts of African spiritualities that emphasize the connection between a deity and all forms of life, hence the title *God Among Us!* Ntila has stated that the bee is a family symbol and it makes an appearance in a few of her digital collages, including *I'll Take It from Here* (2021), in which a bee perches on the bright red fingers of a many-faced being, and *Bees in the Trap* (2021), which depicts a matriarchal figure holding a large white flower amongst the petals of which giant bees buzz. The family scene depicted speaks again to the bee as Ntila's family emblem, a depiction perhaps of a harmonious connection with ancestors.

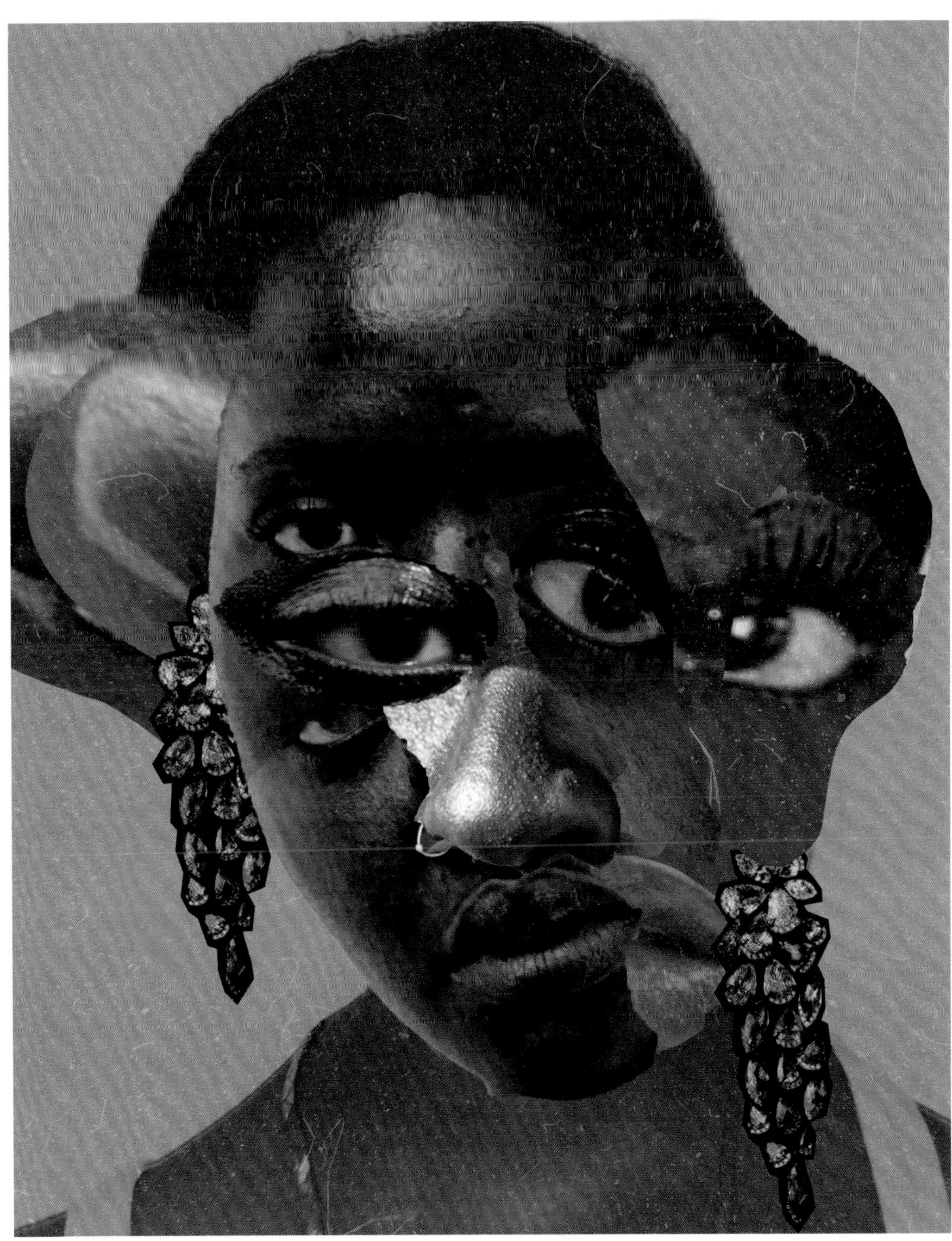

Jabulani, 2021

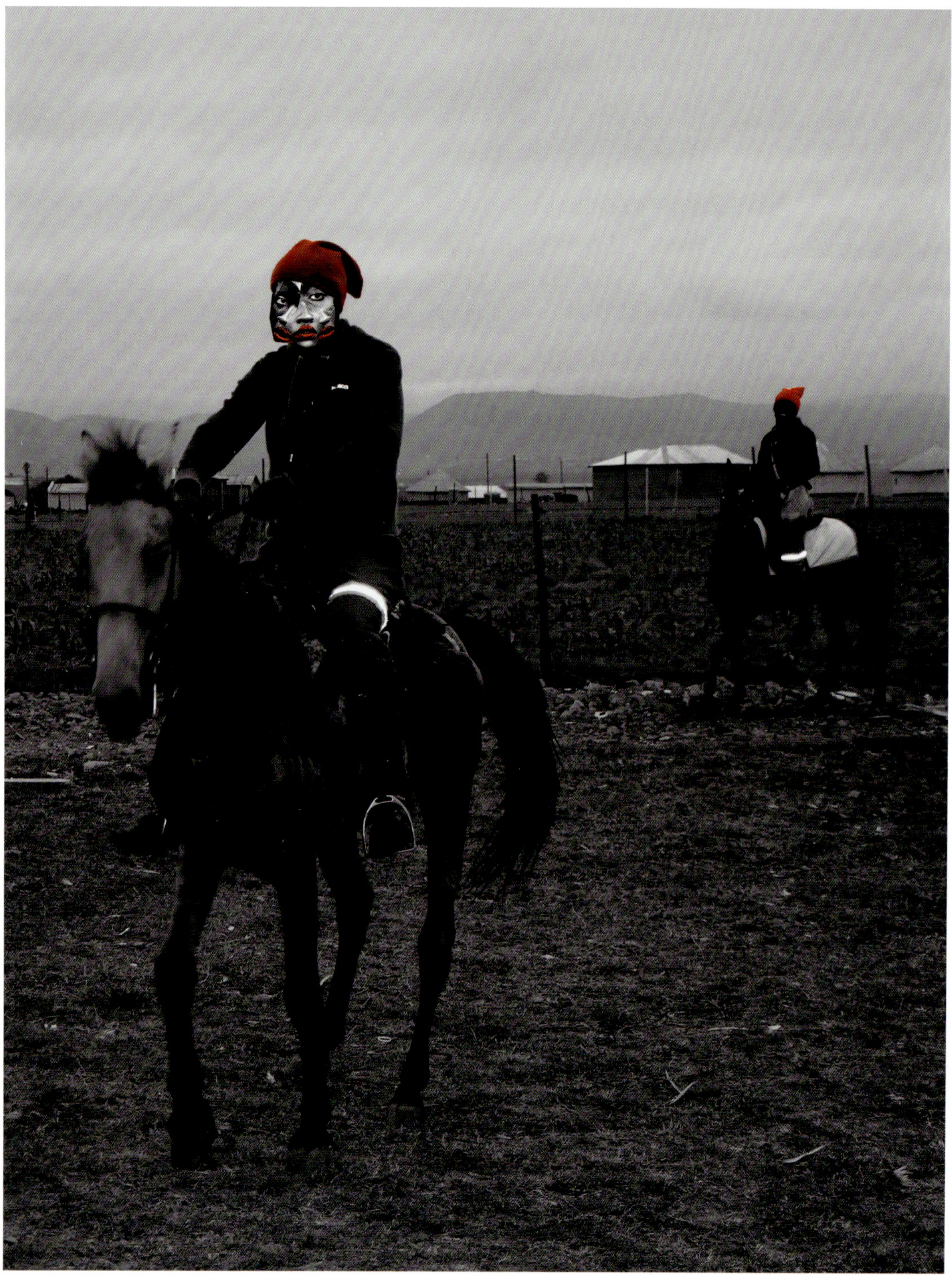

Two Man Show, 2021

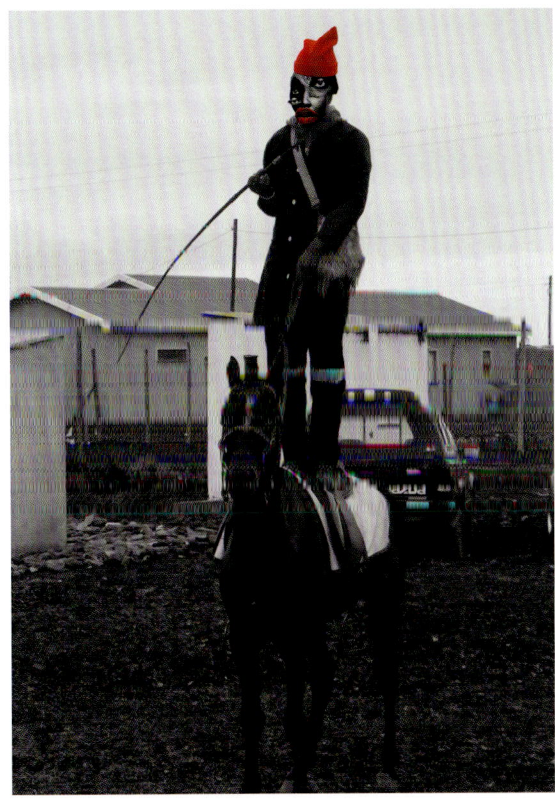

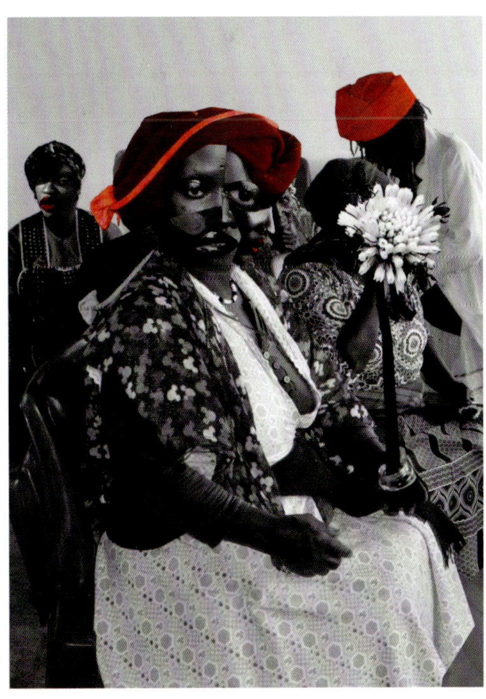

From top:
Get Off Your High Horse, 2021
Bees in the Trap, 2021

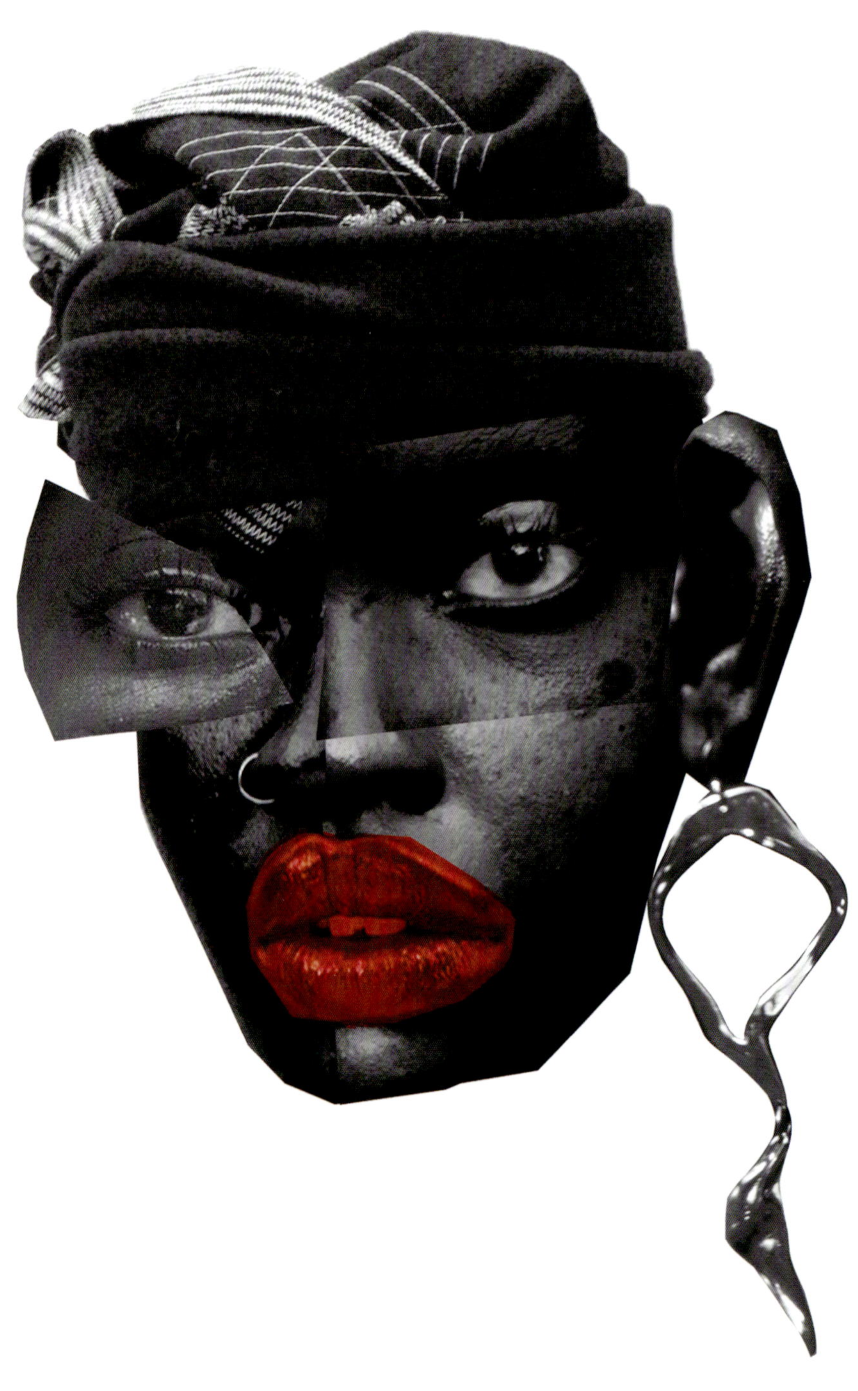

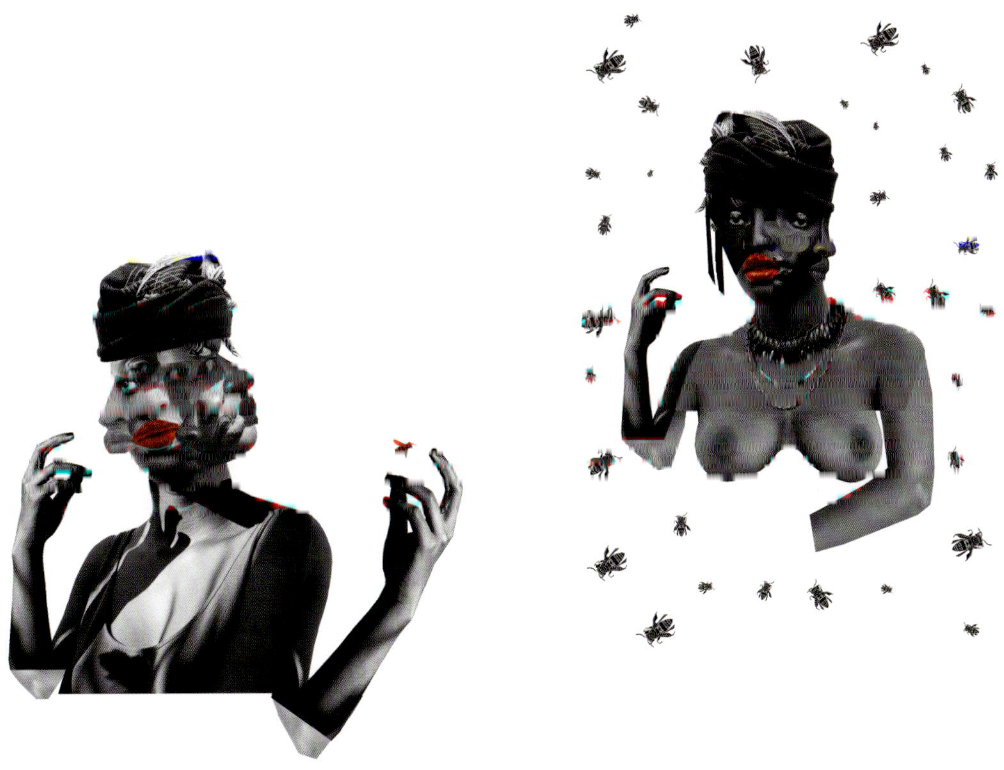

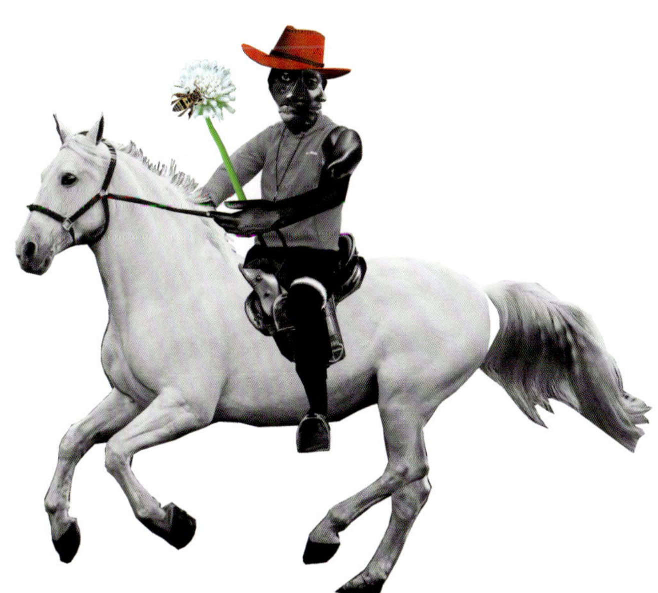

These pages, clockwise from left:
Chandelier, 2021
Zandisile, 2021
Sweet and Tender, 2021
Take Me Where Your Heart Is, 2021

Jodi Minnis

Rejection and Reclamation

Part of Bahamian multidisciplinary artist Jodi Minnis's work over the past few years has involved "rejecting and reclaiming" the offensive caricature and stereotype of the "mammy" figure.[35] Probably most recognizable in the context of American cultural history, the "mammy" is a racialized trope that imagines older Black women as gleefully subservient and unsexed mother-figures. In the context of Minnis's background, the "mammy" figure is embodied in the character of the "Bahama Mama", which the artist explores through photography, sculpture and painting. Minnis created a small sculpture – a saltshaker, in fact – in the image of the "Bahama Mama" with a voluptuous bosom, dark skin, red lips, a polka-dot headscarf and a rolling pin in her hands. In *Bahama Mama Army 1* (2020), part of her photographic series on this subject, a group of unpainted figurines stand in formation with their backs to the camera, save for one which is painted and facing forward. You can see the whites of her eyes, which have no pupils, and the rolling pin is wielded more like a weapon. In *Guards* (2020), four unpainted figurines stand, rolling pins in hand, their headscarves transformed into glittery head coverings that completely obscure their faces. The idea of the non-threatening domesticated and servile figure is transformed into figures that are unknowable and potentially dangerous.

> "The idea of the non-threatening domesticated and servile figure is transformed into figures that are unknowable and potentially dangerous"

Minnis also took photographic self-portraits, transforming herself into the "Bahama Mama". Showing her dressed in a red headscarf, barefooted and wielding a rolling pin as well, the photographs explore the line between the offensive stereotype and the real Black women it reduced. In *No* (2019), the rolling-pin-as-weapon is activated, the utensil large enough to block out Minnis's face and blurred from motion as it seems to come down on the viewer's face with the swift rebuke of the work's title.

Fish (2019) is a painting that, while not stated by Minnis to be explicitly part of the *Not Your Bahama Mama* series, feels like a defiant response to that image. In another self-portrait that bears a similarity to the "Bahama Mama" images with the polka-dot headscarf and very dark skin, Minnis evokes neither domestic servitude nor somebody battle-ready. Instead, the subject indulges in a meal of fried fish, made for *herself*, not anybody else. Her eyes look directly at the viewer as her tongue pokes out to savour white flakes of fried fish. In two photographs that accompany the painting to form the series, *I Fried Fish for Me*, Minnis documented the act of gutting and seasoning fish in preparation for the meal, taking "the communal activity of cleaning and frying fish and [making] it a singular action for the benefit of one".[36]

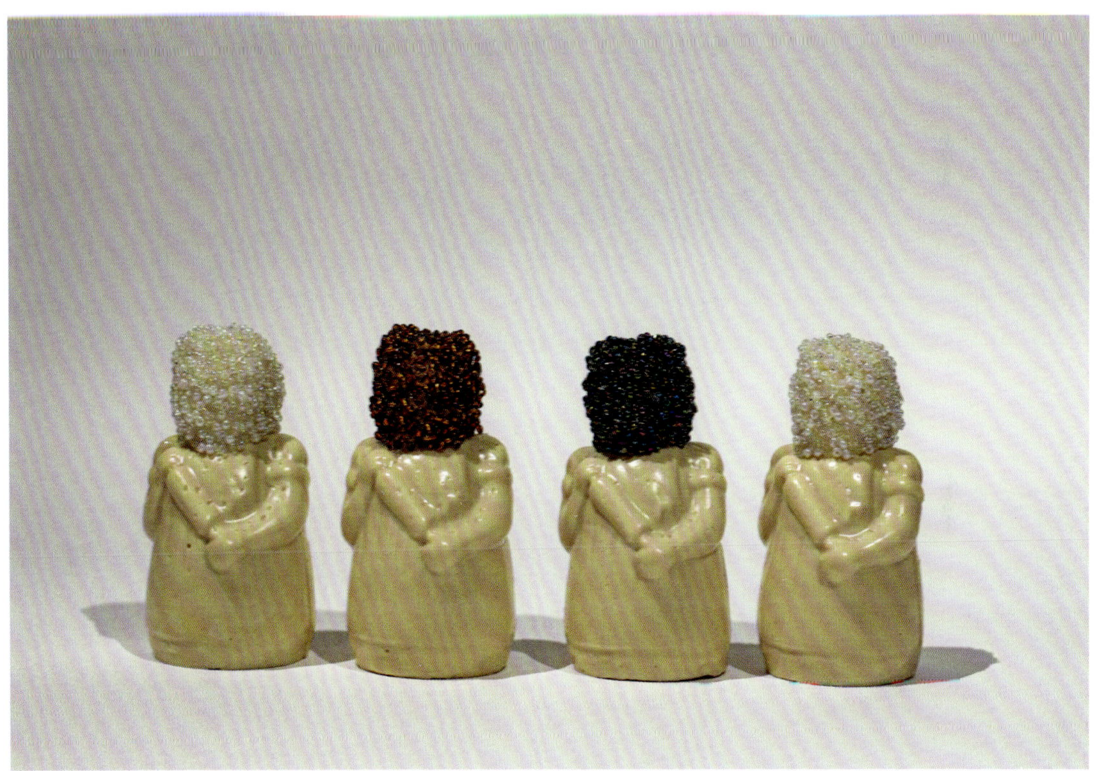

Bahama Mama Army 4, 2019

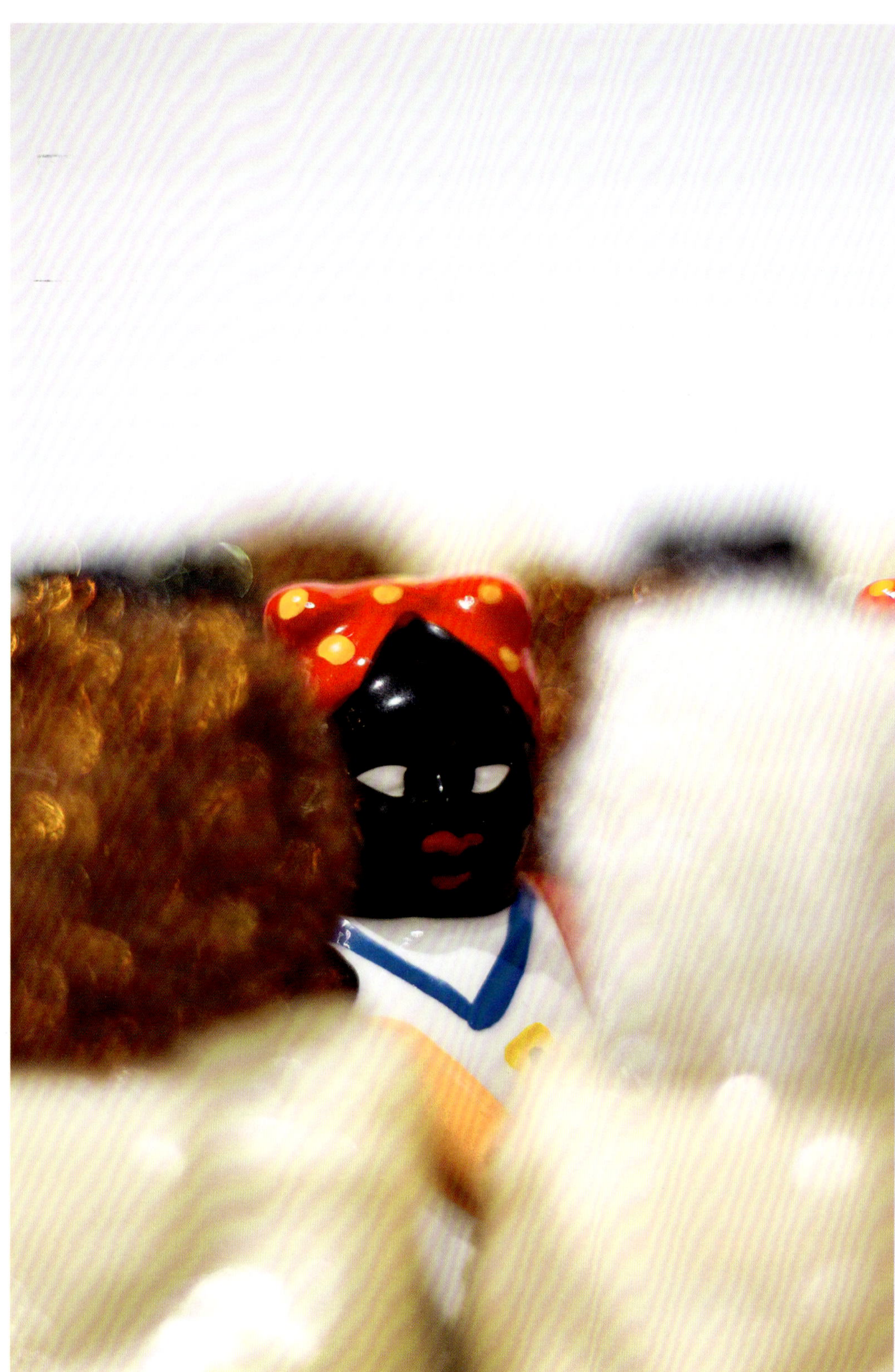

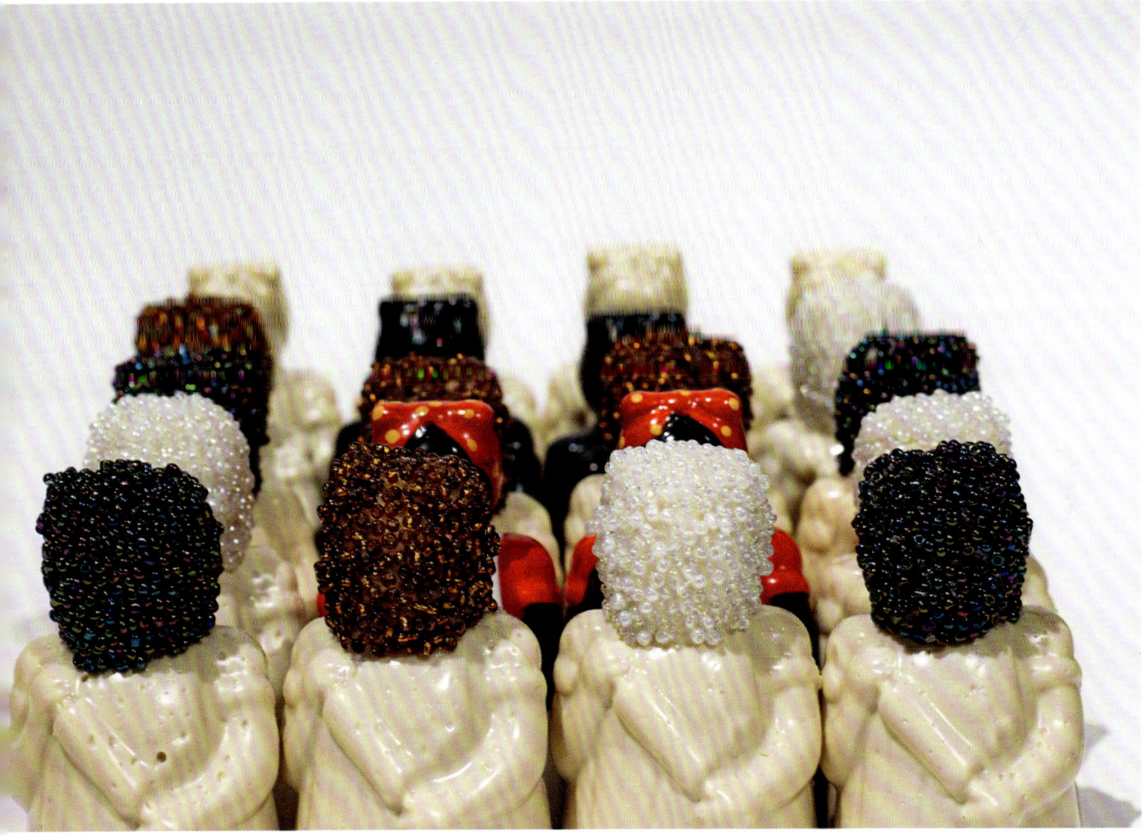

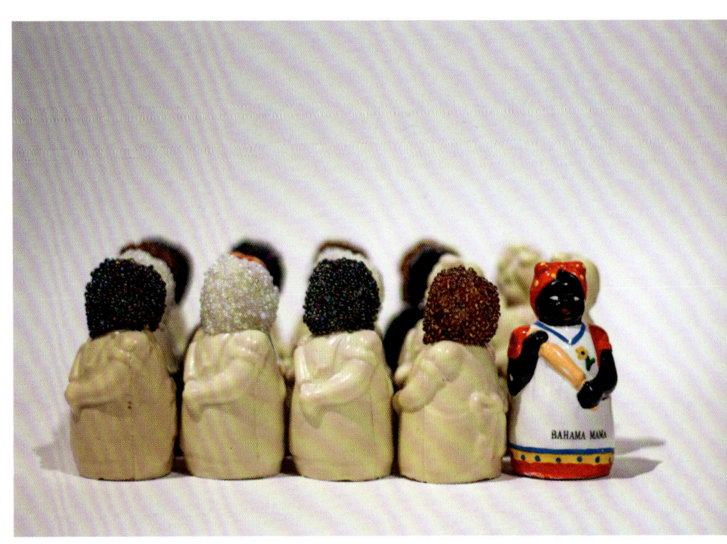

Opposite: *Protect Her*, 2019
This page, from top: *Bahama Mama Army 2*, 2019
Bahama Mama Army 1, 2019

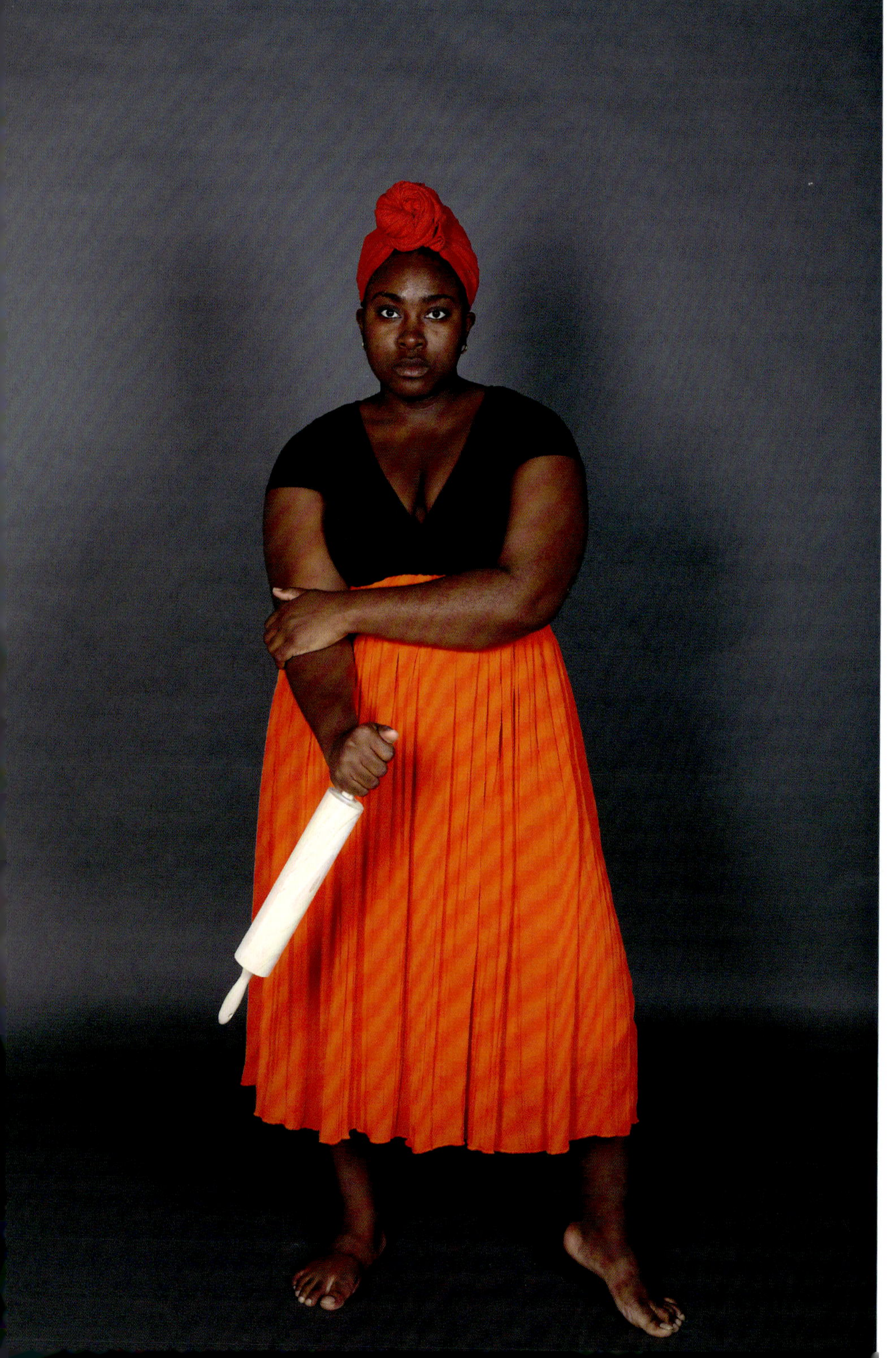

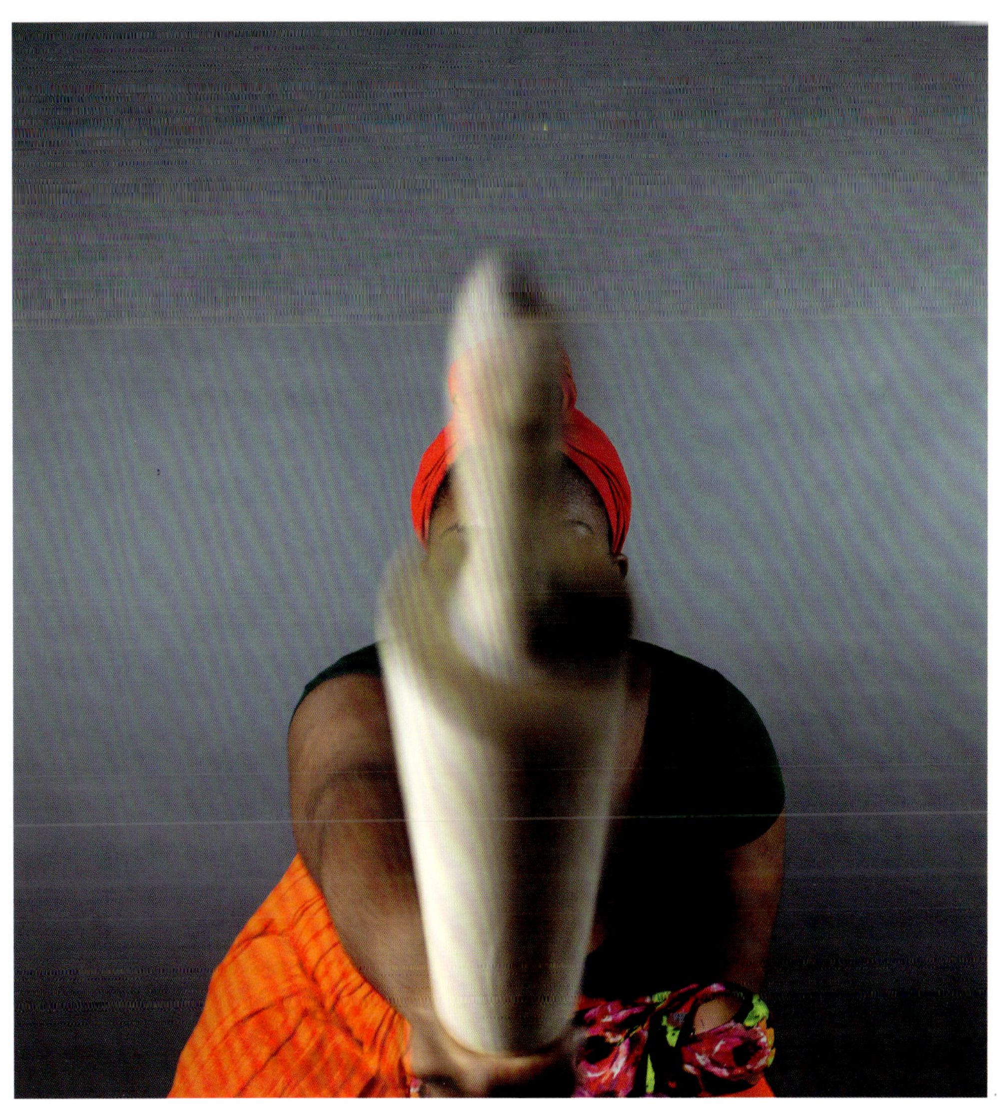

Opposite: *NO*, 2019
Above: *No*, 2019

Délio Jasse

Between Reality and Memory

Délio Jasse was born in Angola and lives and works in Milan, Italy. He has also lived in Portugal, which was the colonial power in Angola, so much of Jasse's work seeks to explore the contradictions of colonial rule through the everyday images taken during those times. The archive, both as a concept and as an endless repository of material, is the foundation of his work. He uses found photographs and techniques such as screenprinting to explore the concept of memory too – not just personal but also collective and cultural memory.

His 2018 *Nova Lisboa* – Portuguese for "New Lisbon" – transforms archive photographs from the 1960s into black-and-white screenprints overlaid with brightly coloured prints of official documents. New Lisbon was the colonial-era name of the city in Angola which is now called Huambo. The photographs are dominated by men in well-cut suits. Children wear prim dresses. Cars gleam. The images evoke Americana-style nostalgia: the white-picket-fence dream with a slight edge of cool made safe by an emphasis on the familial.

But Jasse interrupts that white middle-class fantasy with reminders of the colonial enterprise that built the world of these families and intentionally excluded the majority Black population. Works like *Serie No Name* (2018),

> "Jasse interrupts that white middle-class fantasy with reminders of the colonial enterprise that built the world of these families and intentionally excluded the majority Black population"

in which one disconcerting image depicts an imploring Black woman serve to highlight and interrogate this relationship between these two demographics.

The effect of the overlaid printing, which looks like stamps and immigration documents, places the works in this space between the real and the fictitious, "neither reality nor memory", as Jasse described them in an interview with *Aperture*. Jasse also wanted those printed images and texts to depict the "nonsense" of official documents, saying, "You are not who you are just because a document states it." The artist moved to Portugal from Angola when he was 18 years old and lived without citizenship for a while because of lost documents in his old home and the complicated bureaucracies of his new one.

Serie Black Portrait – part of the *Nova Lisboa* series – similarly transforms found passport photographs into silver gelatin prints depicting their smartly dressed male subjects with stamps in gold running across their silhouetted faces. You can make out the signatures, the dotted lines with faint, barely legible text. The stripping of identifying characteristics, replaced by stamps and scribbles, speaks to the attempt to equate identity with official documents against which Jasse protests.

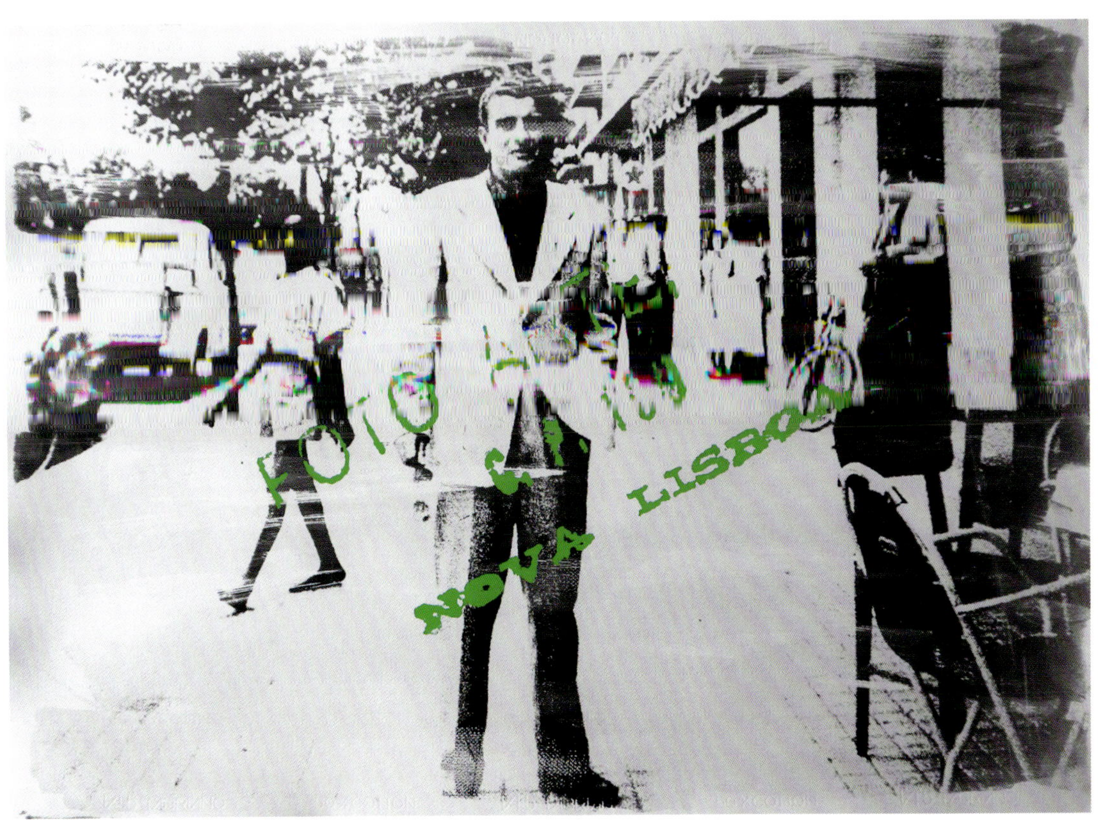

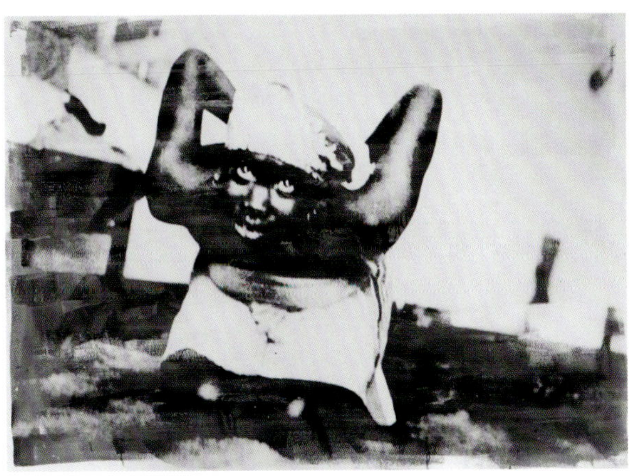

This page, from top: From *Nova Lisboa #1 #2*, 2018
Untitled, 2018
Following spread: *Pontus*, 2012

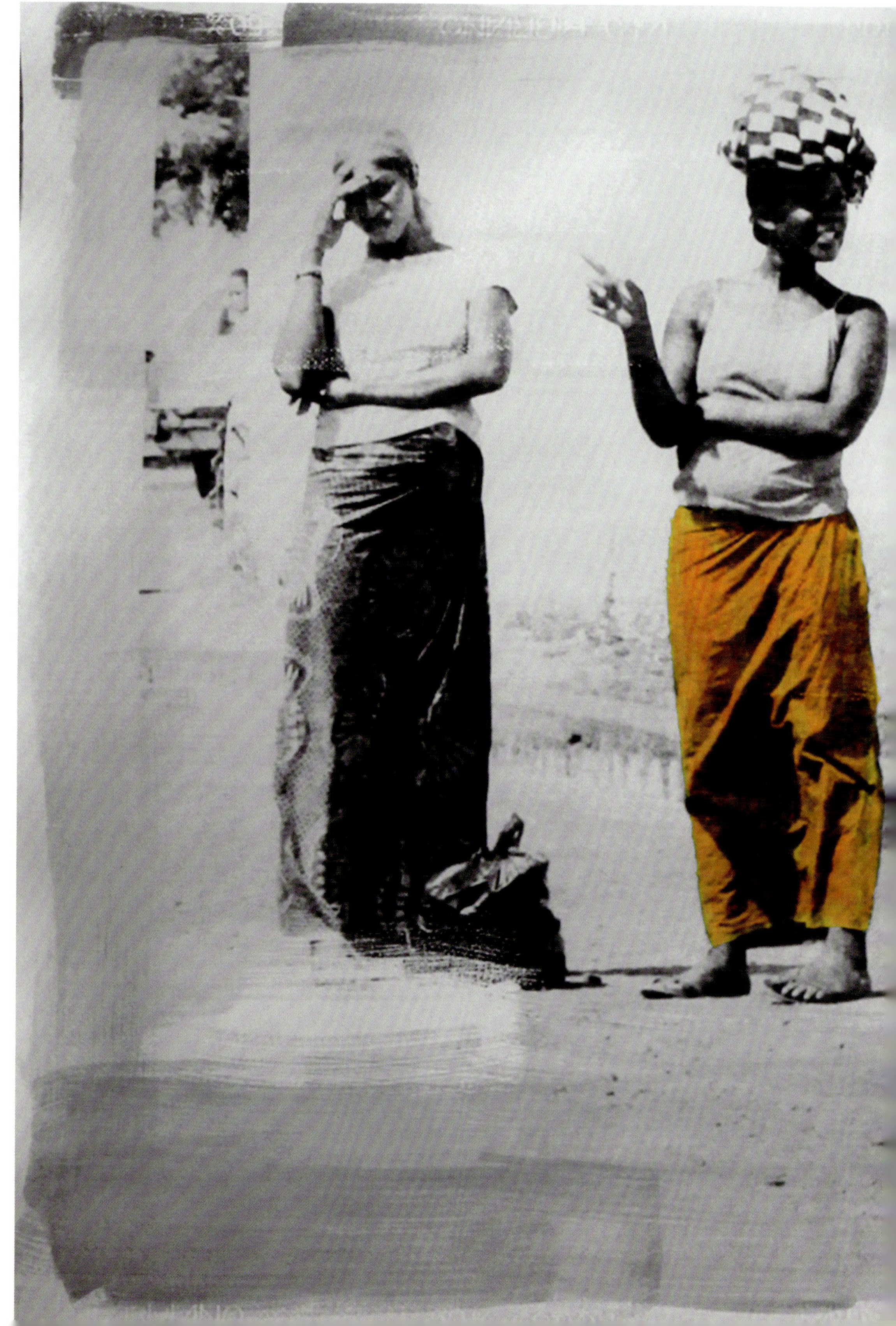

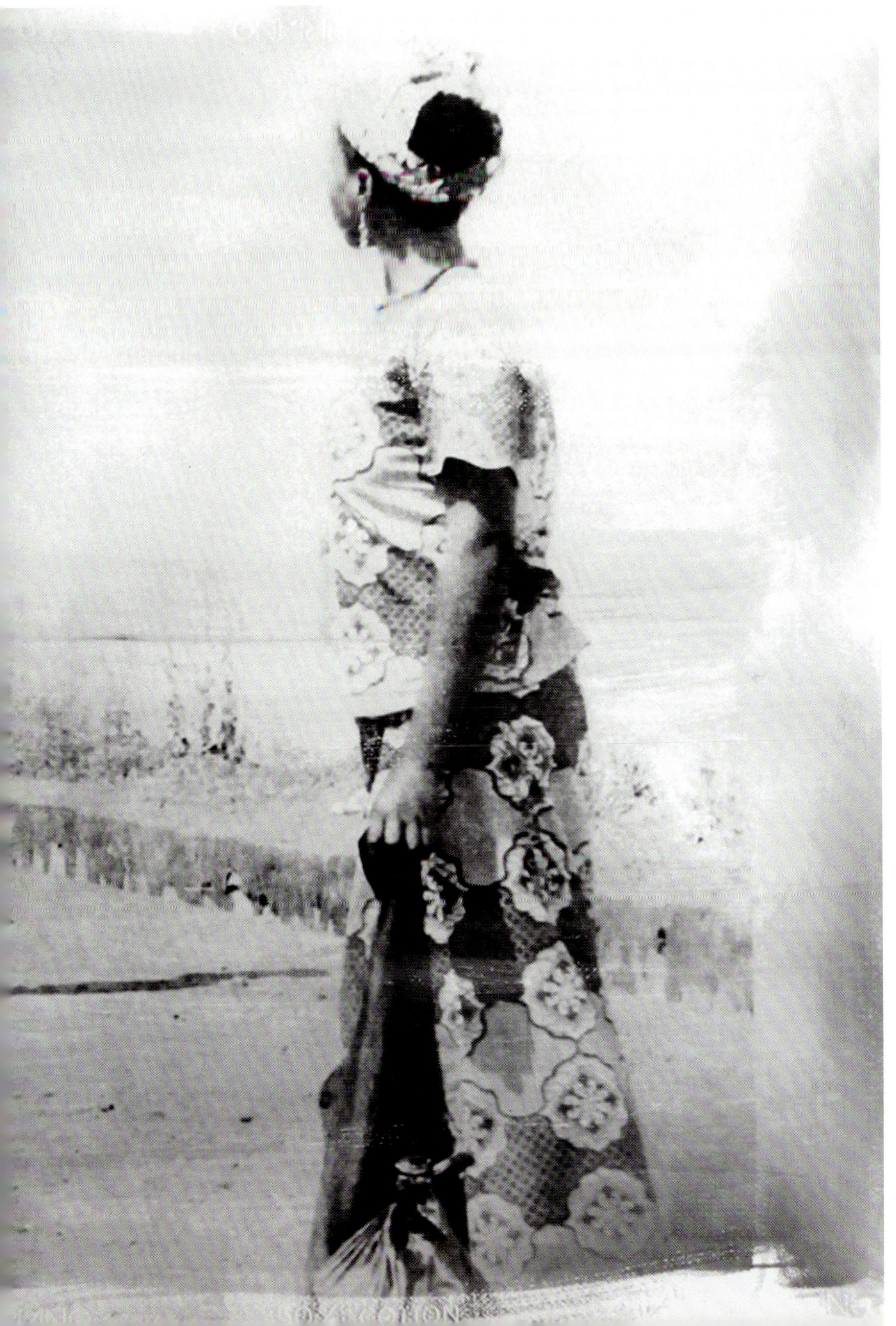

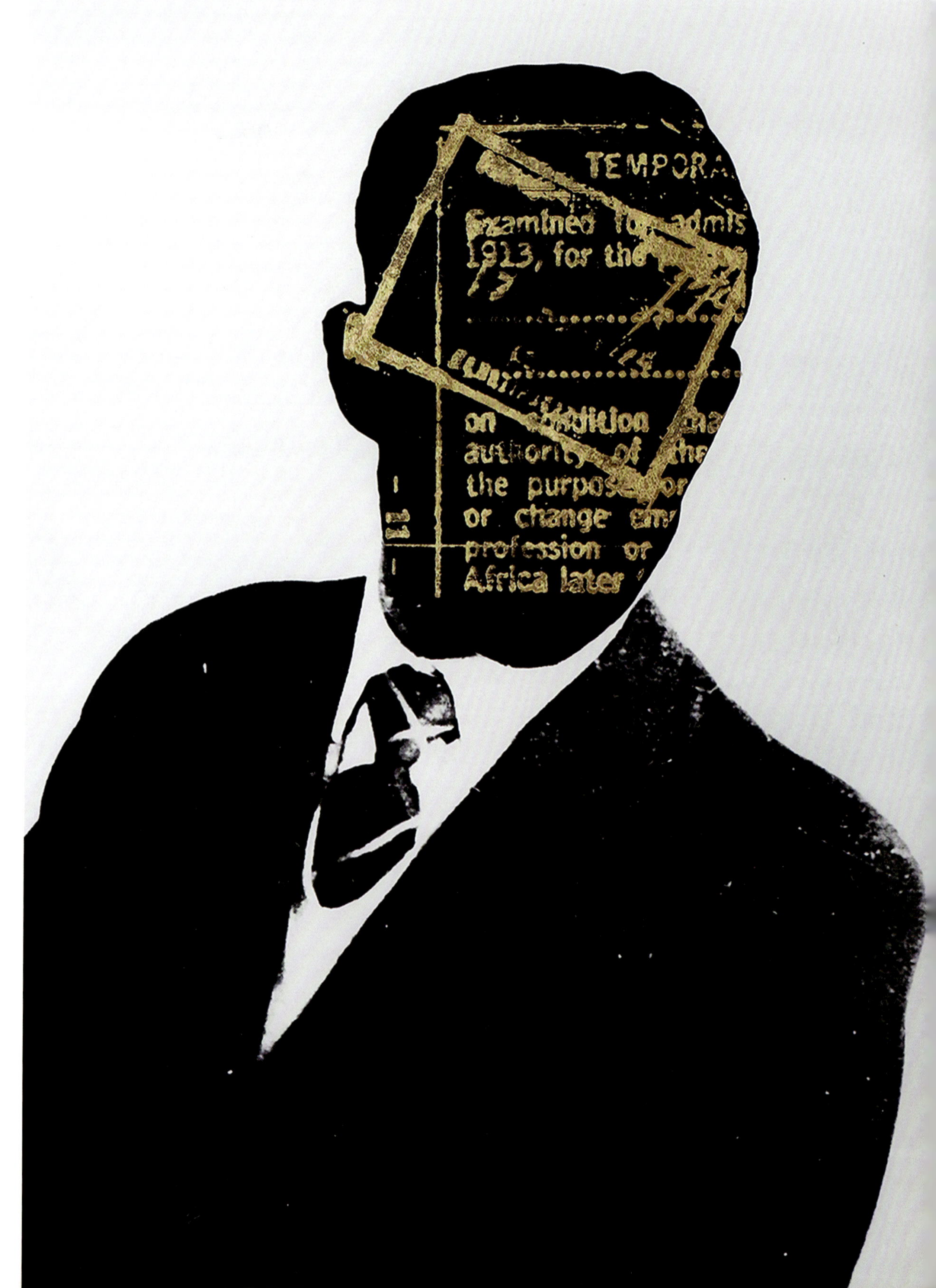
TEMPORA
examined for admis
1913, for the
on
authority of the
the purpose or
or change em
profession or
Africa later

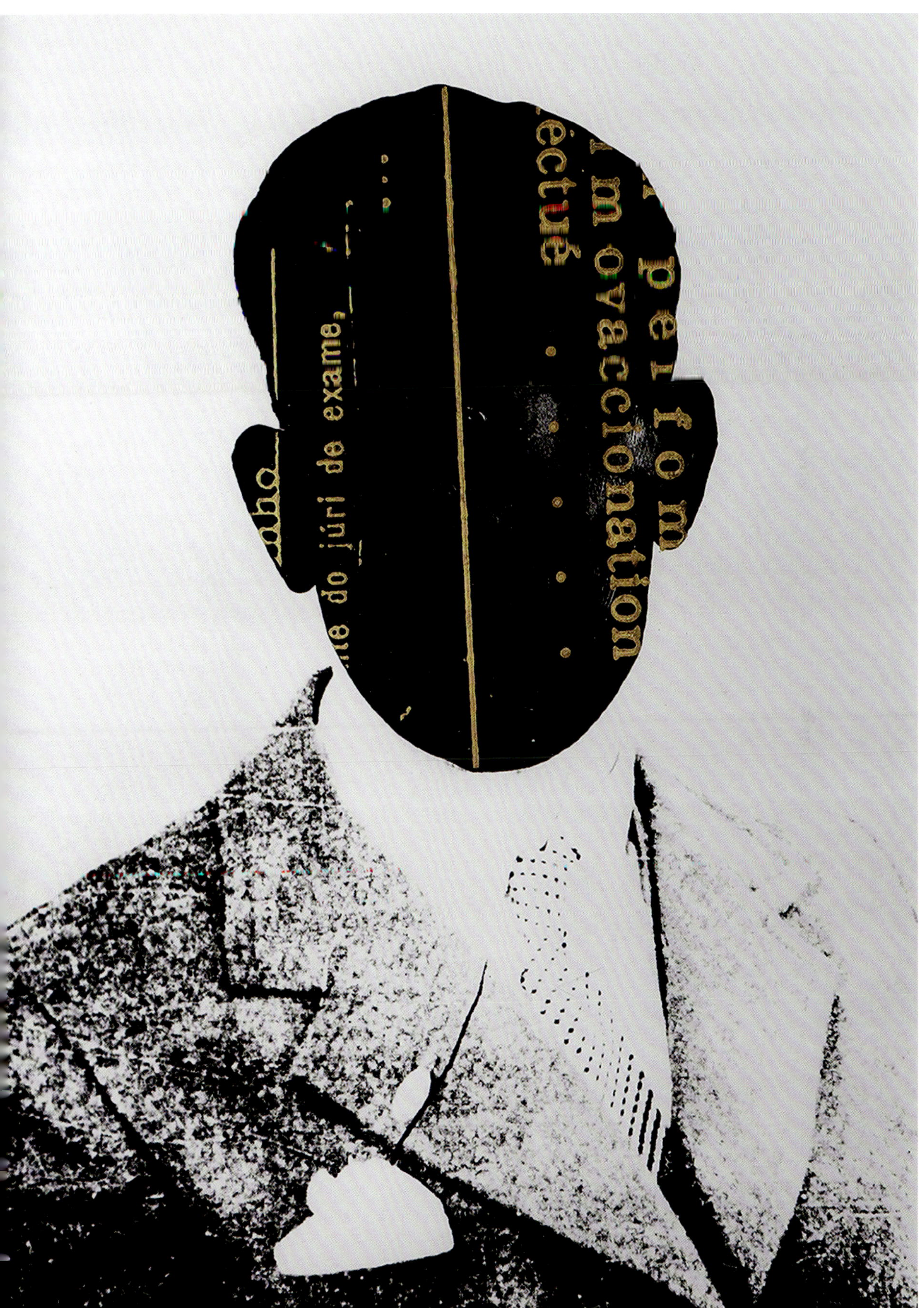

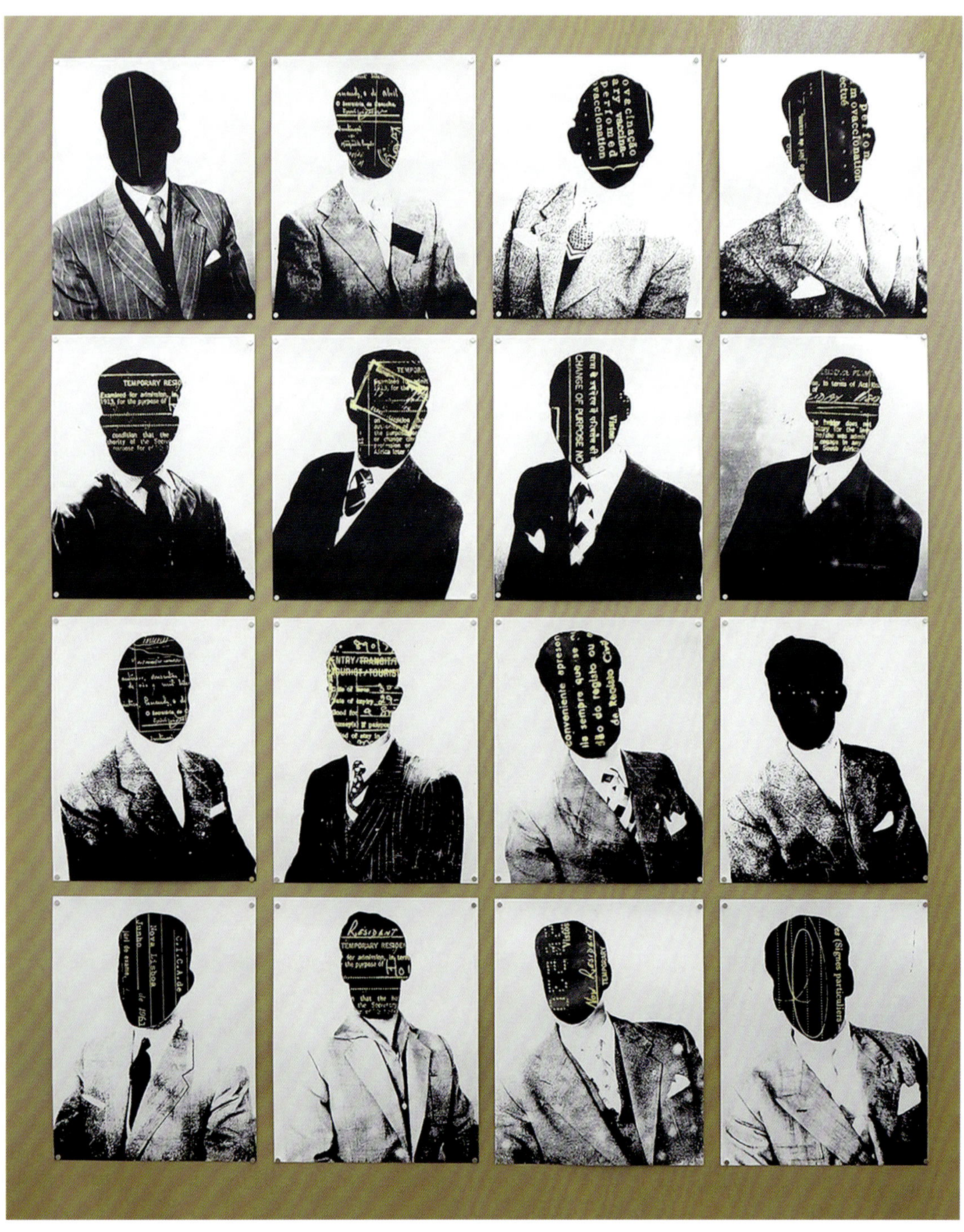

Previous spread and these pages:
All from *Serie Black Portrait*, 2018

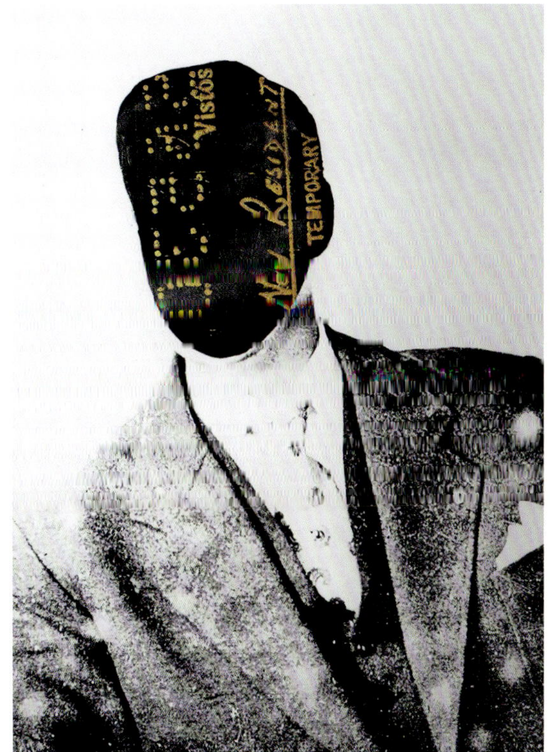
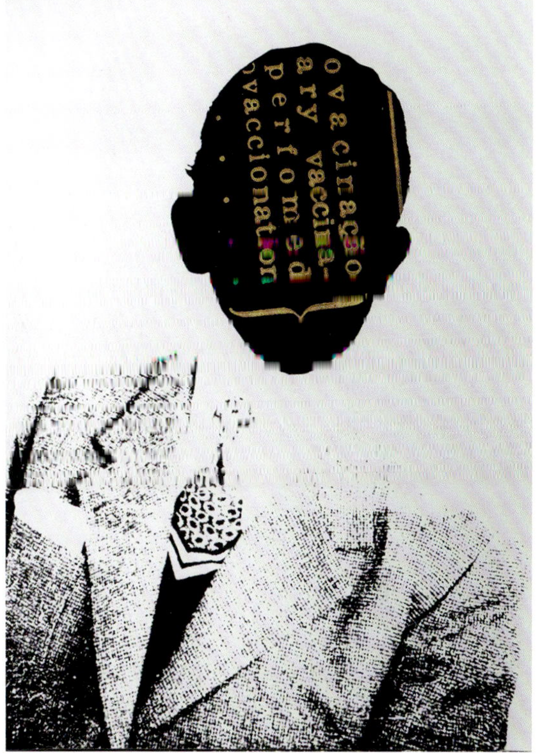
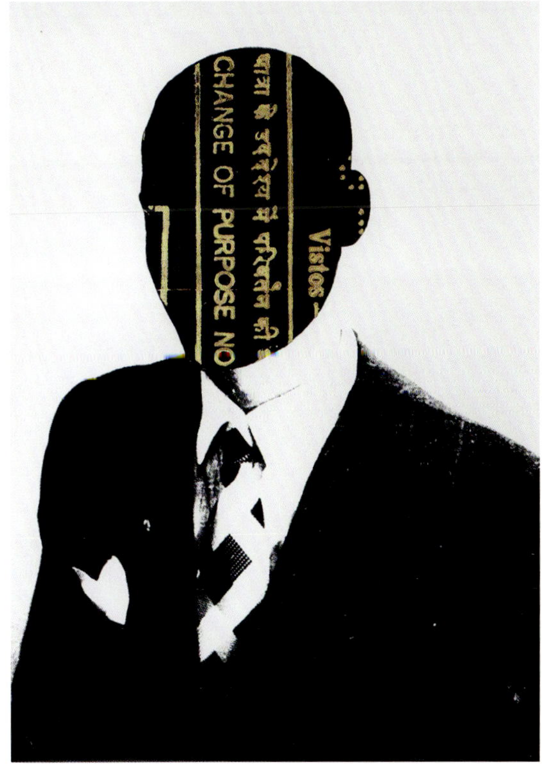
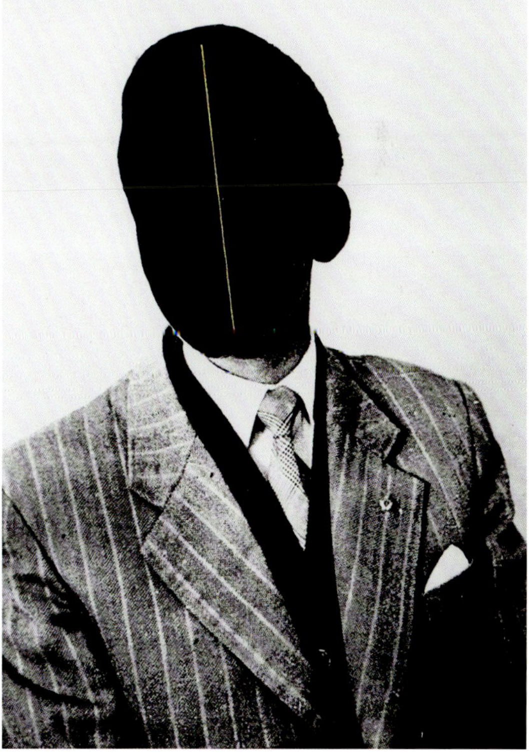

Joana Choumali

Seeking Solace

After initially becoming interested in photography as a child, Côte d'Ivoire-based artist Joana Choumali took up the practice in earnest in 2011 to explore Africa's past and present. *Hââbré – The Last Generation* (2016), for example, is a portrait series in which Choumali documents the dwindling practice of scarification, the ancient act of making permanent, sometimes patterned incisions in the skin. Her subjects are men and women who had emigrated to Côte d'Ivoire from Burkina Faso, where *hââbré* means both "writing" and "scarification" in the Kô language. They are all photographed against the same teal-blue backdrop, an abundance of light illuminating and drawing focus not just to the scars but to the whole of their faces, highlighting these figures as likely the last generation among whom facial scarification will be prominent.

Following a deadly terrorist attack in 2016 in Grand-Bassam, a town to the east of Abidjan where Choumali is based, the artist began to add another dimension to her photographs: embroidery. She found the process therapeutic, another method of nonverbal communication to express the trauma, grief and melancholy she was witnessing in the city in the aftermath of the attacks but which was going unsaid due to a sense of cultural "taboo". The resulting series, *Ça Va Aller* – from the French, meaning "it will be okay" – depicts solitary figures around the town photographed discreetly by Choumali on an iPhone. Those images were then embroidered with brightly coloured cotton, wool and lurex thread, the woven lines sometimes seeming to emanate from the figures, like physical manifestations of unspoken emotion. In some works, the embroidery embellishes the image, the photograph still mostly visible. In others, the embroidery dominates, transforming the image into an almost tapestry-like piece. There is a simultaneous simplifying into shapes and blocks of colour and the addition of intricate detail on the surface.

For Choumali, art and healing are connected. Her mixed-media creations are an expression both of the attempt to find solace and regain hope in the act of making as well as the end result being something that might offer that comfort and hope to its viewers. Choumali's more recent works have also featured embroidery on photographs as well as photomontage and collage. Her series *Alba'hian* – which means "dawn" in the Agni language of Côte d'Ivoire's Akan people – grew out of the artist's 5am walks around several African cities including Accra, Ghana; Casablanca, Morocco; Dakar, Senegal; and her hometown, Abidjan. Choumali deftly translates dawn light into thread with mixes of gold, pale blues and bright pinks. Her subjects are larger than life, giants towering over her cityscapes and beach scenes, emphasizing the "magic" in "magic hour".

> "Choumali captures the dwindling practice of scarification, the ancient act of making permanent, sometimes patterned incisions in the skin"

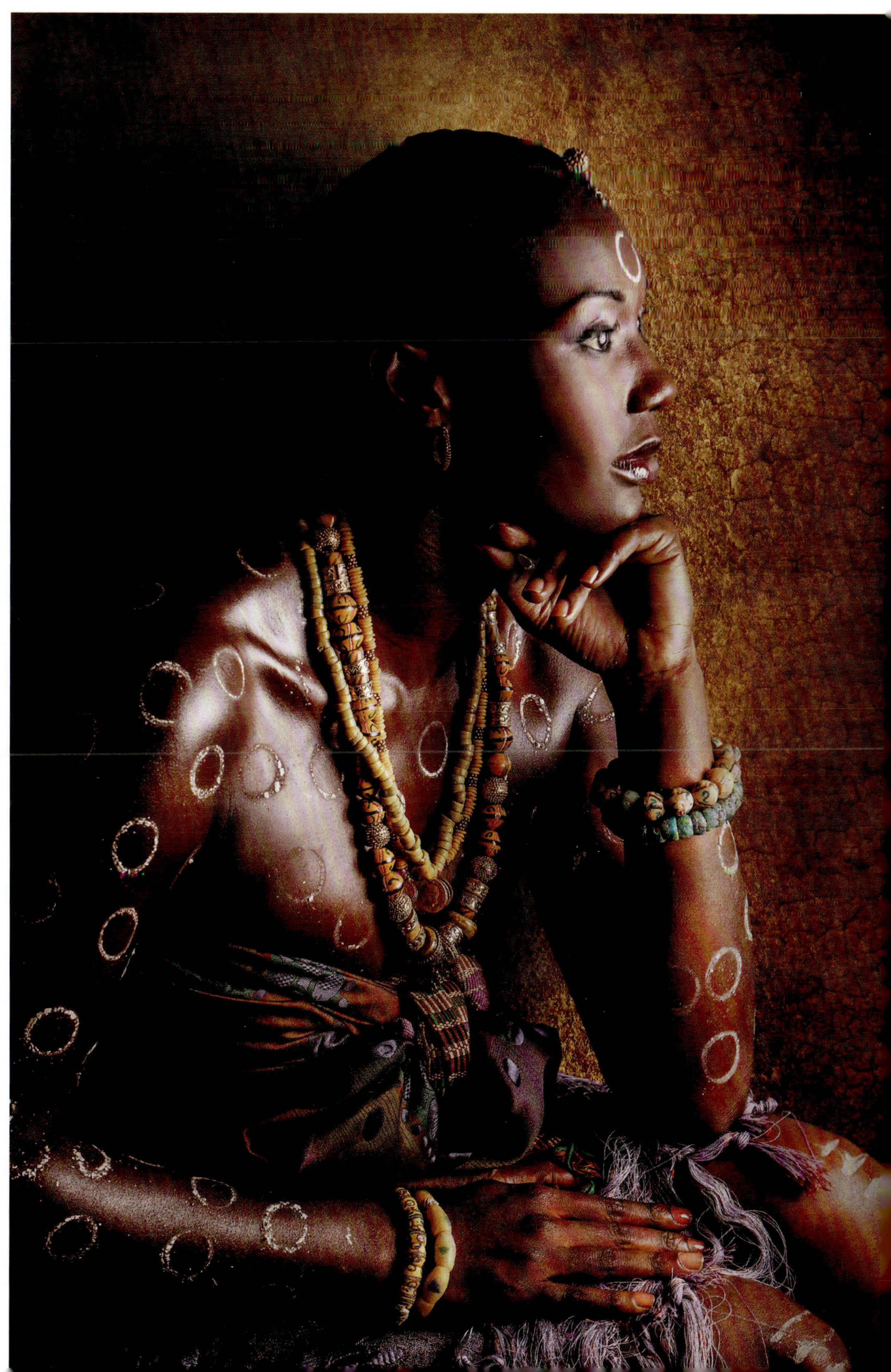

 As We See It

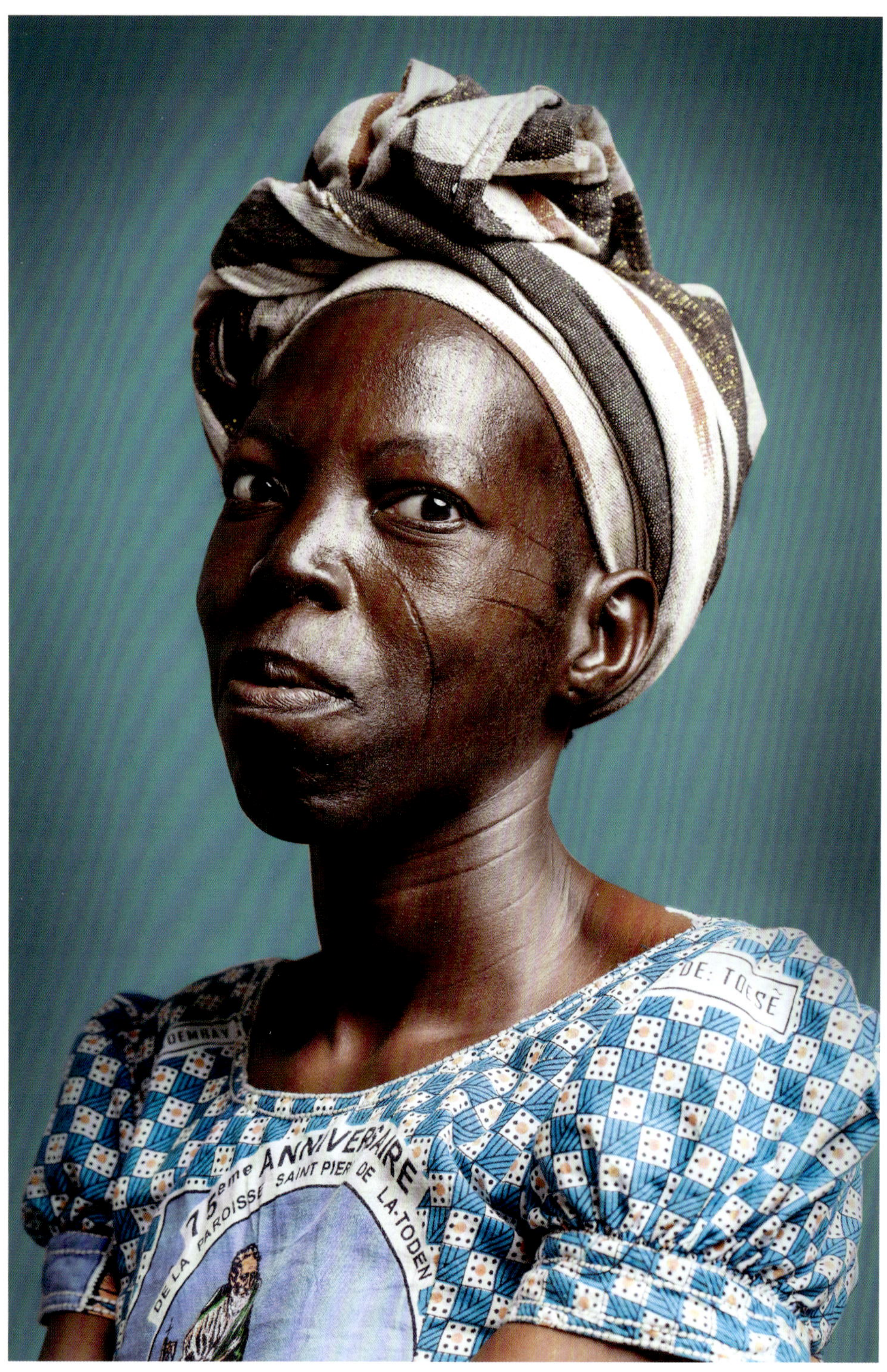

Mrs Martine from *Hââbré, The Last Generation*, 2013–14

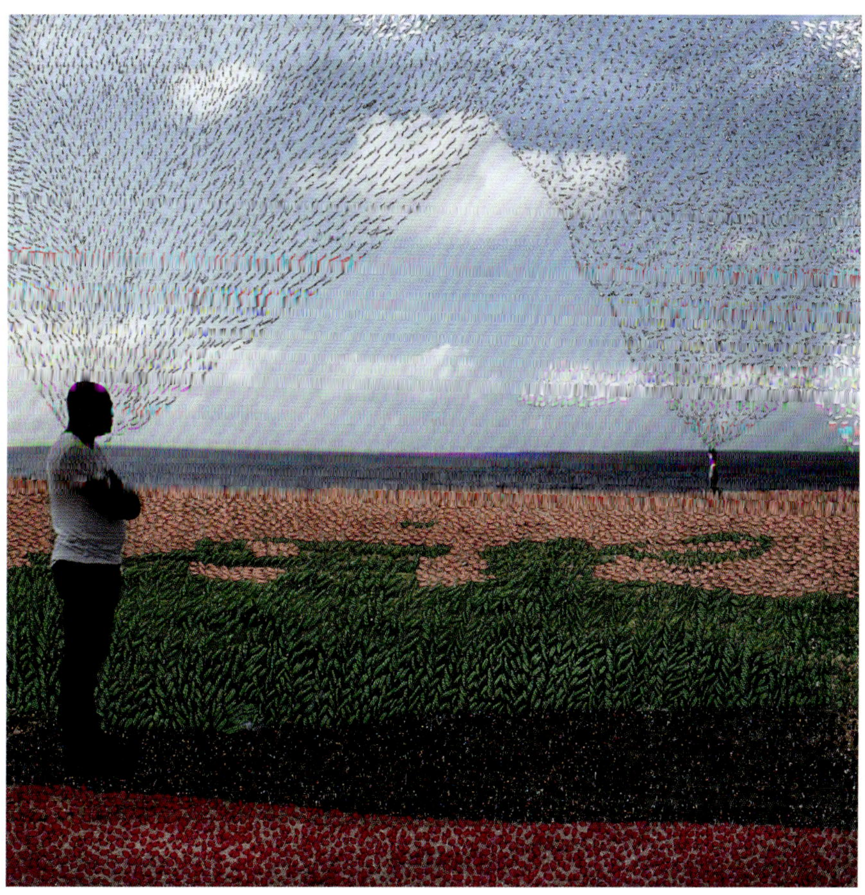

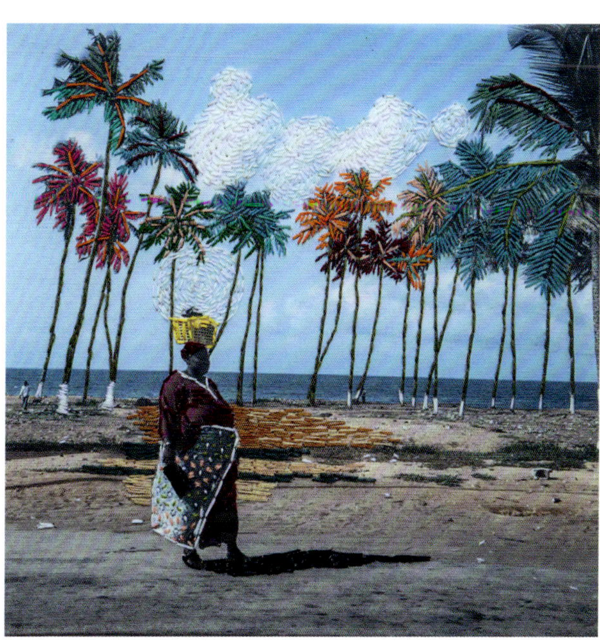

Previous spread:
Akan Attie, from *Resilients*, 2014
This page:
Untitled, from *Ça Va Aller*, 2018
Untitled, from *Ça Va Aller*, 2018

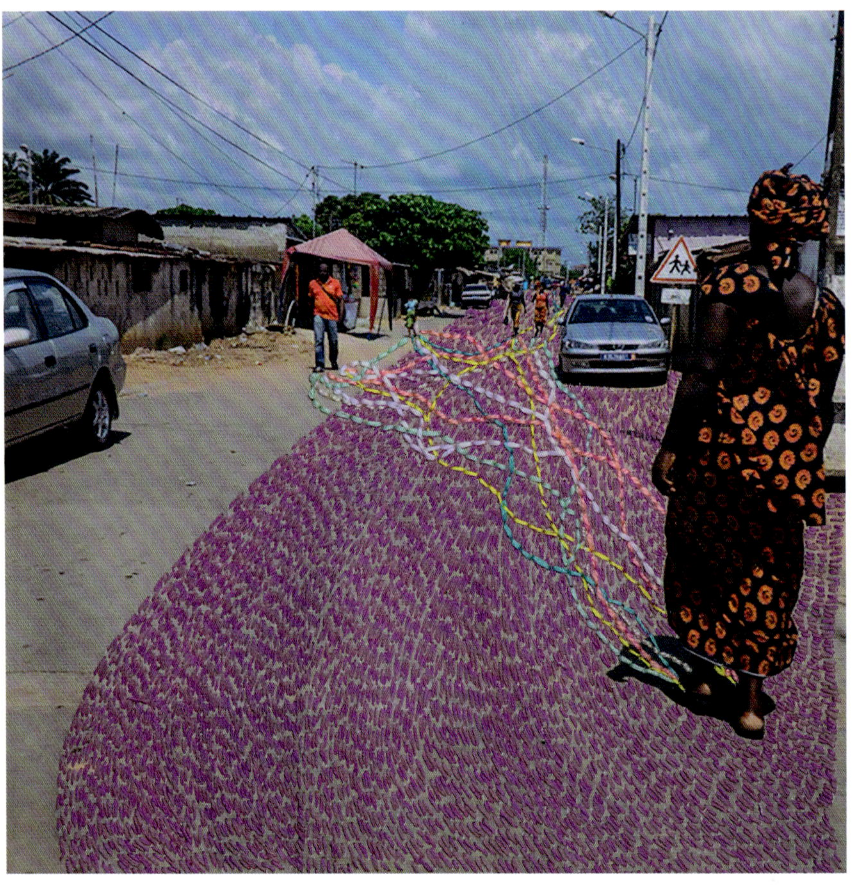

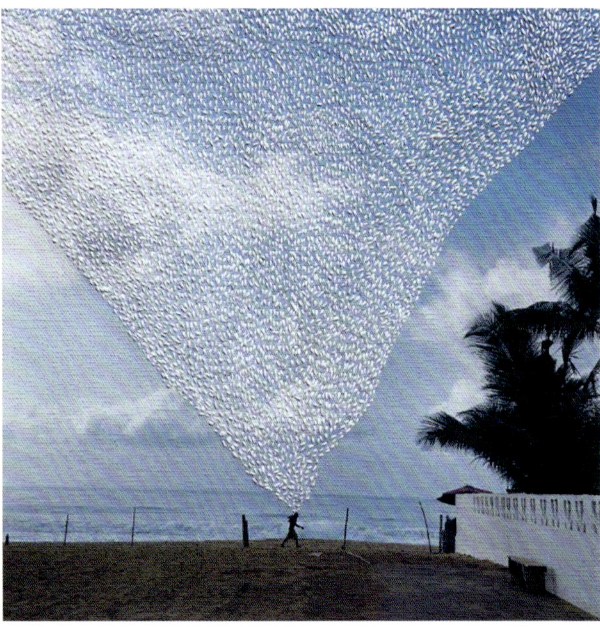

This page, from top:
Untitled, from *Ça Va Aller*, 2019
Untitled, from *Ça Va Aller*, 2018
Opposite:
From *Hââbré, The Last Generation* 2013–14

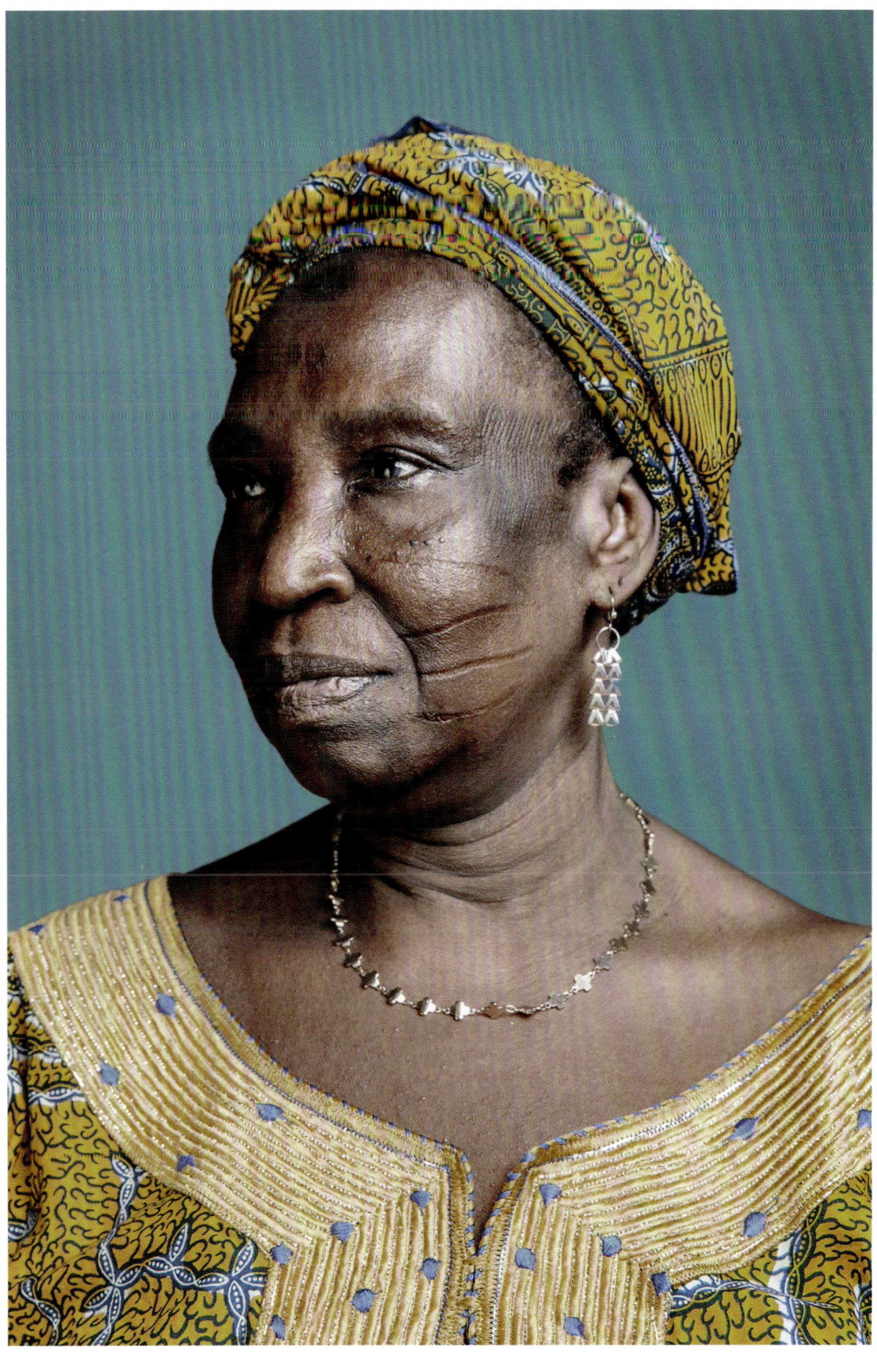

Emma Prempeh

Compressing Memory

Fabric plays a significant role in London-based artist Emma Prempeh's explorations of memory and familial relationships. *Red, White, Blue and Brown* (2020) depicts the artist's mother in her first flat in Brixton, south London, in the 1980s. She sits barefoot on a vibrant red carpet, looking over her shoulder with a smile and a wine glass in her hand, toasting the viewer. The title references the colours of the Union flag in conjunction with the colour of the artist's mother's (and her own) skin in a way that brings to mind Chris Ofili's *Union Black* (2003), which reimagines the UK's national flag in red, black and green, the colours of the Pan-African movement. Prempeh herself is of Ghanaian and Vincentian heritage, both places being former British colonies.

Behind the subject hangs a white embroidered curtain that Prempeh has attached to the canvas, which lends the work a physicality; the potential of touch feels like a bridge between the viewer in the present and the subject in the past. The white curtain appears again as a bridal veil in *Hindsight* (2020). The earthy browns, beiges and creams – a colour palette which dominates Prempeh's work – provides the viewer with an oscillation between a sense of the cocooning warmth of nostalgia and the elusiveness and haziness of memory.

In an interview with *She Curates*, the multidisciplinary artist described her work as the "attempt to depict things that are essentially intangible through paint; trying to evidence my perception and experience of time".[37] In *Windows of Emotion* (2020), Prempeh once again incorporates textile into her work. The piece depicts a young Black woman looking wistfully out of a window-like space built out of imitation gold leaf. She is covered in a blanket, also attached to the canvas, on which Prempeh has printed diary entries. The fascinating tension in Prempeh's art comes from the depiction on the canvas of the difficulty of her task. Faces are blurred, eyes and mouths sometimes difficult to distinguish. The darkness of the canvases seems to present memory as a chasmic space in which things could be irrevocably lost, a void that threatens the very physical integrity of her subjects. Figures constructed out of imitation gold leaf in *Forgetting* (2020) and *De Speeltuin* (2021) show their cracks and peels, in a state of liminality, on the verge of either disintegration or materialization.

> "An embroidered curtain that Prempeh has attached to the canvas lends the work a physicality; the potential of touch feels like a bridge between viewer and subject"

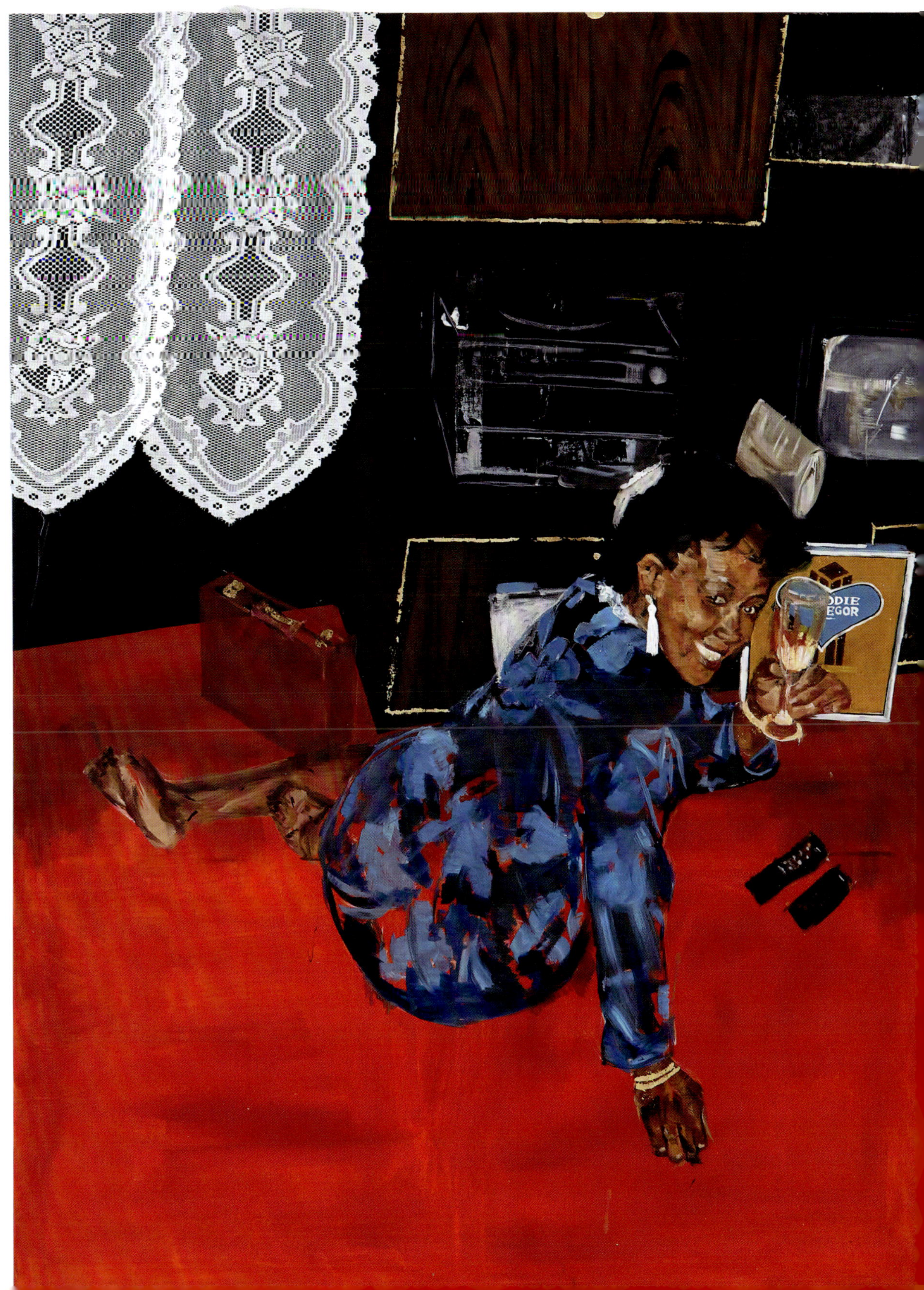

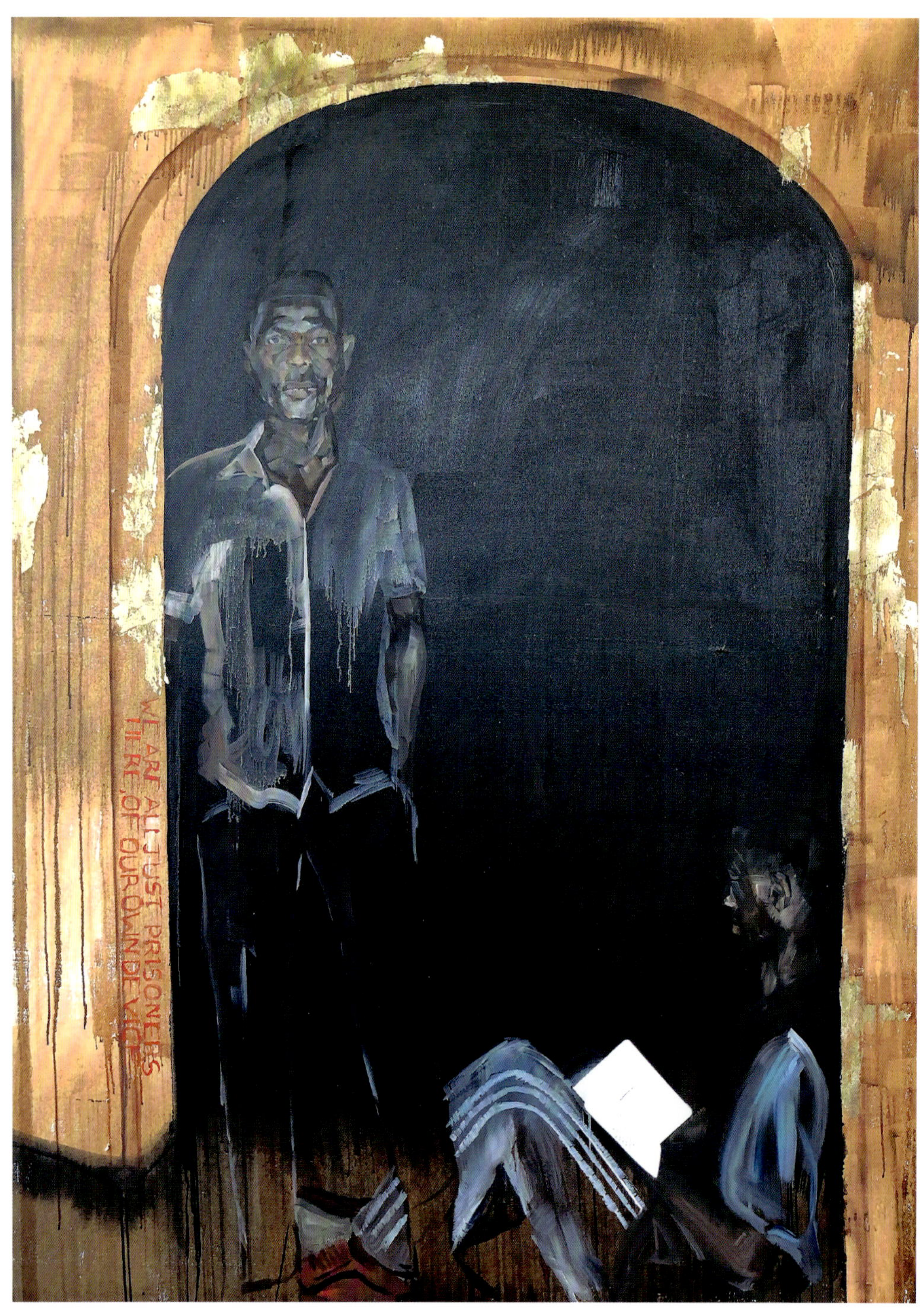

Previous spread: *Red, White, Blue and Brown*, 2020
Above: *Staring at the Sun*, 2021

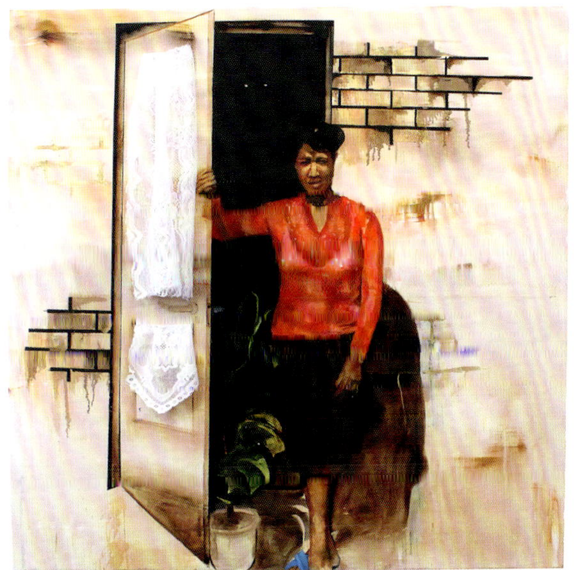

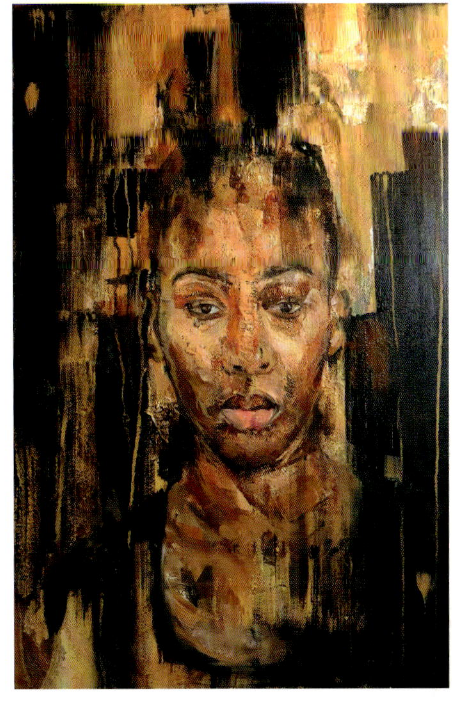

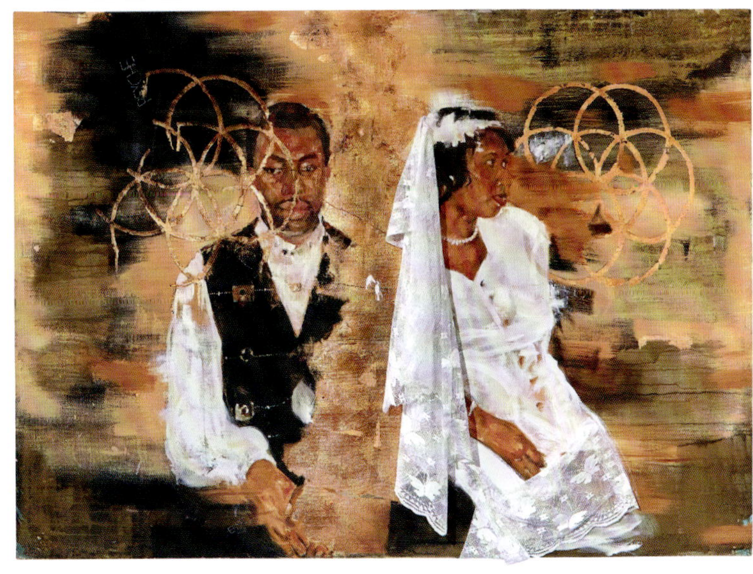

This page, clockwise from top left:
The Arrival, 2021
February Blues, 2021
Hindsight, 2020

Further Reading

Books

Addy, Campbell, *Feeling Seen: The Photographs of Campbell Addy* (Prestel, 2022)

Campt, Tina M., *Image Matters: Archive, Photography, and the African Diaspora in Europe* (Duke University Press Books, 2012)

Campt, Tina M., *A Black Gaze: Artists Changing How We See* (MIT, 2021)

Campt, Tina M., *Listening to Images* (Duke University Press Books, 2017)

Eshun, Ekow, *Africa State of Mind: Contemporary Photography Reimagines a Continent* (Thames and Hudson, 2020)

Gilroy, Paul, *The Black Atlantic: Modernity and Double Consciousness* (Verso Books, 1993)

Gilroy, Paul, and Stuart Hall, *Black Britain: A Photographic History* (Saqi Books, 2007)

Godfrey, Mark, and Zoe Whitley, *Soul of a Nation: Art in the Age of Black Power* (Tate Publishing, 2017)

Ijewere, Nadine, *Our Own Selves* (Prestel, 2021)

Pitts, Johny, *Afropean: Notes from Black Europe* (Allen Lane, 2019)

Sargent, Antwaun, *The New Black Vanguard: Photography between Art and Fashion* (Aperture, 2019)

Sargent, Antwaun, *Young, Gifted and Black: A New Generation of Artists: The Lumpkin-Boccuzzi Family Collection of Contemporary Art* (D.A.P., 2020)

Sealy, Mark, *Decolonising the Camera: Photography in Racial Time* (Lawrence and Wishart, 2019)

Walsh, Lauren, *Through the Lens: The Pandemic and Black Lives Matter* (Routledge, 2022)

Publications/Websites

blackartmatters.com
homebyrm.space
iniva.org

nataal.com
@seeinblackproject

Endnotes

1. www.thefader.com/2019/12/04/ghana-scene-profile-darovibes-amaarae-joey-lit

2. www.vogue.co.uk/article/nadine-ijewere-interview

3. www.itsnicethat.com/news/nadine-ijewere-beautiful-disruption-c-o-berlin-photography-250521

4. www.out.com/fashion/2017/3/05/gay-photographer-campbell-addy-exploring-his-religious-roots-his-first-solo-show

5. www.newyorker.com/culture/photo-booth/scenes-from-a-new-york-city-protest-of-the-police-killing-of-george-floyd

6. www.cocobuttershutter.com/c6da892c10-gallery

7. www.invisible-borders.com/black-portraitures-whose-black-is-it

8. www.emekaokereke.com/as-we-recede

9. www.friendsoffriends.com/art/emeka-okereke-on-countering-western-hegemony-through-trans-african-exchange/

10. www.thephotographicjournal.com/essays/dream-to-me

11. www.nataal.com/girma-berta

12. www.nataal.com/kenny-germe

13. www.officemagazine.net/naima-green-radiating-nature

14. www.nytimes.com/2019/06/15/opinion/photography-nature-green.html

15. www.itsnicethat.com/articles/ articles/david-nana-opoku-ansah-photography-220720

16. www.vogue.co.uk/arts-and-lifestyle/gallery/youngphotographers

17. www.theguardian.com/artanddesign/2020/jul/17/dariocalmese-vanity-fair-first-black-cover-photographer

18. https://i-d.vice.com/en_uk/article/dyzw3m/these-photoscelebrate-the-beauty-of-black-life-in-the-bahamas

19. www.thelovemagazine.co.uk/article/davey-adesida-how-do-you-sleep-at-night-knowing-that-you-only-hire-your-white-friends

20. https://artsandculture.google.com/story/black-lenses-matter-takeisha-jefferson-what-we-see/ AUhJ-PANKWVbq?hl=en

21. www.smh.com.au/culture/art-and-design/australia-has-never-been-secure-or-comfortable-for-me-atong-atem-20200616-p55384.html

22. www.smh.com.au/culture/art-and-design/australia-has-never-been-secure-or-comfortable-for-me-atong-atem-20200616-p55384.html

23. https://nataal.com/atong-atem-at-red-hook-labs

24. https://nataal.com/atong-atem-at-red-hook-labs

25. www.youtube.com/watch?v=P3-HvzW05ew

26. www.itsnicethat.com/articles/donavon-smallwood-langour-photography-100321

27. www.youtube.com/watch?v=ySJEKbLI7Ns&ab_channel=NikonUSA

28. www.lensculture.com/ articles/rahima-gamboeducation-is-forbidden

29. www.bombmagazine.org/articles/at-the-rivers-edge-allison-janae-hamilton-interviewed

30. www.brooklynrail.org/2021/04/art/Allison-Janae-Hamilton-with-Yasi-Alipour

31. Monster Theory: Reading Culture, University of Minnesota Press, 1996

32. www.pilarcorrias.com/news/7-interview-with-sedrick-chisom

33. www.hyperallergic.com/670057/what-does-it-mean-to-create-afrofuturistic-art

34. www.contemporaryand.com/magazines/lunga-ntila-seeks-god-among-us-in-her-body-of-work

35. www.jodiminnis.com

36. www.jodiminnis.com/ifriedfishforme

37. www.she-curates.com/interviews/artists/emma-prempeh

Picture Credits

9 © Ronan Mckenzie. Asahi Sano (Hair Stylist), Ammy Drammeh (Makeup Artist), Jonathan Johnson (Casting Director) 10 © David Nana Opoku Ansah. Art Director @orlandofficiale, Creative & Styling @kusikubi, Models @muminjangani @benjaminmensah_, Production Company @luduproductions_, Producer @instabryte, Makeup @Sachaokoh using @soaesthetics, Hair Stylist @hamidvijay, Photo Assistants @friday_boi @commonjuls, Styling Assistants @brimah @prince_b07, Production Coordinator @nana_poley, Production Assistants @ayineme_ra @rooky_rider 11 © Ronan Mckenzie 13 © David Nana Opoku Ansah. Art Director @orlandofficiale, Creative & Styling @kusikubi, Models @muminjangani @benjaminmensah_, Production Company @luduproductions_, Producer @instabryte, Makeup @Sachaokoh using @soaesthetics, Hair Stylist @hamidvijay, Photo Assistants @friday_boi @commonjuls, Styling Assistants @brimah @prince_b07, Production Coordinator @nana_poley, Production Assistants @ayineme_ra @rooky_rider 15–19 © Prince Gyasi, courtesy Nil Gallery 21–23 © Nadine Ijewere/ Trunk Archive 25–27 © Campbell Addy/Trunk Archive 29–33 © Chris Facey 2020. Christopher Facey, all rights reserved 35–39 © Emeka Okereke 41 © 2018. Courtesy the Artist 42, 43 above © 2017–18. Courtesy the Artist 43 below © 2018. Courtesy the Artist 44 © 2015. Courtesy the Artist 45 © 2018. Courtesy the Artist 47–49 © Braylen Dion 51–55 Courtesy of the artist and Addis Fine Art 57–61 © Kenny Germé. Photo styled by Edem Dossou 63–67 © Naima Green 69–73 © Mikael Owunna (www.mikaelowunnastore.com) 75 © David Nan Opoku Ansah 76–77 © David Nana Opoku Ansah. Art Director @orlandofficiale, Creative & Styling @kusikubi, Models @muminjangani @benjaminmensah_, Production Company @luduproductions_, Producer @instabryte, Makeup @Sachaokoh using @soaesthetics, Hair Stylist @hamidvijay, Photo Assistants @friday_boi @commonjuls, Styling Assistants @brimah @prince_b07, Production Coordinator @nana_poley, Production Assistants @ayineme_ra @rooky_rider 78–79 © David Nana Opoku Ansah 81–85 © Lebohang Kganye 87–89 © Dario Calmese/Trunk Archive 91–93 © Melissa Alcena, courtesy Tern Gallery 95–97 © #ThursdaysChild x Trunk Archive/Davey Adesida 99–103 © Takeisha Jefferson 105–107 Courtesy of Atong Atem and MARS Gallery 109–111 © Donavon Smallwood 113–119 © Henry J. Kamara 121–125 © Zithelo Bobby Mthombeni 127 © Ronan Mckenzie 128, 129 Ronan Mckenzie. Asahi Sano (Hair Stylist), Ammy Drammeh (Makeup Artist), Jonathan Johnson (Casting Director) 130–133 © Ronan Mckenzie 135 above © Rahima Gambo/Tatsuniya Art Collective 135 below, 136–137, 138 above © Rahima Gambo 138 below © Rahima Gambo/Tatsuniya Art Collective 139 © Rahima Gambo 141–145 Courtesy of the artist and Marianne Boesky Gallery, New York and Aspen. © Allison Janae Hamilton 147–149 Courtesy of the artist and Pilar Corrias, London. Photography: Adam Reich 150, 151 Courtesy of the artist and Pilar Corrias, London. Photography: Christopher Burke 153–157 © Lunga Ntila 159–163 © Jodi Minnis, courtesy Tern Gallery 165 © Délio Jasse. Courtesy the artist and Jahmek Contemporary 166–167 © Délio Jasse. Courtesy the artist and Tiwani Contemporary 168–171 © Délio Jasse. Courtesy the artist and Jahmek Contemporary 173–177 © Joana Choumali 179–181 © Emma Prempeh 187 © Jodi Minnis, courtesy Tern Gallery

JACKET
Front © Kenny Germé. Photo styled by Edem Dossou
Back (Clockwise from top) © David Nana Opoku Ansah. Art Director @orlandofficiale, Creative & Styling @kusikubi, Models @muminjangani @benjaminmensah_, Production Company @luduproductions_, Producer @instabryte, Makeup @Sachaokoh using @soaesthetics, Hair Stylist @hamidvijay, Photo Assistants @friday_boi @commonjuls, Styling Assistants @brimah @prince_b07, Production Coordinator @nana_poley, Production Assistants @ayineme_ra @rooky_rider; © Zithelo Bobby Mthombeni; © Joana Choumali

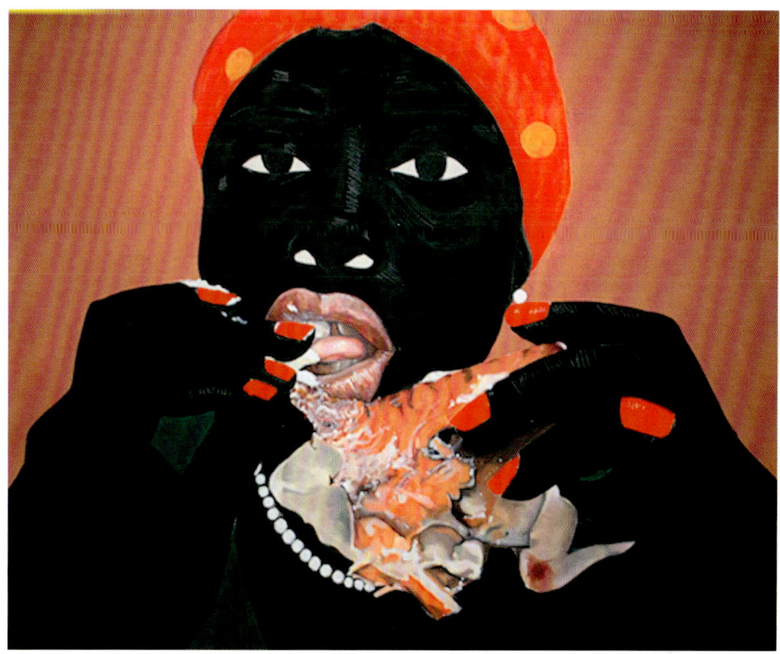

Jodi Minnis, *Fish*, 2019

Index

Acknowledgements

I'd like to thank all the artists featured here for their beautiful, inspiring and thought-provoking work and, along with their galleries and agencies, for making the images available. I'd also like to thank everybody at Laurence King for the opportunity to write about those that are creating rich, nuanced representations of Black life.

To those I owe a text message or an email, so sorry! To my mum and sister: thank you so much for your support both practical and emotional while this book was coming together.

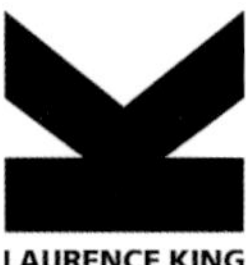

LAURENCE KING

First published in Great Britain in 2023
by Laurence King Publishing
an imprint of The Orion Publishing Group Ltd
Carmelite House, 50 Victoria Embankment
London EC4Y 0DZ

An Hachette UK Company

10 9 8 7 6 5 4 3 2 1

A CIP catalogue record for this book is available from the British Library.

ISBN 978 1 786 27958 3

Design by Mariana Sameiro

Front cover: Kenny Germé, *The Godfather,* 2020, Highsnobiety
Back cover, clockwise from top: Joana Choumali, *Mrs Martine*
from *Hââbré, The Last Generation*, 2013–14
David Nana Opoku Ansah, from *We Are All They*, 2020
Zithelo Bobby Mthombeni, *Tolü Makay*, 2020

Origination by DL Imaging, UK
Printed in China by C&C Offset Printing Co. Ltd

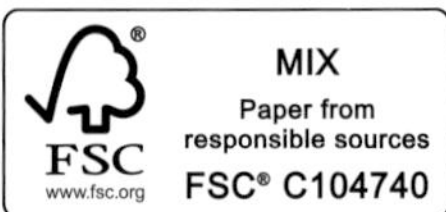

www.laurenceking.com
www.orionbooks.co.uk